This Red Planet

How Jürgen Klopp's Liverpool FC Enthralled and Conquered The World

Paul Tomkins

Praise for Paul Tomkins and The Tomkins Times since 2009

"[Paul Tomkins' work is] … phenomenal. Absolutely quintessential reading for Liverpool fans."
The Redmen TV

"The Tomkins Times is an indispensable website whose diagnosis of all things Liverpool is beyond compare."
LFCHistory.net

"The best Liverpool FC writer, bar none."
Vic Gill, Bill Shankly's son-in-law and former LFC trainee.

"Perhaps the most intelligent guide to LFC available on the internet."
The Independent on Sunday

"Gold-dust analysis"
John Sinnott, BBC

"[Football analysis] is best left to the professionals, like the admirable Mr Tomkins."
The Daily Telegraph

"An ingenious and intelligent look beneath the surface to reveal what the headlines too often don't tell us. Fascinating."
Jonathan Wilson

"Another triumph of impeccable research, Pay As You Play brings much-needed factual insight to a discussion previously dominated by half-truths."
Oliver Kay, The Times

"Liverpool do happen to be blessed with supporters whose statistical analysis provides a lucid interpretation of where the club's strengths and weaknesses lie, accessible through the Tomkins Times website."
The Independent

"To end loneliness, you need other people – plus something else. You also need to feel you are sharing something with the other person, or the group, that is meaningful to both of you."

Johann Hari, **Lost Connections**

For Siân

Paul Tomkins is the author of over a dozen football books, an academic study on the role football finances play in success, and the novel *The Girl on the Pier*. In addition, he was a columnist on the official Liverpool website between 2005 and 2010. In 2009 he set up the website *The Tomkins Times*.

www.TomkinsTimes.com

Contents

Introduction

"It is not the man who has too little, but the man who craves more, that is poor."

Seneca

The best in the world. That's what the aggregate of three major, highly-respected rankings systems said: Liverpool were the best team in the world, at the point 2021/22 concluded.

As its global fanbase swelled to anywhere between 100-500 million fans – or *seven billion*, if you listened to Pep Guardiola – Liverpool's cosmopolitan team, led by the peerless Jürgen Klopp, racked up all manner of records: rising, in 2020, to be rated the 4th-best team *in European history*; and then, in 2022, taking a chase for the ever-elusive quadruple 21 days longer than any previous attempt in English football, and months longer than the club's previous best attempt.

In between, a deadly pandemic brought the planet to its knees, and Liverpool suffered all kinds of losses, big and small. But the club and the city rose again, as it had before; and as life, in general, suggests we all must, with the ebbs and flows of fortune.

This is a book about remarkable success – a remarkable *team* – but also deep, dark struggles; it is a book about football, but also community; about Liverpool, and about the world; about failure and success.

Nothing is ever more important than football, until all the *really important* stuff happens.

#1
'Just' two trophies for the 2021/22 season, but various records, and despite a narrow and undeserved Champions League final defeat amid the chaos of Parisian police brutality that sapped the travelling Kop of its usual indomitable spirit, Liverpool ended the season ranked the #1 side in the world yet again, ahead of Manchester City in second place and, some distance behind, Real Madrid in third.

Since the start of the 2018/19 Premier League season, Man City had accrued 358 points to Liverpool's 357, yet that difference of one point came as City won three titles to the Reds' one. Plus, of course, the Reds made it to three times as many Champions League finals, and unlike City, *actually won one*.

Indeed, as of June 2022, the average of *three* different sophisticated ranking systems 'agreed' that Liverpool were the best: as well as the Club Elo Index, there was the *538* Power Rankings and UEFA's own coefficient: Manchester City edged the Reds minimally in the *538* model, but were a fraction behind them in the latter. Averaged out across all three, and Liverpool are top. From the Elo, *538* and UEFA coefficient, the rankings were: Liverpool first (1st, 2nd, 2nd), to average 1.7; City second (2nd, 1st, 3rd), to average 2.0; and Bayern Munich third (3rd, 3rd, 1st), to average 2.3; with Real Madrid a fair distance behind – even after getting lucky against the Reds in Paris to gain another European crown (indeed, their ranking shows that, overall, they were not an especially great side, but did get a couple of great *results*).

Playing electrifying football, Liverpool won a barely comprehendible *forty-nine* games in 2021/22, more than any in its history, and many more than other notable historically great sides, such as Arsenal's Invincibles, Manchester United's treble winners and anything Chelsea have ever produced.

If the Reds had won their two domestic cups by the narrowest manner possible, they lost the 2022 league title and Champions League by equally tight margins. All four trophies came down to the slimmest of differences; all four went to the wire. The cup finals went beyond 120 minutes, but the league season – 3,420 minutes long – was still a possibility to be Liverpool's after 3,405 minutes (and even then, another goal for Aston Villa at the Etihad, after the full 3,420 minutes, would have given it to Liverpool). The Champions League, when reaching the final, lasts at least 1,170 minutes, and the Reds needed just one goal in the final moments to take it to extra-time, which would have been the least they deserved after absolutely battering the Spanish champions for most of the match.

You get nothing for being ranked no.1, of course; but it does highlight both the quality and consistency of Klopp's Liverpool, given the rolling Elo system awards more points for wins based on opposition quality, and includes European results too; as well as the other two ranking systems having their own built-in depths.

Remember, the Reds ranked 33rd in Europe on the Elo Index when Klopp arrived in 2015.

In the end, the open-top bus parade around Liverpool at the end of May 2022 wasn't to celebrate winning the biggest of trophies, but to appreciate a cup double and the remarkable efforts to try and land a quadruple (as well as to highlight the women's team's well-deserved promotion). Sometimes you can be close *and* enjoy a cigar.

Remember: teams are not always duly rewarded for their brilliance, but they are *remembered* for their brilliance. They are *loved* for their brilliance.

Unification

Above all else, football *unifies*. Of course, it divides too, but at its best it brings everyone together, from different countries, religions, races, political leanings and sexual identities. And this is a big Red planet.

Under American ownership, Liverpool had a German manager, corralling an Egyptian goal machine, a Dutch defensive rock, and a Brazilian trio of guts and guile and glue-like gloves. There was a Senegalese scorer, a Spanish maestro, a French *substrat rocheux* and a cavalier Colombian; a German-Cameroonian cool-cat, a Greek madman, a Guinean grafter; a Japanese marksman, a Belgian cult hero, a Portuguese poacher, and a laid-back Irish custodian; plus a batch of Brits who brought Mackem might, Yorkshire-hewn grit, Scottish indefatigability and Scouse skill.

Now, to go forward, there's a tall Uruguayan goal-getter, in Darwin Núñez; a Portuguese-Brit lock-picker in Fábio Carvalho; and an Aberdonian full-back flyer in Calvin Ramsay; as well as others who will emerge from the academy, as they have done with regularity in recent seasons.

Genesis

I started writing this book in earnest – after a couple of years of research – in January 2022, when it seemed that the Reds' league season had fallen apart.

I'd very publicly written off the Reds' chances of the title when 11 points behind, and then the gap rose to 14 points. It seemed a chasm, for a team then out of form, against a team that rarely slipped up. I didn't enjoy being proved right in the end, but I did enjoy *almost* being proved wrong.

I never make assumptions about the Champions League, as you can get knocked out despite being the better team (as various teams found when playing Real Madrid), and the FA Cup had not been something Klopp could ever really focus on, beyond playing some kids when going out in the early rounds (or beating Everton).

So, with the season – to my eyes – likely to peter out, I chose to finally focus on the story of modern Liverpool FC: how, across the world, communities are united by this passion, in an age where division is almost built into the daily way of life. And, a book about how to enjoy these remarkable rides, when at times they seem to rid us of our sanity.

Just as he tends to, Jürgen Klopp put a gigantic spanner in the works – and revived the season to the point where I had no idea if somehow I'd end up writing about a quadruple (even if it such an unlikely achievement was never even in Liverpool's own hands, once they could 'only' draw at Manchester City in April). In the end, the Reds fell agonisingly short, but they added *reams* to the folklore, if just two trophies to the cabinet.

As such, this book focuses more on 2021/22 than I intended, as *so much happened*.

Indeed, so much happened that I had essentially written *two* books concurrently, and even then, the ideas could be expanded further. It proved the most difficult book I've ever written, as I had so many things to focus on, and there were so many (genuinely) must-win games for Liverpool that it took a toll on my ongoing health issues.

I had also wanted to visit more Liverpool fans outside the UK, ever since meeting up with the Icelandic supporters' club (and the lovely *LFChistory.net* guys) in Reykjavík in 2015 (when starting the research for my soon-to-be-finished second novel), or the Westport group in Ireland, who invited me out to their event in 2005 (along with Jonathan Swain, who assisted me on my first book). In the end, connecting to people around the world online has been the most practical way, when these days even getting to Anfield can be a challenge for me.

With so much content left over, I will put extra chapters onto *The Tomkins Times'* (TTT) website and Substack, as well as expanding myriad ideas and big themes – connection, our mental health as football fans, the divisive nature of social media, the things that diminish our joy, and how we can find fulfilment in following our team – that were only half-formed by this summer. (I almost had a meltdown when I saw that 2022/23 starts in *July*. I love football, but at times it feels like too much of a good thing; especially with rivals' games, spread across the week or the weekend, creating a constant state of tension.)

As ever, none of my books are ever definitive accounts, but this, like the others, can hopefully provide some unique insights, and give a flavour of what went on. I offer my own perspectives, albeit honed and shaped by the environment, which includes the various bright minds of TTT, as well as the odd scrap of inside information.

While a standalone volume in its own right, *This Red Planet* is perhaps best seen as the third instalment in the unofficial trilogy of *Mentality Monsters* (2019) and *Perched* (2020), which, amongst other things, cover the procurement and development of (most of) the squad and coaching staff that achieved so much from the run-in of 2020/21 through to the consistent excellence of 2021/22 (with the possibility of a quadrilogy *one day*, given that Klopp's work is not done, and he extended his contract to 2026).

In a couple of places I revisited, rewrote and reworked my own pre-existing articles, but most of it is confined to the second chapter, which seemed a good semi-starting point for this book: just how *insane* 2020/21 had been, in terms of terrible luck, Covid lockdowns, and the lowdown on what I (correctly) thought were fixable problems, that everyone else seemed to be missing. It's worth noting that not one single BBC pundit, out of the 20 asked to pick their top four in order for 2021/22 ahead of the first game in August 2021, listed Liverpool as potential champions; yet seven went for Chelsea. Three of the 20 pundits were ex-Liverpool players, and only Danny Murphy and Mark Lawrenson had Liverpool finishing 2nd (Stephen Warnock said 3rd); the other 17 said 3rd, 4th or in the case of Jermaine Beckford, *not even in the top four*, and thus behind Everton, his choice for 4th (and thus, Everton got one more vote than Spurs, who finished there). The aggregate predictions had Manchester City as champions, Chelsea 2nd, Manchester United 3rd and Liverpool 4th.

This perhaps shows how little outsiders understood Liverpool in 2020/21. But once I've reminded people of the various reasons, that I diagnosed at the time, for that team unfairly judged as 'failing', I'll move on to this past season, and all the broken records, the brilliant performances, the trophies won, the methods deployed, and along the way, some perspectives from fans around the world, who shared in the delights.

As a bald, bespectacled football writer with a big nose once said, teams are not always duly rewarded for their brilliance, but they are *remembered* for their brilliance.

We Choose To Go To the Moon

"We choose to go to the Moon in this decade and do the other things, not because they are easy, but because they are hard."

John F Kennedy, 1962

"I choose to stay in my bedroom."

BigDickLolz69, 2022

Moonshot

Liverpool never set out to win the quadruple. No one does. Just as no one sets out to win all 38 league games, or run around the world non-stop, without refreshments. Some things have never been done, and for good reason. A team just tries to win each game at a time, as managers will say; even if they have to plan further ahead (maybe two or three games, maybe more in a less direct way), and manage a busy schedule and which players will be in the red-zone for injuries. Then, once the 'potential' tag – treble, quadruple, unbeatables – sticks, and that team understandably falls a little short, it becomes a way to call an outstanding achievement a failure.

Prior to the 2022 FA Cup final, Klopp told the press: "If we are all only happy when we are really winning when your race finishes what life would that be? When I say 'Enjoy the journey' I mean it.

"We only cause ourselves problems as human beings. For example: 'Don't come home without a Quadruple' – you will never be happy. If that is the only way to satisfy you, then that is really difficult.

"[But] let's give it a go. Football games are sometimes decided by single players, most of the time they are decided by the whole performance and we can work on the whole performance and have world-class players – and we will have world-class players.

"It is not what other teams are doing and it's like 'Gah, they signed him'. I never thought that to be honest. When they took a player from me and put him there, in Germany quite frequently, it gives them 20 per cent and us minus 20 and that's not cool. But as long as they don't pick from us I'm fine.

"It has never been done before [the Quadruple] so it's like the first step in whichever island, we're the first team to give it a try and that's what we do.

"If you had said at the end of the season you will be in all finals and two match-days before the end we are three points behind City, I'd have said 'nah, I can't see that happening'. Not all together in the same season.

"But the boys did it and that's really special, but we know the decisive part is coming now. You can see it – warming up is finished. Now we have rhythm finally, now we can go for it."

The four-trophy sweep didn't come to pass, but boy, *how close*.

"I could have gone to Bayern [Munich] a few times," Klopp also said, prior to the victory over Chelsea. "I could have won more titles in my life. I would say there is a good chance at least of that. I didn't do it. I had a contract here and I never did it. That's completely fine.

"The world is not full of winners, the world is full of triers hopefully. And I try and, sometimes, I win with some other people together. I am happy with that."

NASA

That the quadruple was even possible related to a dozen years' work, from the point FSG (then NESV) bought Liverpool in late 2010, and a project started to be shaped, in essence, once Michael Edwards was brought to the club in 2011, along with Ian Graham, by Damien Comolli. Mistakes morphed into moonshots.

It was Edwards and Graham who helped bring in the best players in those early years, and who confirmed that Jürgen Klopp should be the manager to be approached in 2015. John W Henry handed over control to a more football-astute partner in Mike Gordon, and he became FSG's go-to man; the one who went out and procured the German, after Manchester United had failed, a year earlier, with a cringeworthy pitch to the Borussia Dortmund manager.

Few successes occur overnight. We often only see the *fruits* of ten years of striving, when someone hits the big-time. We don't see the striving itself.

NASA going to the moon took a decade-or-so, in addition to all the technological work that had taken place up until 1961, including taking German rocket expertise honed in the 1940s via the horrors of war. From 1961, dozens of unmanned and then manned missions built up the experience necessary to make that final tiny step for mankind. Progress was made, incrementally. Rockets exploded along the way, and astronauts died.

A few brief examples, via a list of the programme's launches, is worth quickly summarising, to show the iterations.

Saturn I, October 27, 1961. Test of Saturn I first stage S-I; "dummy upper stages carried water".

QTV Little Joe II, August 28, 1963. Little Joe II qualification test – the "launch escape system".

Saturn I, September 18, 1964. "Carried first programmable-in-flight computer on the Saturn I vehicle; last launch vehicle development flight"

Saturn IB. August 25, 1966. "Suborbital flight to Pacific Ocean splashdown. CM heat shield tested to higher speed; successful SM firings."

Apollo 1. February 21, 1967. Saturn IB. "Never launched. On January 27, 1967, a fire in the command module during a launch pad test killed the crew and destroyed the module. This flight was originally designated AS-204, and was renamed to Apollo 1 at the request of the crew's families."

Apollo 4. November 9, 1967. "First flight of Saturn V rocket; successfully demonstrated S-IVB third stage restart and tested CM heat shield at lunar re-entry speeds."

Apollo 9. March 3, 1969. "First crewed flight test of Lunar Module; tested propulsion, rendezvous and docking in Earth orbit. EVA tested the Portable Life Support System (PLSS)."

Apollo 10. May 18, 1969. "'Dress rehearsal' for lunar landing. The LM descended to 8.4 nautical miles (15.6 km) from lunar surface."

Apollo 11. July 16, 1969. "First crewed landing in Sea of Tranquility (Tranquility Base) including a single surface EVA."

In between: various other test flights, going further, or trying something different. Several further astronauts died.

None of these things were easy. None could be achieved overnight. And none could be done without a huge amount of teamwork. NASA estimates that nearly *half a million* men and women across the United States were involved in the Apollo programme. It was about the least-easy thing humankind had ever done (unless you're a crazy conspiracy theorist who thinks it was filmed by half a dozen people in a Hollywood basement; or a crazy activist who thinks it a shameful example of the evils of colonialism, presumably displacing all the indigenous Clangers in the process).

I mention all of this, as it feels like Liverpool have spent their past dozen years on various missions, all barely possible, but some inexplicably achieved. To win the quadruple, however, would have been like the Apollo mission, back in 1969, boosting from the moon, orbiting Mars, slingshotting Saturn, and depositing a kidnapped President Nixon into the gaseous hellscape of Jupiter, where he probably belonged.

The whole Liverpool/Klopp project looked in jeopardy at various points between March 2020 and March 2021, when football was mothballed due to Covid on the brink of title success, over £100m was lost due to empty stadia and television deal repayments, and then the team, replete with a few ageing players, appeared to be on its knees due to a run of injuries and illnesses. It felt nearly broken. That Liverpool were able to 'go again' from March 2021 onwards, to the degree they did, was itself a minor – maybe even a *major* – miracle.

Before getting onto the actual football that gave so much joy, it's important to establish the *context* of what was achieved.

Richer Rivals

In the dozen years since Liverpool Football Club gained new owners (from the brink of bankruptcy), Chelsea continued to spend big, and Manchester City further skewed the difficulty levels.

Newcastle United joined the party in late 2021, so by the time the Reds went to St James' Park in the run-in to 2021/22, the Geordies had gained the richest owners in world football, and already spent almost £100m in the January window (a record, albeit not when adjusted for inflation), to make the task of the visitors all the more difficult. Just to make it even harder, BT Sport had managed to schedule this away game for 12:30pm on the Saturday, having just shown Liverpool on Wednesday night in the Champions League semi-final first-leg against Villarreal, ahead of showing them again on Tuesday night. No wonder Jürgen Klopp was always unhappy about how hard the broadcasters make it (in contrast to other countries), even if, of course, their money helps to make the Premier League the strongest in the world.

There is a sense in English football of the smaller clubs – and even the broadcasters – wanting to sabotage the bigger clubs, as seen with the retention of the three subs rule, which had been expanded to five subs all over Europe. Yet there seems to be no distinction between big clubs that are well run and big clubs that are badly run or financially doped.

Bizarrely, during Sky's commentary for Liverpool's penultimate game, Martin Tyler said that they "support the underdog", then literally mumbled something not even half-arsed when Takumi Minamino scored; genuinely sounding like someone had died. Yet with Southampton having nothing to play for, and Manchester City the title favourites, he seemed to be talking down a title race, with Liverpool needing a win to take it to the last day of the season. Instead, rather than just do his job of making goals at both ends feel exciting, he sounded crestfallen. (Manchester City fans don't like him either; maybe he should return to not worrying about who he is perceived to support or favour, and just sound like someone *enjoying* football, like Peter Drury and others.) A few weeks earlier, Tyler had decried the big clubs wanting and finally getting five substitutes (for 2022/23), when it took *at least* 14 clubs to vote in favour of it – presumably as the 'little 14' saw how many injuries they were clocking up. It was not a decision made by the Big Six.

In England, the 'little 14' tend to vote to do anything to hold the bigger clubs back – as they had initially on the five subs ruling used across Europe – whilst also keeping the Championship clubs locked under a trapdoor and in financial peril, as they did with the outrage over Project Big Picture (PBP). The greed is no more exclusive for the Big Six – lost in the future over PBP and the European Super League (ESL) – with almost everyone in the Championship gratuitously overspending in the desire to get rich via promotion, and the teams in the bottom half of the Premier League playing dull survival football just to retain their place on the gravy train. (Which isn't to say PBP and ESL weren't flawed in other ways.) The game's finances are in a mess, from top to bottom, with just a few sensible, sustainable clubs (including Liverpool), and a few with owners so rich that, while they remain in charge, will always be able to dole out problem-solving money.

Going back to April 30th, Klopp had to rest Mo Salah, Fabinho, Trent Alexander-Arnold and Thiago, amongst others, at Newcastle; and rest even more at Southampton, which was scheduled just days after the cup final.

Newcastle had won their previous four league games, as part of a run of wins that extended to 10 in 2022 alone, to take them from bottom to above mid-table; indeed, only Liverpool had won more points than Eddie Howe's men in the year so far. This was not a good *time* to be facing the Geordies, in any sense; with the lunchtime kickoff just another spanner in the works.

Yet it proved a relative stroll, with 24 shots by the Reds to just four by the hosts (a shot-count that would be eerily replicated in the Champions League final), to gain a 1-0 win marred by poor finishing, but never allowing Newcastle a sniff of goal. Joe Gomez excelled at right-back, and James Milner, who spent the mid-part of his career on

Tyneside, patrolled the midfield some 20 years on from his Premier League debut.

I've written for 18 years – it first struck me in 2004 – that the week of the six-day Champions League semi-final/league game/semi-final (or the same sequence with the quarter-finals) is often the breaking point of many ambitious and indeed, *superior* teams, when going for both domestic and European honours; back then, it was for Arsenal's 'Invincibles', caught out by an improving Chelsea side pegged as underdogs, who themselves were caught out at that point in 2005, in some game where some bloke who drinks Sangria managed by a fat Spanish waiter (according to rival fans) upstaged the dominant domestic team of the season in Europe, on the way to glory in Istanbul.

But so far, not Liverpool. In 2019 and in 2022, these pinch points did not prove costly, even if a fresh Spurs did spoil the party days *after* Liverpool reached the Champions League final with a second victory over Villarreal. (This was the second time Spurs denied the Reds, after an extended period to prepare for the game.)

While this game came too soon, Newcastle represent a serious new danger: another stomach-churning finance machine that could squeeze a properly-run club out of the top four places, so that outrageous wealth – from vile regimes – begets more outrageous wealth, as well as the trophies adored by sportswashers. It's depressing, and yet, at the same time, a *challenge*.

Statistical Contortions To Pretend City Aren't Much Richer Than Liverpool

Sometimes you'll read a sentence *so bad* that, even when trying to take it easy for a while after a testing winter (as I am), you end up writing a piece to counter it. This, courtesy of the *Manchester Evening News*, may as well have been written in Abu Dhabi:

"Liverpool won the title for the first time in 30 years after recording the biggest transfer spend in a calendar year in English football history, in 2018."

Now, I hate net-spend arguments, as I've noted many times, and made clear in the book *Pay As You Play* from 2010. But gross-spend arguments – as this is – are the *worst*.

Net-spending arguments can be twisted by arbitrarily (or sneakily) moving a cut-off point; for instance, only start counting the day *after* Man City spent £100m on Jack Grealish, and suddenly *they didn't spend any money at all on Jack Grealish*.

Hey presto! (Yet he was magically there all along.)

Everton massively outspent Man City in the first half of 2022, so Everton should be better, right? No, because gross spend is dumb, and net spend is semi-dumb. Inflation-adjusted XIs (the '£XI', as I dubbed it), are what counts, along with inflation-adjusted squads. That's the average cost of the team over the course of the season, in what would today be 2022 prices; as such, you can compare a team from 1993, 2006 and 2019 and all will be in 2022 money, so all can be compared on an equal footing.

Indeed, net spend in *the calendar year*, before the summer 2022 window opened and they spent big, saw Man City having raised £43m on Ferran Torres. You wouldn't say City's chances were nosediving in 2022 as they were -£43m on outlay for the months January-May. That made them the 'poorest' team in England, based on that wayward accounting. In truth, they were just offloading one more luxury asset.

Gross-spending arguments take the same flawed approach and make it even worse, by ignoring what money came in. It ignores the sell-to-buy that all clubs, unless financially doped, have to live by. Both net and gross calculations also tend to ignore inflation, which means that a massive historical but still relevant spend – say five years earlier – could be trumped, but the original cost far more in 'real' terms due to the fact that transfer prices generally rise.

So, in 2016/17, the average price of a Premier League player was 18x what it was in 1992, when we began our index (not that *football* began then, but we had to start somewhere). But this season, the average price has risen to 30x what it was in 1992 (having actually fallen to 27x in 2020/21). So an £18m player in 2017 effectively cost £30m in the current market. Average prices sometimes fall, but the general trend – in line with rising income in football – sees them increase.

When Klopp said at the time Paul Pogba joined Manchester United that he'd never spend €100m on a player, it was a time before a 66% price hike in Premier League transfer fees. Pogba's fee now equates to almost £150m, and in addition to the drain of massive wages, he walked away for free. As such, £64m rising to £85m (€100m) for Darwin Núñez was not *astronomical*. Indeed, in the Premier League era, Andy Carroll remains the Reds' most expensive signing in 2022 money, at £135.5m.

Both net and gross spend arguments ignore the state of a club *before* the arbitrary cut-off point: did they need to spend money, or had they spent the past few years shelling out tons to perfect their squad?

The key fact to all this – to counter the distortions from the *Manchester Evening News* – is that in 2018, Liverpool sold Philippe Coutinho to Barcelona for £142m; as well as offloading Danny Ward for £12.5m and Ragnar Klavan for £2m, while losing Emre Can (who needed replacing) on a free transfer. (All fees listed when discussing prices relating to TPI are the *maximum* amount payable, so including clauses that may or may not be triggered, but which are in the initial contract.)

That's £156.5m *recouped* during 2018.

The money was reinvested in Virgil van Dijk, £75m, in January 2018; and in the summer, Naby Keïta (£52.7m), Fabinho (£43m), Xherdan Shaqiri (£13.5m) and Alisson, (£64.4m). That's £248.6m, which is clearly huge; but less than £100m *net*.

One of the reasons for co-creating the Transfer Price Index with Graeme Riley in 2010 was to look at how much *teams* cost (the team that plays, and the overall squad), based on transfer spending, adjusted for football inflation. (Andrew Beasley is now helping to track the data, and Daniel Rhodes is creating some Tableau vizzes for *The Tomkins Times* to help present the information; albeit I don't like filling books with tables and graphs.

These were the top four inflation-adjusted squad costs in 2021/22:

1 Manchester City: £1,300.2m. (Or £1.3 *billion*.)
2 Manchester United: £1,148.7m.
3 Chelsea: £1,018.6m (including £228m out on loan).
4 Liverpool: £784.8m.

As you can see, City's squad cost was 65.6% more expensive than Liverpool's, and the £XI was 47.2% higher. Based on the talent that *started games* (which factors in absences due to injury, as well as those not selected to start for other reasons) the £XIs were:

1 Manchester City: £705.4m
2 Manchester United: £537.5m
3 Liverpool: £479.2m
4 Chelsea: £353.1m

Wages are obviously another big factor, and City obviously top the wage-bill chart, too, albeit Liverpool, with a lot of bonuses built in, also carry a big wage bill. Wage analysis can be more accurate than the £XI if based on company accounts, but often until then, wages can be wildly varying rumours, and a club's official wage bill is usually at least a year out of date. (It can also include hundreds of office staff, with Liverpool apparently employing 686 people in 'admin and commercial', three times as many as Manchester City, who somehow make more money.) What we've shown for 12 years is that the £XI often tracks with league position to a fairly strong degree, even if there will be outliers, good and bad.

The sale of Coutinho was seen by a lot of Liverpool fans as a sign of impending doom. Less than three years earlier, Liverpool had lost Raheem Sterling to Man City (at what works out now at well over £100m), having had Luis Suárez pilfered in 2014; and now the club were losing another key player.

That's where Liverpool were between 2010 and 2018 (and indeed, a process that began *before* 2010, under the shambolic ownership of George Gillett and Tom Hicks): unable to retain their elite talent, as they didn't have the financial power to pay mega-wages, but instead had to manage the wage bill in a way that maintained unity. In order to buy, some selling was usually required. Also, the Premier League was lagging behind *La Liga's* giants until fairly recently, which made losing players to Real Madrid and Barcelona a constant threat. European rivals will still occasionally do so. Even now, Bayern Munich have snaffled Sadio Mané, but only at a price Liverpool agreed to, at a time Liverpool agreed with (i.e. a player aged 30, entering the final year of his deal and seeking a bumper final payday).

What has changed is losing contracted players to English rivals. A year after a neck-and-neck title race in 2014, Liverpool lost a key player to Manchester City. Liverpool's rise under Klopp and FSG has seen that threat diminish.

When Raheem Sterling moved to City – essentially taken against Liverpool's will – the average price of a Premier League player was £7.4m; now it's £18.1m. Sterling therefore cost almost £120m with inflation. Kevin de Bruyne – a player who can be misleadingly represented as a cheap buy – works out at £133m; while the recently retired Sergio Agüero cost £177m – albeit the only City player to rank in the top 20 in the Premier League era, which is comprised almost entirely of Chelsea and Man United players from 2001-2016. If you were to only look at net or gross spending since Pep Guardiola arrived at City, it would not include the £250m of talent in Sterling and de Bruyne, as well as the players who helped win titles up to 2021, such as Agüero. The starting points were radically different, with so few of the players Klopp inherited worth keeping long term (or 'poached', in the case of Philippe Coutinho).

What City have, with so few homegrown and free players, is a squad packed with expensive players, many of whom cost big money a few years ago, but that big money, as an illusion, seems smaller now unless inflation-adjusted. (City, in contrast to other big spenders over the years, simply don't have many cheap players at all.)

For instance, it would be crazy now to say that Stewart Downing was a cheap signing for Liverpool, because a decade ago, *£20m was a lot of money*. Right now, £20m is peanuts. Yet from 2012, with inflation, it now equates to £93m; someone who cost c.£30m in the 2000s – as a few players did for Chelsea and Manchester United (Andriy Shevchenko, Wayne Rooney, Rio Ferdinand, Michael Essien, Didier Drogba and a bit later at £50m, Fernando Torres) – is now the equivalent of around £200m (which is where the 'actual' European transfer record maxed out just a few years ago, before the biggest signings abated, in part as FFP partially applied the handbrake).

Perhaps what has changed is a greater number of expensive signings, and fewer *super-expensive* signings; certainly in the Premier League, with excesses curbed by FFP. When we devised TPI in 2010, FFP had yet to take hold. Now it would seem unthinkable to spend £200m on a single player and stay within the allotted budget if building a *team* rather than just a vanity project around one individual; but that's essentially what was happening in the 2000s. Chelsea had a number of £200m players, as did Man United.

The most recent signing in the TPI top 20 is Agüero, at 7th, while Man United's procurement of Paul Pogba and Anthony Martial both make the top 20. Otherwise, even £100m last summer is not as outlandish, *relatively speaking* (and the whole point of adjusting for football inflation is to make things relative), as the deals taking place prior to FFP.

(For the sake of this book, '2022 money' is based on transfers in the summer of 2021 and January 2022; before the next season of signings takes place and concludes at the end of January 2023. Also, our inflation model only focuses on Premier League signings to calculate present-day money, so cannot accurately measure overseas spending – but the European transfer market still generally operates in the same way, certainly at the top end.)

Football – amongst the sensible clubs – has also become less about superstar individuals, and in fairness to Man City, they are a prime example of a system of interchangeable players, who almost all cost a *lot* of money, rather than marquee players.

Even now, the few players who *might* cost £200m are retained by the big clubs that own them, or are about to be available in the summer on free transfers or reduced buyout clauses. Indeed, holding onto such players – as PSG have done with Kylian Mbappé – is almost the same as paying £200m, as they did for Neymar (and almost as much for

Mbappé), as they are essentially writing off £200m; only an oil state could afford to do that.

Manchester City have 17 players who cost at least £33m in the TPI model; they have 15 players who cost £46m or more; 13 players who cost £56m or more; 11 players who cost £62m or more; six who cost £80m or more; and three who cost £100m or more.

That's the crux.

City's 17th most expensive player (İlkay Gündoğan) cost £33m, roughly the same as the Reds' 11th most expensive; yet the biggest indicator of the gulf is that Liverpool's 15th most-expensive (Andy Robertson) cost £11m, whereas City's cost £46m. Only Phil Foden was free, otherwise there's Oleksandr Zinchenko (and reserve keeper Zack Steffen, who played one league game); the next-cheapest are £39.3m, £46.1m and £47.7m.

If you compare the £XIs by position – averaging out the costs of the different players used from 1-11 by the old numerical system from back to front – then there are eight where City's players cost more, two where Liverpool's cost more (goalkeeper and left centre-back) and one where the price was the same (centre-forward). Alisson was far more expensive than Ederson (by £46.3m), but even Virgil van Dijk 'only' cost £18.8m more (in 2022 money) than the average of the various City players fielded at left centre-back. (Liverpool's other three centre-backs, in 2022 money, cost just over £41m combined.)

The differences in the other direction – City's players averaging out as more expensive – were, from right-back forwards, to the tune of £53.6m, £50.1m, £32.9m, £27.0m, £11.9m, £28.1m, £39.0m and £15.7m. City had Foden to Trent Alexander Arnold in the homegrown stakes, and Zinchenko, who cost about the same as Kostas Tsimikas, but that was it; there was no Joël Matip (free), James Milner (free), Curtis Jones (second academy graduate to play more than a handful of games), Harvey Elliott (cheap), Joe Gomez (cheap) and Andy Robertson. There were no *gambles* in the City squad. Each signing was a kind of luxury. When Liverpool pay bigger wages (albeit still just over half of what City's top earners receive), it's because those players have proved themselves to deserve pay-rises, along with performance-related bonuses. City can pay more initially, and then reap the rewards of the quality they pay for.

It seems a little sad that so much time is spent on analysing the finances of football these days, but the reason I focus on it is because it clearly makes a difference. When City's clear financial advantages are obfuscated, it needs addressing. And how City are financed is also somewhat unsporting.

Apex Predator

For all City's mega-spending since 2008, how many of their best players were whisked away from them at their peak? None. (Leroy Sané *might* qualify, but he was going to be sold the previous summer anyway.) Ferran Torres went to Barcelona, but only as City were willing to sell.

Imagine losing Kevin de Bruyne to Real Madrid, or Ederson to Barcelona, two or three years ago, and having to replace them, with the 50-50 chance that the replacement won't be a success. Imagine that, a few years before that, David Silva and Vincent Kompany were bought by rivals when at their peak. City have never had that issue in the modern age.

Yes, City will give their players the chance to always play in (if not *win*) the Champions League, and will challenge for the title. But an unseen sign of their power is how they can fend off all predators. They are the top of the food chain, and how they do it – indeed, how they got their money to start with – isn't always palatable.

City are a super-smart operation with a world-class manager, albeit one who left Germany having bored the Bayern Munich hierarchy. City don't *have* to entertain neutrals, but there *is* something sterile about them, as noted by several people in the media that got the blue half of Manchester so riled. They stack the deck in their favour, that it stops feeling like *sport*. As many noted (and I'll cover later in more detail), only Liverpool keeping an unexpected pace with City made the league feel competitive.

Guardiola won more in Germany than Klopp, but Dortmund were literally bankrupt when Klopp arrived, and what he achieved – against all odds – will be remembered for longer, as Bayern are a monster of a machine, who were chugging before Guardiola arrived and chug exactly the same after. Guardiola changed the style, but essentially added nothing new. Indeed, managers before and after him won the Champions League with the club, and a lot of observers, including some of Bayern's hierarchy, found his football duller. Klopp took Dortmund from near collapse to back-to-back league titles and a Champions League final with a young, inexpensive team, who played exciting football. I've never quite understood the accusations that Guardiola's sides are *dull*, but the reduction of risk can add to that impression. He is indisputably an elite, generation-defining manager; the best in the world – *until* 2019, when Klopp's deeper, tougher-won achievements, with a broader skillset, saw him rise to the pinnacle.

Klopp has taken Liverpool much further, from a starting point of mediocrity, than Guardiola has taken City (albeit he *has* improved them, clearly), whose players had mostly already won the Premier League by 2016. That said, Guardiola, domestically at least, can't easily take City any further than he already has done. He's already broken all kinds of records (albeit Liverpool's 97- and 99-point seasons remain more incredible based on the budget and the starting point, and the 97- and 92-point seasons when also reaching Champions League finals are unique in European football history). Guardiola also had less scope to improve City, whereas Klopp was taking over a side that, for 15 months, had forgotten how to win, how to score, and how to defend, and whose few best players were soon injured or snaffled.

Adam Lallana spoke to BBC Radio 5 Live's *Football Daily* podcast towards the end of 2021/22, and explained how Klopp keeps everyone happy: "I know how difficult it is when you're not playing or not in the squad, it's tough because you want to play, and you're paid to play. But football is a team sport and everyone is needed and they had to put in a big shift. That's the culture and mentality of the group. You keep training hard and trying to show why you deserve to play – and hopefully you get your chance. Klopp is the best motivator I've ever spoken to, within a minute of speaking with him, you want to be fighting for your life for him. That's the genius in him."

"His empathy, his human nature is unbelievable," said Tim Hoogland, who played for Klopp at FSV Mainz, and who said that 14 years on he still hears from his old boss. "That's something that hasn't changed from when he was my coach in 2008 to now. His human skills were way above everything I've ever seen in football. It's not something you see very often."

Klopp is also incredibly *smart*, in a whole host of ways. He is the ideal person to bring together all the different disciplines at Liverpool, in a way that possibly no one else could.

It's hard to say that Liverpool can easily capture hearts and minds, given the enmity that exists in football fandom, but I think a neutral (or if the labels were removed from both clubs like unmarked cans in a taste test) would put Liverpool's European and Premier League ride of 2018-2020 above any period of Man City's dominance given the more thrilling and unexpected nature of it; just as Leicester's league title trumps anything else in terms of expectations; just as the *nature* of Istanbul in 2005 tops anything anyone can do, as an underdog 3-0 down at half-time. The same would apply to Liverpool's quadruple chase, which far outstripped any City season for excitement, even if the end results were 'just' the two domestic trophies.

Alas, Liverpool could not ride out Covid in the way that City or Chelsea, with their petrodollar ways, could (although Chelsea had a rude awakening in 2022). That's a fact of life. Liverpool have turned many cheap and mid-priced players into world-beaters (this is the model), but to pay them all the going rate would cripple the club.

The wage bill, with sensible bonuses, already has little room for leeway, but even to give Mo Salah £400,000 a week – as he seemed to be seeking in the summer of 2022 – would mean he would be on *double* what everyone else was getting, and would likely see £100,000 added to the demands of all players to follow. That's how wage structures spiral out of control. That Sadio Mané will be paid almost that much by Bayern Munich will only strengthen Salah's claims (as others arrive in the Premier League on almost £400,000 a week), but Liverpool's response is to pay Darwin Núñez a 'mere' £140,000 a week; which itself is more than Luis Díaz and Diogo Jota are paid, but still less than the existing key men (and all three combined will earn less at Liverpool than Mané alone will at Bayern, albeit Jota and Díaz will surely get pay rises whenever they sign a new deal). Núñez could have got far more at Manchester United, but he made a footballing decision, not a financial decision; as did Virgil van Dijk, when arriving on a wage that did not match the transfer fee.

Liverpool also cannot find themselves with souped-up sponsorship deals that make them the biggest earners in the world. City, for all their intricate brilliance, continue to do it with *all the money*, and in that sense, you almost can't blame them. (You *can* blame them for any financial chicanery, mind, that has been exposed several times by *Der Spiegel* amongst others. As was reported, "Manchester City owner Sheikh Mansour bin Zayed al-Nahyan would allegedly 'rather spend £30m on the 50 best lawyers' and sue Uefa 'for the next ten years' than accept their punishment," in relation to breaking FFP rules.)

As I always said about José Mourinho: let's see how he does *without the money*. It's like the fastest person in a cycle race – while the rest may take EPO and pedal away as hard as their legs will pump, they're competing with the guy on the rocket-boosted Kawasaki Ninja.

Even with a big budget at Manchester United, *some* money at Spurs and a fair chunk at Roma, Mourinho is diminished by both time – staler ideas – and the lack of having *twice as much money as everyone else*. His Chelsea squad from a decade and a half ago still remain by far and away the costliest in English football, when adjusted for inflation. City can take comfort from the fact that they didn't distort the market in quite the same way as the arrival of Roman Abramovich. (Mourinho is now down to finishing 6th in *Serie A* after a big spending spree at Roma, crowing about winning a brand new European competition created *specifically* for the mediocre sides. This is not *Sassuolo*, even if the Roma fans did enjoy the ride, and that's fair enough from a fun perspective – but not an achievement perspective.)

Another example: *uninflated*, Tanguy Ndombele (£65m at the time) cost Spurs more than any fee Man City had paid for a single player up to that point; yet to claim that therefore Spurs were a richer club than City would be madness. If you take inflation into account, City have spent that type of money or much, much more on many, *many* occasions. And they still benefit from several of those players; indeed, 11 at £62m or over when adjusted for inflation. Yet this is the logic Man City's mouthpieces seem to use to obfuscate their spending.

As many have noted, the only thing keeping the Premier League title race interesting is Liverpool's amazing overachievement on what is a sizeable but, by comparison to City, much smaller budget. (Again, Liverpool are not *poor*, and FSG invest all the money back into the team via transfer fees and wages, with the latter increasing in line with increased revenues from over-performance on the pitch, to create a virtuous circle.) Maybe Liverpool make it more interesting for City, too. Yet the neutrals can see the relative shallowness of City's achievements; often only enjoying the fact that the generally disliked Liverpool (due to decades of dominance two generations ago) are the team being denied.

Dan Kilpatrick of the *London Evening Standard*, who usually covers Spurs, wrote in late May, "… apathy is an increasingly common response to City's relentless quest for perfection and growing dominance of the Premier League leads to bigger questions about the impact of state-backed sportswashing projects on the game.

"Put simply, it is harder to be emotionally invested in a club when the odds are so overwhelming stacked in their favour by virtue of pouring a state's resources into the sport. While impressive and a result of more than wealth alone, City's sporting achievements appear lacking in both jeopardy and the sense of strife and a journey which characterises, say, Liverpool's successes.

"Guardiola has claimed that most would prefer Liverpool to win the league. On this, he is surely mistaken, although not for reasons he would care to admit. The majority of rival supporters would prefer City to be champions, purely because their unparalleled financial might makes their feats seem inevitable and even meaningless.

"While it would be unbearable for many to see Liverpool win another title, let alone a quadruple, City are easier to ignore.

'They inspire so few real emotions in many supporters, they have actually become a useful vehicle in denying rival clubs the title. Manchester United fans are largely happy that City stopped Liverpool winning another league; Arsenal fans supported them over Tottenham in the 2019 Champions League quarter-final."

Kilpatrick then takes a deserved dig at an infamous Liverpool FC marketing slogan, which I always found crass, but even then, he sees some truth to it: "Liverpool understandably antagonised with their slogan 'This means more', but in the context of their rivalry with City, there is truth to it.

"There is an authenticity to Liverpool which makes them emotionally arresting, and that simply does not exist with their title rivals, so Guardiola has it right in one sense (that a majority seem more appreciative of Jürgen Klopp's side) but wrong in another (that this results in a desire for Liverpool to better City).

"City inspire a kind of apathy of hopelessness in most supporters, which is obviously not a healthy attitude on the part of football fans.

"This is one of the most alarming consequences of sportswashing projects: they are robbing the game of the meaning and emotion on which it is built."

Miguel Delaney wrote in the *Independent* a few days earlier that, "The Catalan [Guardiola] has spent the last few weeks complaining that more people wanted Liverpool to win the title, but it's hard to think that is true. The debate around the [Liverpool fans'] booing of the national anthem at Wembley fed into the fact there does remain a resistance to the Anfield support. Many neutral fans would have preferred City preventing Jürgen Klopp's side winning the title, the domestic treble and a possible quadruple."

As an aside, this resistance to Liverpool and their fans was later seen in the dumbly tribal online reactions to their outrageous treatment in Paris, which included the tear-gassing and pepper-spraying of children, just for *queuing to get in*; yet again blamed when clearly innocent, albeit this time it took social media (one of its few positives) to reveal the 'truth' rather than 30 years of requests, protestations and inquests. It's yet more ammunition to the sneering 'it's never your fault' brigade.

Delaney continued: "That would have been too much for many to bear. City winning the title, though? That's just something that happens now, to a super-funded level that is by this point as akin to an industrial process as sporting perseverance. The money makes it easier to accept as inevitable, so it consequently leaves many football fans fairly emotionless.

"That only points to bigger discussions over the very nature of this sportswashing project, that have only grown in recent years. This is not to repeat arguments that are by now well rehearsed, but it does mean City are curiously fitting champions in that regard.

"This has been the most geopolitical of seasons, and they are the most geopolitical of winners. It just emphasises what is happening to the wider game, as made clear by the futures of Erling Haaland and Kylian Mbappé.

"Consider some of the scenes on Sunday, that themselves evoked key themes from the season.

"Premier League chief executive Richard Masters was there to present the trophy, at the same time as his competition continues an investigation into City over potential rule-breaking. Masters had earlier presided over a hierarchy that just waved through the Saudi takeover of Newcastle United, as soon as issues relating to broadcasting piracy were finally resolved. You couldn't have a clearer indication of the priorities.

"The recent controversy over Newcastle's third kit [in Saudi national colours] only made farcically obvious the absurdity of that decision, particularly the ludicrous talk of 'legally binding assurances' over separation of the Public Investment Fund and the Saudi state, but that was already long after the Chelsea situation [Roman Abramovich being sanctioned by the UK government after the war in Ukraine] illustrated some of the dangers of all this."

Later in the piece, Delaney added, "The Premier League is currently in a position of unprecedented financial strength, with that largely built on the glamorous image of being the most unpredictable league in the world. The wonder is how long that view will actually persist, as City claimed their fourth title in five years. It is a little disconcerting to think that it would have been five from five had it not been for Liverpool appointing a genius.

"Jürgen Klopp has reshaped the reality of the game, but that has in turn kept the illusion of competitiveness. Even Liverpool, an undeniable super club who are on the brink of their seventh Champions League, have had to push themselves past their limits to keep up with City. And it still wasn't enough.

"The gap of a point is at once a tantalising illustration of how close Liverpool again came but also a show of how City will almost always be ahead."

Eamonn Sweeney in the *Irish Independent* was scathing about City, in an article entitled *A classless man in charge of a classless club run by classless people*.

"Manchester City won the title race but Liverpool made it great.

"Without Jürgen Klopp's side the Premier League would be *Ligue 1*, a championship entirely dominated by a behemoth overpowering all opposition through financial might.

"The football authorities owe Liverpool a debt of gratitude for making the Premier League look more open than it actually is. But all the Sky Sports PR guff about the greatest league in the world can't disguise the fact that this race never includes more than two horses – 18 points separated second and third place this season. Four years ago when City also pipped Liverpool, that gap was 25 points."

Regarding the final game of the season, as the title lay on the line, he said: "… The differing reactions of both sets of fans when their teams struggled in the second half showed why this is so. Anfield was a seething cauldron of anxious excitement with supporters trying to lift their team over the line by force of will.

"The prevailing note at the Etihad, on the other hand, was a kind of sulky disbelief. 'Why is this happening? We didn't pay for this kind of thing.' The contest between City and Liverpool is a contest between the synthetic and the organic. And we live in a synthetic age."

He ended with, "City are the perfect champions for the neoliberal era, true believers in the creed that money makes its own morality. They are football's Facebook, its Twitter, its Airbnb, its Amazon, its one-percenters. But they're not Liverpool and they never will be."

Also from Ireland, where the writers often seem freed of the backslapping and kowtowing seen by some of the English media, Tadhg Coakley, author of *The Game: A Journey Into the Heart of Sport*, wrote in the *Irish Independent* about the soul-sucking nature of sportswashing in general.

"… Kylian Mbappé's disgusting signing-on fee of €150m and an annual salary of €100m, after tax, to stay with Paris Saint-Germain. PSG are owned by the state of Qatar which will host the Fifa World Cup later this year at an estimated cost of €200 billion, but the real cost is in human lives: thousands of migrant workers have died building the infrastructure needed to host the event.

"Sports fans know about the corruption, sexism and inequalities in sport but still we consume it in huge gulps. Why?

"Could it be what French academics Jean-Marie Brohm and Marc Perelman refer to as the 'opium of sport', how it facilitates 'the narcotisation of the conscience'? Is sport really what they refer to as an infantilising drunkenness or narcosis, a type of fiddling while Rome burns (or while the planet is being destroyed by man-made emissions and Ukraine is being bombed to obliteration by Russia before our eyes)?

"Perelman says that sport is society's only project steamrolling modernity, eliminating all obstacles. Society has no other project, he says, except barbarian sport. Everybody is flocking to it and everybody is joining in. This is difficult to disprove.

"The Premier League is the most popular sports league in the world. It is shown live in 212 territories to 643 million homes with a potential TV audience of 4.7 billion people. I'm one of those people, my home is one of those homes.

"In India, 93 per cent of people (1.28 billion souls) self-identify as sports fans, while 70 per cent of people in the USA follow sport and devote an average of 7.7 hours a week to it. In 2016, the financial value of sport was estimated to be $500bn in the United States and $1.3 trillion worldwide.

"The question is: given that sport facilitates such appalling and damaging behaviour, should we avoid it altogether? By our involvement in sport, are we somehow condoning or facilitating so many abhorrent actions? Would we be better off without sport in our lives at all, so we could better manage climate change, the inequalities in Irish society and the crisis in Ukraine?

"But wouldn't that deprive our children of all the joy and togetherness they will experience this weekend and every weekend in Ireland? And the volunteerism in clubs and communities up and down the country which is such a font of wellbeing, good mental health and helping to avoid isolation?

"Perhaps instead of scrapping sport, we should put it in perspective. The French philosopher Pierre-Henry Frangne says that 'sport can only be ethical and virtuous through the moderation of our approach, through the restrained nature of our relationship with it, through the purpose which we confer on it – since it has none of its own, being just a game, a futile activity, even a derisory one'.

"We have to be more like the children Eduardo Galeano eulogises in the epigraph of his book *Football in Sun and Shadow*: 'The pages that follow are dedicated to the children who once upon a time, years ago, crossed my path on Calella de la Costa. They had been playing football and were singing: We lost, we won, either way we had fun.'"

Another Irish journalist, Ken Early, wrote in the *Irish Times* on the eve of City landing the 2022 title, that "Most of us don't watch football for technical quality or tactical intrigue. We're watching because we want to feel something – and the risk of defeat adds savour to the joy of victory. In the simplest terms, we like a bit of end-to-end. No coach despises end-to-end more than Guardiola. His teams are designed to exert the maximum of control and allow the absolute minimum of randomness and uncertainty.

"City are also the best-resourced team, so they have the best technical players, playing the most careful, disciplined, risk-averse football. It's a style better adapted to winning titles than admirers. They would be more charming as a wasteful giant. Look at the joy Manchester United have given the world these last several years. Lurching from crisis to crisis, they continue to be more watchable than City's vastly superior team."

He continued, "… But of course the main problem is, and always has been, the money. City represent the ruthlessly efficient application of overwhelming financial firepower and there simply is not a lot of magic about that story.

"They will soon celebrate their fourth title win in five years, which is not an unprecedented level of dominance: Aston Villa did it in the 1890s, Arsenal in the 1930s, Liverpool twice in the 1970s and 80s, Manchester United three times in the 1990s and 2000s. City fans rightly point out that all of these dominant teams were underpinned by considerable economic clout. But in no previous case was the financial superiority as overwhelming as it is now." [I'd argue that, actually, adjusted for inflation, Chelsea circa 2004-2007 were more financially overwhelming, but the general point stands.]

"For example, during the Liverpool-dominated 1970s eight other teams broke the British transfer record: Tottenham, Arsenal, Derby County, Everton, West Brom, Nottingham Forest, Manchester City and Wolves."

"Money was spread around more evenly, nobody had a decisive financial advantage. Contrast with the weekend, when City's starting XI included nine players who cost £47 million (€56 million) or more – that is, each of these nine was more expensive than the record signing of every English club outside the big six. Is it surprising that nobody can give them a game?

"Last week it was reported that City have leapfrogged apparently much-better-supported teams like Manchester United, Real Madrid, Barcelona and Bayern to become the world's top-earning football club. The news was a reminder that there is one thing City are good at making you feel, and that is the helplessness that comes from knowing that you live in a world where the richest will always get their way, and if you don't like it they will spend £30 million on the 50 best lawyers in the world to sue you for the next 10 years, as someone once said. In that sense at least, City have captured the spirit of the age."

Returning to Delaney's article, he referred to the way discrimination is now being used, somewhat disgustingly, as a smokescreen for legitimate criticism of sportwashers.

"Guardiola even seemed to propagate one of the more cynical new lines of defence that has developed over the last while. That was the portrayal that Abu Dhabi is unfairly seen as more problematic than many from elsewhere.

"'When you put something here [sponsor] it's overpaid, but other [clubs] the money comes from the USA but the money is correct, even if it's higher.'

"It was difficult not to feel that this was of a theme with a more overt line, stated by chairman Khaldoon al Mubarak after City won their own domestic treble in 2018/19. *Liga* president Javier Tebas had referenced 'petrol money and gas money', and Khaldoon responded: 'There's something deeply wrong in bringing ethnicity into the conversation. This is just ugly. The way he is combining teams because of ethnicity, I find that very disturbing to be honest.'

"Tebas had not brought ethnicity into the conversation, though. He had simply made reference to 'state-run clubs', and the reality that the economies of those states – and their immense wealth – are built on fossil fuels.

"Such a defence consequently feels a highly cynical attempt to shut down fair criticism of the nature of these projects, not least because some of the main problems with these states are human rights abuses against their own populations."

Finding the Joy
Can Liverpool fans keep enjoying it, though? I spoke to many, all over the world, for the writing of this book. The consensus seemed to be that the football is great, largely down to Klopp – and that the modern game is fast and exciting – but the wider context is not so pleasant.

Norwegian Jan Ove Knudseth said, "The ongoing war in Ukraine, the sanctions against Abramovich and others, the World Cup to be held in Qatar, Newcastle's new owners receiving a warm welcome to English football and probably a lot more crazy things I don't know about makes it a little bit hard to enjoy football to be honest. The obvious corruption, hypocrisy and double-standards on display in football's governing bodies is disgusting. I quietly enjoy Liverpool FC, and little else about football I guess."

Andrés da Silveira Stein, half-Uruguayan and half-Brazilian by parentage but born in Mexico City in the late 1970s, finds the new media landscape has actually made it easier to be a Liverpool fan.

"I enjoy it more now than when I was young. When I was young I was doing a lot of other things, and access to English football wasn't easy. Football is now one of the few things I do outside of trudging –

working, bah, you know the drill – and because I understand more of the nuances of football, and I can appreciate more what we are doing and achieving over the field. Also, have you *seen* how Liverpool is playing? How can I not enjoy this immensely?"

Erin McCloskey, an American in New York married to a Liverpudlian, and whom I've known online since the start of TTT, said, "What I most enjoy is Jürgen Klopp! Every time he speaks, I'm proud to have him. He's so smart. He's so kind. He's so cool. I adore him in a football sense, but I love it even more when he speaks about the world and current events. He's compassionate and thoughtful, and isn't afraid to offer and explain his opinions.

"The most important thing for me is that I can feel proud of the club. I don't want a dirty oligarch or some dubious oil money, even if it has been proven to purchase success. I want to like the people associated with the club – owners, managers, players – even if it means not achieving the same levels of success. Obviously I want us to win. I want us to be good. I want us to be *great*. But not if it means selling our soul. Pride > Success."

Not all early visits to Anfield go smoothly, for those lucky enough to do so. According to subscriber *Snatch*, "My older brother took me to Anfield as a birthday present. I hated the experience, it was frightening. My mother was not impressed when she found out." It was April 1950, and he was seven years old. "Fortunately I was not permanently damaged, although it was not until I was at secondary school that I went as a regular."

Getting back to 2022, Puvan Selvam travelled from Singapore to Liverpool in late May, just to savour the atmosphere in the city during the final league game and the Champions League final.

"Right before our last Premier League game against Wolves," he told, me, "when the dream of a quadruple was still on, I had a mad image of how crazy the parade would be if we actually did it. And by then it had been confirmed to take place. So I decided to head to Liverpool, catch the Champions League final at a local pub and be in the city centre during the parade. Booked my tickets, managed to convince work on taking some off days and I was off.

"I was conflicted between watching the Champions League final in the city vs. Anfield itself. I opted for the latter, and ended up watching it right next to the stadium in a beautiful pub called The Church. The atmosphere was electric. Though I had to sit there for almost five hours just to keep my seat and view of the screen. Made a couple of friends, some who had travelled from London or Newcastle. But no one mad enough to travel from Singapore to watch it in a pub at Anfield! Just to be there though to hear the songs sung in full voice, was worth it.

"The night ended depressingly of course, and I was in no mood for a parade. But once I got to the city centre, I remember the sun had come up and fans were already out and about from 2pm. What an atmosphere! It was another long wait in the cold, and though the red flares made it extremely difficult to see much of the players I did manage to catch glimpses of many of my favourite players.

"I'm so grateful that I had the chance to do this and though we didn't win the big two, and that slightly underwhelmed it, the chance to watch the match and parade at the heart of Liverpool was an experience that has left me wanting more. I'll be back, and this time I hope it will be a mad title party."

Long-time TTT contributor Abhimanyu Vinay Rajput (*El Indio*) did the same, travelling from his native Bangalore. He watched the title-deciding game in a pub with author and TTT editor Chris Rowland, who would be missing his first European final, having previously attended every single one from 1976 to 2019, and wrote a book, From *Where I Was Standing*, about his experiences at Heysel in 1985. As Abhi put it, "We wandered off past the Shankly Hotel and into the Victoria Cross in Sir Thomas Street, just round the corner from the Cavern Club, where the crowd was gathering as we ordered our first round there. We met an Irish Red who was excited about us winning the league, and had planned to travel to Paris as well."

I too had been hoping to meet Abhi, Chris and one or two others, but my chronic health issues kept me away. The pair met up again for the Champions League final six days later, after Abhi had spent the intervening time touring Britain.

"We called at a Greek restaurant for some solids ahead of the liquid refreshment that lay ahead, before deciding we would watch the game in the Fly in the Loaf in Hardman Street. We got lucky when a group of lads left, leaving a small table we could stand at and put our drinks on – space was already at a premium, and all the seats were taken, it was standing room only. We were in the Fly in the Loaf three hours before kick-off, and it didn't feel any different from attending a match at the stadium. Everyone was in high spirits, and the collection of songs were brilliant – the Gini song, a rousing, passionate *You'll Never Walk Alone*, the Suárez one (*Just Can't Get Enough*), *Allez Allez Allez* and others. We kept our hold of the table by taking turns to go to the toilet – by now it was getting very crowded in there!"

The game ended in disappointment, but like Puvan from Singapore, Abhi wanted more.

"On our way back, there was quite a queue at Central Station to get back to our hotel, but it all seemed orderly. We had another round of drinks at the hotel bar with Chris going with beer and a whisky chaser, but I chose initially not have any before deciding on Gin and Tonic. We spoke about what could have been and tried to discuss Paul's old articles about Stoicism. That helped me recall a conversation from a movie called *Bridge of Spies* where the Russian spy recalls a story about an unremarkable man who stood up to the beatings of the local police. But because he never gave up the police gave up on beating him. We hoped that we would be back next season with similar zeal, and a commitment to be in with a shout of the Holy Two: Premier League, and Champions League."

As frustrating as many aspects of modern football can be – not least the financial doping and sportswashing – there is still so much to treasure about being a Liverpool fan, especially right now. It's just a shame that the team hasn't quite hauled in the trophies it deserves, but it's won a few, as well as plenty of plaudits, and yes, millions of hearts and minds.

Someone who won't give up is Jürgen Klopp. In 2022, the German told journalist Melissa Reddy: "All of us expect that relentlessness from ourselves. None of us are free of defeats, which means we are really used to it as humankind.

"My idea of life is I don't expect anything, I don't take anything for granted – as long as I have a chance, it was always enough for me. And we have the chance obviously to react so let's give it a try. So we felt already how rubbish it feels when you lose so you have to work to get the other feeling.

"When we sang the song [after the Champions League defeat to Real Madrid in 2018] in my kitchen that we'll bring the trophy back to Liverpool and then we actually did it, I think it was pretty special. By the way, this morning my phone reminded me of that memory with a picture of Peter Krawietz and another friend of mine holding a vase pretending it was the trophy. That's when we started creating the song, but it's a good example."

Financial Foul Play
While Liverpool have some of the expertise you'd usually only find at NASA – a small group of physicists who try to find ways to gain advantages playing football – the club is more like 1960s Argentina or Portugal trying to create a space programme to go up against the Americans.

Liverpool have individual owners; Manchester City and Newcastle are owned by *sovereign states*.

Of course, a club like Manchester City won't be short on its own intelligent analysts (one of *The Tomkins Times'* original subscribers, Lee Mooney, eventually became City's senior data scientist, having joined them in 2013 in a role with youth team analytics – but thankfully left the club in 2019, and as such, he is now fully forgiven). But for now, Liverpool have to find ways to outthink and outfox the bigger, financially-doped rivals. The trouble is, the richer rivals also do a lot of things to create marginal gains. It just has to be that Liverpool try to be smarter, off the field and on the training ground, to narrow the gap. A few years ago, prior to winning the title, it was appointing Thomas Grønnemark as a throw-in coach; mocked by the old guard, it proved less about hurling the ball further, but throwing it *smarter*. The old way was just to 'hit the line' – throw it upfield, to gain yardage almost – but that often gave away possession; indeed, at the time, Liverpool were the worst in the top flight for keeping the ball from throw-ins (not helped by being a small team, so hitting the line is a bit futile). So Liverpool worked on ways to throw *infield*, or backwards in order to move forwards. Now many clubs do the same, making it less unique; you don't get long with an innovation before others are copying; and doubtless Liverpool also pay attention to other clubs' innovations. You'd be foolish not to. Yet the Reds take analysis to a whole new level.

American William Spearman is Liverpool's lead data scientist, and unlike Liverpool and football fan Mooney, he arrived in his position via a much weirder route: via the European Organisation for Nuclear Research (CERN).

In an interview with the official Liverpool FC website in 2022, Spearman said, "Unlike many people working in football, I grew up being really bad at most team sports… I still am, and that's probably not a surprise given that I am one of the nerds of the place!"

"I was much more focused on individual sports and science and maths. I was in my early 20s when I first got interested in team sports and I started watching American football. I had friends in Boston and I became a huge fan of the New England Patriots.

"The thing I'd really enjoyed about physics was working on a problem that there's no established solution for. But towards the end of my PhD, I found myself repeating the same type of analysis others had done previously.

"I wanted to work in an area that wasn't as established, so sports data seemed really interesting to me. I was very interested to learn about the work being done in American football and baseball and then I got my first taste of proper football data and that was just fascinating.

"For example, with baseball there have been advanced statistics around for 40 or more years because it's a simpler game with a clear outcome to every play, but with football there is an elegance that is much harder to quantify.

"It's a much more complex sport and that's what makes it much more interesting to me."

Spearman explained the difficulties of analysing football. "You've got 22 players on a large field. There is a high degree of coherence to their interactions yet it is individual brilliance that is often decisive.

"In American football the play starts and stops and you can measure what happened at the end of it. But in football, goals are relatively rare so you have to try to quantify how you get to those places where you can score.

"You look at things where you don't have a distinct outcome, you look at things where it's not clear if it was good or bad. It's just a beautiful game and you can enjoy it on so many levels. Just watching it, it's great seeing the fantastic goals and the great passes, but it just has so much depth to it.

"As I started playing with the data and watching as a fan I fell more in love with it and over time it became the primary sport I was interested in, pretty quickly supplanting my initial interest in American football."

On a whim (as you do), Spearman created a model relating to 'pitch control'. "Over a weekend me and a friend decided to look at space, because football is a game of space, and we ended up putting together a model of pitch control," he says. (Clearly space is where the club's astrophysicists *should* be looking.)

"I looked and I hadn't seen people doing something particularly similar. I showed it to some of the football analysts at Hudl and they thought it was fascinating and suggested I present it publicly.

"That's actually how I met Ian, Tim [Waskett] and Daf [Dafydd Steele, both of Liverpool's research department] for the first time, in 2016 in London…"

"I was extremely nervous because I was in a room with people from Liverpool, PSG, Barcelona and whatnot; people who know more about football than I could ever possibly know!

"I was getting up there showing stuff that I'd largely just worked on for fun for a week or so. But it was something people were really interested in, despite the fact that it was pretty early doors.

"I realised then that by coming at this from a new perspective we can really develop some interesting ideas on the mathematical modelling side with the data. It was really exciting."

Pitch control, he explained, is "basically … the regions of the pitch that one player or a team are in control of.

"So, if a team were to try to pass to that point, that team would be in control. It shows how you can close off space, how you can create space with runs.

"It's the fundamental notion of how you control space and how space is valuable. We call it 'off-ball scoring opportunity', which is an extension of the idea of pitch control."

"… With the tracking data I'm able to answer a lot of the same questions as you can with event data, but usually with a lot more context.

"For example, in event data you can't really say if a back-pass was a good idea or not because the ball is moving away from goal, which doesn't look good. But the tracking data will tell you whether the player was under pressure at the time. Was he opening up a passing lane forward by passing back?

"You're able to get the context that provides much more clarity."

The article also explains that "Spearman deciphers tracking data on Liverpool and opposition players in games, writes a statistical view of every match and delivers this to the club's analysts, who in turn present their report to Jürgen Klopp and his coaches."

This seems vital: the decoding of complex data into everyday language that can be understood by non-quants. This is where someone like Michael Edwards and, as of the summer of 2022 (albeit he built up to the role in the second half of 2021/22), Julian Ward, can help as Sporting Director: bringing the various disciplines and odd bedfellows together.

The article continued, "Spearman also works on bespoke data projects with coaches and analysts, and the data produced by his model is consulted and evaluated during the Reds' player recruitment process."

"I work in the scouting office," Spearman noted, "and having conversations with the very smart guys there has really helped my understanding of the game and the development of the model too."

There are other ways where Liverpool are looking to get ahead. In late 2020, with the Reds' reigning champions, Ben Rumsby wrote in the *Telegraph* about "artificial intelligence specialists DeepMind and the Premier League champions' in-house research team have joined forces in a move that could lead to football clubs' selection, tactics, transfer policy, and even training techniques, all being dictated by machines.

"DeepMind and Liverpool have recently co-authored research on the potential use of AI in the game, which states their 'overlying goal' would be the development of just such technology.

"The research, entitled *Game Plan: What AI can do for Football, and What Football can do for AI*, envisages the creation of an Automated Video Assistant Coach (AVAC) to analyse match footage and 'accordingly advise coaching staff' – including while a game is still ongoing."

The article notes that, "The credentials of Liverpool's contributors to the research into AI and football are almost as impressive.

"Ian Graham, William Spearman, Tim Waskett and Dafydd Steele are widely regarded as the best team of their kind in the English game following the record-breaking run that saw the Anfield club crowned champions of England for the first time since 1990.

"Graham, Liverpool's director of research, has a PhD in theoretical physics from Cambridge University, Spearman is a Harvard University graduate who worked at the European Organisation for Nuclear Research, Waskett is an astrophysicist who specialises in coding, and Steele is a chess champion.

"The quartet were already at the cutting edge of the use of AI within the game and are now looking to boldly go where no-one has gone before."

It's clearly not going to turn players into robots, but will help to see things in a clearer light.

"In one example of what AI methods could do, the researchers combined statistical analysis with game theory to devise penalty-kick strategies based on individual playing styles, including how they move on the field. In another example, they used computer vision and statistical analysis to compute the best predicted trajectories for players to take as they ran down the field and looked for situations in which a player's actual movements deviated significantly from this predicted trajectory."

This is all cutting edge stuff, but it still needs the humans to decode it, to explain it, to coach it, and ultimately, to *play* it. Until we pay to watch robots, and unless we're seduced only by PlayStation football, it's still 11 vs. 11.

With one game of the 2021/22 season left, Jeremy Wilson wrote in *The Telegraph* about the technology Liverpool now employ to reduce injury risk (albeit it can't predict a flying idiotic goalkeeper with little arms). "Invented by the artificial intelligence company Zone7, who are based in California's Silicon Valley, Liverpool have been using cutting-edge computer algorithms that both detect injury risk and recommend preemptive action.

"It all helps to explain why manager Jürgen Klopp chose to rotate nine key players in beating Southampton on Tuesday night, barely three days after needing 120 minutes to win the FA Cup.

"It perhaps also helps to explain how Liverpool have slashed their number of lost days this season to injury by more than a third and retained such remarkable performance levels across 61 games.

"The Liverpool men's first-team squad have been using Zone7's technology since the start of this current 2021/2022 season. The platform analyses comprehensive player information, including in-game and training data, as well as biometric, strength, sleep, flexibility and stress levels to create risk signals and practical interventions, all aimed at improving performance while lowering injury rates."

Wilson spoke to Tal Brown, the chief executive and founder of Zone7, and explained the CEO's history: "... Brown was a first-class graduate of computer systems engineering at the University of Warwick before starting his career in the Israel Defence Force's Intelligence Corps. His team have long been designing predictive software in other industries, ranging from cyber security to financial services, and began working in football four years ago. They duly gathered millions of hours of data from more than 30 teams worldwide, including Getafe, Glasgow Rangers and Hull City.

"In its quest to identify patterns that might get missed by purely human analysis, the algorithm provides information at various levels, from football as a sport through to teams and individual players. It is designed constantly to update and improve with new data."

Brown told Wilson: "The software can simulate optimal scenarios on a day-by-day basis so that the players are trending towards their peak and injury risk is minimised. Sometimes risk may mean a reduction in workload – less running of a specific type like sprinting. Sometimes a player can be undertrained and additional work may be required."

Zone7's philosophy, Brown told the newspaper, has been to also employ people with experience inside professional football, so as to make sure people understand the game, and that the information is rendered comprehensible. "These are Premier League veterans – it's not just a couple of people from Silicon Valley running around with spreadsheets. It was a long process to create adaptations that make the software usable in a football environment. Football is not stock trading and neither is it anything else out there on a professional or human experience."

As noted in the piece, "According to Premier Injuries, a company which analyses injuries across England's top-flight, Liverpool have recorded vast improvements this season. They have so far lost 1,008 days to injury, compared to more than 1,500 in 2020/21. Crucially, the days lost to what are deemed 'substantial injuries', which are those lasting more than nine days, have almost halved from 1,409 to 841."

More commonly cited were German neuroscientists *neuro 11,* who joined in partnership with the club in 2020, but only really got going in 2021, after Covid restrictions ended. Co-founders Dr Niklas Hausler and Patrick Hantschke said that they try to help athletes improve precision and get 'in the zone' by reaching their optimal mental state, achieved through the addition of brain activity-scanning skull masks, commonly seen on the AXA training ground for set-piece takers (but also, anyone else interested).

While it helped during the season, and with penalty shootouts, the set-piece delivery in the Champions League final – on the biggest of big occasions – let Liverpool down, with the clear aerial dominance over Real Madrid totally untapped.

One thing *neuro 11* cannot do is totally eradicate nerves – like AI, they cannot make players less *human* – but over time, it will surely be more of a help than a hindrance, in becoming a bit less fallible.

Struggle

The *struggle* keeps things interesting, but also, there does remain a sense of injustice at how the big trophies go to sportswashed clubs. We need to embrace the struggle, for now at least.

Cheats and bullies are harder to beat, but doing so provides the sweetest victories.

As Viktor Frankl, the famous holocaust survivor turned psychiatrist, philosopher and writer, said: "What man actually needs is not a tensionless state but rather the striving and struggling for some goal worthy of him. What he needs is not the discharge of tension at any cost, but the call of a potential meaning waiting to be fulfilled by him."

Climbing Everest

In May 2022, TTT subscriber Murtaza Khan wrote on the site:

"To climb Mount Everest, you need a Sherpa. A true battle-hardened hero. The knowledge and experience required to build as safe as relatively possible path to the peak. I recall a visit to the Himalayan Mountaineering Institute in Darjeeling, located in the Eastern cradle of the Himalayas, a few years ago. The Institute was set up to commemorate the first successful ascent of Everest by Tenzing Norgay and Edmund Hillary. Perched on top of a hill the 'climb' up there was tiring, for me at least.

"During the visit we met a young woman who had scaled Mount Everest. She was no taller or bigger than my 12-year-old sons yet had scaled the gargantuan rock. Her achievement was punctuated by the Sherpas, who guided her and her group. It was amazing to our boys that 'a girl climbed a mountain'. Their mum told them with the right mindset and people anything was possible in life. That finding the right 'sherpa' could help seed and grow success. Wise words from my better half. They often are.

"When you look at Jürgen Klopp it's not a giant leap to imagine him in his mountaineering gear. His face weathered, eyes beaming and that spontaneous smile against the Himalayan backdrop. Where he leads you follow because he has inspired and motivated you to do so. There is no compulsion, I feel, with the German. His tradecraft has not been welded together in heavy metal rather human nature.

"I used the term *Gesamtkunstwerk* on how the German, like a composer of an opera without an ending, is guiding us up Everest again. The journey is different each time and this season is one you cannot conceivably plan for. But we adapted to the challenge. Any transformation of a team or organisation must have culture at its heart. The footballing *Gesamtkunstwerk* Klopp initiated in 2015 has, with FSG and our people, is reaching its peak again. The German's work of footballing art will never be the prettiest, but its theme of artistic synergies and dysfunction allows Klopp to somehow create something stunning to those who understand its context, timing, and co-contributors.

"The coaching spine running through the club is as strong as ever. If you rewind a few years back Klopp kept reminding us that Jon Achterberg was fantastic. Today the statement is read as fact. Even Cláudio Taffarel's arrival did not raise my eyebrow as it could have once done. Peter Krawietz or Pep Lijnders are the bedrock of Klopp. Krawietz is Klopp's companion whilst Lijnders is a next generation coach. Each contributing to Klopp's *Gesamtkunstwerk* with the young Dutch coach's leadership and vision more and more influential from the outside.

"As Klopp leads us up familiar terrain the evolution of Liverpool is not some grand secret. The Neu Schuhraum is the force of inspiration for the creativity we are incorporating in the team. Their work transformative. It's a higher satisfaction and almost cathartic release viewing his own seven-year work. Now Klopp is staying he will be immortalised at Anfield for generations to come as a seminal piece in

Footballing *Gesamtkunstwerk*. A man who climbs the tallest of mountains with a smile and determination on his face."

* * *

Whether it's climbing Everest or shooting for the moon (not to be confused with a Kepa Arrizabalaga penalty), Liverpool can only keep trying; keep up the struggle. As fans, we need to enjoy the ride; especially as there aren't really any other managers in world football who can do all the things Jürgen Klopp can do, including how his in-check ego allows all kinds of collaborations. It can't last forever, this delicious chemistry. The club will likely be in a position of real strength when he finally leaves, but some of his qualities will be irreplaceable.

The football is often on a totally different level, and we have to embrace that, and try to ignore the laughter from rivals about slipping up, finishing 2nd, failing to land the quadruple, and so on. We have to keep choosing to go to the moon, not because it is easy, but because it is hard.

How the Autopsy of Black Swans Became a Celebration of Overcoming the Odds

In hindsight, 2020/21 was perhaps the most traumatic season for Liverpool FC, and perhaps the city as a whole, since Hillsborough in 1988/89. In the spring of 2022, the *Echo* reported that "More than 1,700 Covid-19 related deaths have been recorded in Liverpool since March 2020." Though not as scandalous or avoidable – or as directly related to attending a football match – more Liverpool fans died than in April 1989; and some of them as a result of attending the Atlético Madrid game in March 2020. Most of the city's Covid deaths occurred during the winter when Jürgen Klopp's mother Elisabeth died, in January 2021, and he could not return to Germany for the funeral due to lockdown restrictions. A month later, Alisson Becker's father, José Agostinho, out for a swim in Lavras do Sul in their native Brazil, tragically drowned, aged just 57; again, Alisson could not attend the funeral.

It's easy to forgot the jolts to society of the first lockdown in 2020 and widespread fear, and subsequent struggles. Even though it ended up being delayed, Liverpool fans at least had the league title to celebrate, even if it couldn't be *properly* celebrated. Perhaps part of the issue with 2020/21 was the sense of a crisis having passed, only to think, *Oh no, here we go again.*

On the pitch, the football was grim. During this time, in an empty Anfield, the Reds – with a home record prior to Covid that proved record-breaking – lost *six* league home games in a row. It felt soulless and depressing, going through the motions in the middle of a pandemic that had only just started to be eased by the first rounds of vaccinations, with stadiums – full at the start of the season – now just endless rows of plastic seats.

Top of the league in early 2021, many months *after* the season-ending injury to Virgil van Dijk, a full-blown injury crisis and Covid chaos precipitated a run of just three wins in 14 games, to drop to 7th by the time Fulham came away from Anfield with three points in early March. Despite beating Red Bull Leipzig home and away, 2-0 each time, a makeshift defence could not keep Real Madrid at bay in the quarter-finals, with the 3-1 defeat at the empty Alfredo Di Stéfano Stadium the sole loss since Fulham's success on March 7th. Even so, Liverpool were ahead in consecutive games against Leeds and Newcastle before Diego Llorente in the 88th minute and Joe Willock in the 96th minute (at Anfield) respectively snatched improbable equalisers. With just four games to go, Liverpool were 6th.

A game against Manchester United in April had to be postponed after rioting, with the Reds' team coach targeted by protesters, in the wake of the Super League proposals and United's own finance-leaching owners.

All in all, it was a horrible time, with solace to be taken from the fact that "football is the most important of the least important things", a quote attributed to just about every football manager in history. It helped that, out of the chaos of the season, Liverpool rallied just enough to secure a top-four place, with some incredible moments even with grounds still empty.

Speaking to a number of local-based journalists including Paul Joyce of the *Times* a year after those darkest moments, in the group's first informal meeting in two years due to Covid restrictions, Klopp summed up how demoralising, depressing and draining the early months of 2021 had proven. He reflected on what was missing. "When you don't have it, you realise. The atmosphere, for example.

Sometimes it is not that good in a stadium. That doesn't really happen for us, but if it is the case you think, 'Why was it like that?'

"But if you have [had] no atmosphere, you take each atmosphere [even if it's not that good]. In some moments, it was the hardest time of our lives – at least our football lives – because you are still Liverpool but with half-cut wings. You try to fly but it is pretty difficult."

With the death of his mother, and the tragic drowning of Alisson's father, it had to be up there with the hardest part of their lives, full-stop; a squad full of players separated from loved ones in other countries and on other continents, and perhaps in the midst of a serious Covid outbreak.

"I am an emotional coach," he continued. "We are an emotional team, we are an emotional club. We are not like a little bit here, a little bit there. We need this extra bit. That was obviously not there and it was not helpful in the most difficult situation we had. Injury-wise, it was absolutely crazy.

"That is why I always say, after winning the Premier League [in 2019-20], winning the Champions League [in 2019], winning other cup competitions, finishing third last season comes next pretty quickly because that was incredible how we did that in the end. We were pretty much on three wheels, getting somehow over the line.

"It was an incredibly intense season and, yes, I was more than happy for a holiday. For the first ten days, I didn't take out the phone one time, or whatever, and ask, 'Could we have this player?' I couldn't have cared less at that moment.

"Why should managers be different [from other people]? But for all of us it was the same. We were all really drained. Just finished. Done.

"I never thought more about football – and I think a lot about football – than in this period. That was really tough, while everyone was talking about the former champions and now the worst-ever defending champions."

The injury crisis was so extreme that even the 3rd- and 4th-choice players were injured in certain positions; at one point, arguably the 7th and 8th choices for centre-back were being fielded. At that point, it becomes almost like roulette.

"… It was so hard. You don't have solutions player-wise because the [injured] players are just not there, so how can we keep the others confident through that and until the moment when we are in a different moment? It's not cool. I would go home and think, 'That's why they pay me that much money.' In other moments I still don't understand why they do it, but in these moments I think, 'Ah, yes, that's why it is.'"

The highs returned in 2021/22; indeed, the run-in to 2020/21 was, as Klopp suggests, a major joy. Yet it's worth noting how much adversity the Reds faced in Klopp's fifth full season, and how – as long as it doesn't totally break you – what almost kills you often makes you stronger.

The Bevy of Black Swans

The "Black Swan": that event so freakishly rare you rarely see them; the term made famous by Nassim Nicholas Taleb.

As I noted throughout a dark season – with some of that analysis revisited here – pretty much the only swans seen at Liverpool Football Club in 2020/21 were of the jet-black variety (with all the sheep mysteriously that colour too; and you couldn't cross a street without seeing a black cat run across your path).

In this bizarro world, perhaps there was also a proliferation of white widow spiders, pale crows and albino jaguars; and of course, throw in some pink giraffes and green elephants, just to make it all the more trippy.

Time was running out – just two games to go after the match at West Bromwich Albion, which, in the 94th minute, stood at 1-1. The Champions League qualification dream was over, with just time for a late corner.

What happened next genuinely rates as one of the greatest single moments in the history of Liverpool Football Club, for various reasons. It was unique; it was late in the game; it proved pivotal; and not only was the goalscorer a 6,000-1 shot, and the situation a 100,000-1 shot, it came with the emotional release of a grief suffered that, due to global travel restrictions, could not be exorcised via normal means.

The cross came in, and Alisson Becker, initially unsure whether or not to go up for the corner, made a late run into the box.

For the first time in nearly 6,000 games of football in Liverpool's history, and perhaps getting close to 100,000 top-flight games in England since the inception of league football in Victorian times, *a goalkeeper scored the winning goal* (as well as, I believe, becoming the first to score at that level with a header – most of them have been either long clearances that caught the wind, or the occasional stab-home in a mêlée. It's also worth noting that, less than a year later, another Liverpool goalkeeper scored the winning penalty in a cup final shootout).

As I wrote, "Indeed, as the corpses of Black Swans littered the Anfield area in this era of plague and pestilence, we got to see something even rarer: a flying Golden Griffin, complete with gloved talons, as Alisson Becker channeled his inner mythic beast to head home the goal that potentially earned the Reds in excess of £50m and, more importantly, the *cachet* of elite football – and most vital of all, the chance to win next year's Champions League (or, to at least enjoy some big Anfield nights that transcend the Europa League)."

In that moment, the last living Black Swans fell from the sky, dropping dead to the ground. It will never be Jürgen Klopp's most celebrated achievement, but it could be his most impressive.

Worth

In the end, Liverpool couldn't quite land the 2022 European crown (not helped by the chaos caused by UEFA, the French police and stadium officials), but came mightily close. Many more great nights were indeed written into folklore, and after the loss of around £100m in income during Covid, the £14m for qualification was ramped up to many multiples of that amount. Excluding all the additional income from ticket sales, etc., the prize money worked out at £72.4m, split as follows:

- Runner-up - £13.93m;
- Semi-finalists - £11.23m;
- Quarter-finalists - £9.52m;
- Round of 16 - £8.62m;
- Group stage wins - £2.51m (x6);
- Group stage qualification - £14.05m.

Diagnosing Disaster

The lessons of 2020/21 were vast and varied. At the time, working out what was going wrong – in a football sense – in a season when so many factors were having an influence was almost impossible. I compared it to trying to diagnose one specific illness from an inexhaustible list of symptoms. I went through the situation at the end of 2020/21, and in this section I revisit, update and expand my May 2021 post-mortem of a season that came back to life just before the tying of the toe-tag (whilst also comparing it to what happened afterwards, in 2021/22). What could have been the endgame instead became a reset.

At the time, people would pick one simplistic (and often incorrect) thing and focus on it; such as: "Thiago slows Liverpool down".

Yet this didn't explain why, during the midseason slump, the Reds were still creating good chances from open play – just a) *missing* them (was that Thiago's fault?); but b) no longer creating them from set-pieces (and he neither took the corners, nor was expected to be on the end of them).

A graphic from a few months earlier (January 2021), at the peak of the 'Thiago slows Liverpool down' nonsense, showed that he made 10 progressive passes per 90 minutes; the next best of all Premier League midfielders were Jordan Henderson and Kevin de Bruyne, at seven each.

To put this in context, in his second season, Thiago rated in the 99th percentile for progressive passes (and the 99th percentile is the highest percentile possible). More surprisingly, he ranked way up in the 98th percentile for progressive carries, which means driving forward with the ball, without necessarily dribbling past players (his dribbling percentile was 62nd). Also 98th percentile was his passes attempted rate, and he had 80th percentile or higher for shots, assists, shot-creating actions, pass completion, tackles, interceptions and aerials won.

Critics saw the addition of Thiago – or rather, his understandably rusty return after several months out after Richarlison had studded his kneecap less than two (extremely impressive) games into his Liverpool career – coinciding with the slump, but didn't note the loss of the third and final major centre-back as a far more decisive moment; especially at a time when Nat Phillips and Rhys Williams had one Premier League start between them. At that point, Liverpool were top of the league.

Both rookie defenders came into the side earlier in 2020/21 and had harrowing games that perhaps suggested they were not ready for the deep end; but while they appeared to be drowning, they were simply learning to swim in a very public pool. They were thrust into a side that had survived the season-ending injury to van Dijk, but once Joe Gomez and Joël Matip also had their seasons ended by early January, Liverpool were almost in a no-win situation.

The choices were: barely-tested rookies; midfield stand-ins; or new recruits who were likely to need time to adapt, and certainly weren't going to be in synch with the Reds' defensive line, drilled to cohesion season after season at Melwood (and then, from November 2020, the AXA training ground). The club also did not want to invest money in a short-term solution that it could not then easily offload if a flop, and where – as when waiting for Virgil van Dijk – someone much better could be available in six months' time. And he was: Ibrahima Konaté. Imagine if Liverpool had plumped for Ozan Kabak on a *permanent* deal instead of waiting for Konaté?

Playing Fabinho (and even Jordan Henderson) at centre-half made sense in that the others did not appear ready; Kabak, who arrived in an emergency loan deal with only an option to buy, was himself only 20, and had to get up to pace with the Premier League with zero time to adjust. (He did pretty well considering, even if he didn't quite convince the higher-ups at Liverpool that he was ready for that permanent deal. My personal concern was that, at 6'1", he was just too short for the Premier League in that position, in a team that needed some tall players to compensate for all the talented smaller ones.)

More strangely, Ben Davies arrived from Preston, but was also only 6'1", and while a talented ball-playing centre-back in the second tier, he had never played a Premier League minute. (Eighteen months on, and, on loan at Sheffield United, he still hasn't.) Liverpool were cash-struck after Covid, and as such, £500,000 for Davies may have been a worthy gamble (at the very least, he could be sold for a profit back to the Championship), and Kabak's option to buy, even at reduced price, was wisely allowed to expire.

Of course, with Liverpool's two giant defenders out, to play the 6'2" Fabinho and the 6'0" Henderson – still below average for centre-backs in the Premier League – removed height and heft from midfield, while keeping them in their normal positions would have helped stabilise in that sense; but relying on Phillips, Williams, Kabak and Davies also felt like the heart of the defence would be weak in one sense or another. Liverpool had fit midfielders, so moving Fabinho – excellent as a deputy in the role prior to 2021 – had its logic, even if it had knock-on effects. Of course, Henderson, having played there quite a bit, lasted just a few minutes of the Mersey derby as a stand-in centre-back in February before *his* season was also ended. At this point it was becoming a farce. Gylfi Sigurðsson scored the game-killing penalty late on, to seal Everton's first win at Anfield since the dawn of the dinosaurs (aka when Duncan Ferguson last played).

Thiago had his ups and downs in early 2021, after returning from near open-knee surgery performed by a snarling Richarlison, but slowing Liverpool down was never true. Yes, he made too many fouls, and at times his lack of pace (and fitness after injury) caused 'optical' alarm – he appeared to be too sluggish – but he always made the ball do more forward-thinking work than any other midfielder in the country. Plus, he returned, after months out, to a side that had already started to struggle. As the season unfolded, he increasingly bossed games. Vitally, as the campaign progressed, he was once again able to have a bodyguard in Fabinho – although he continued to battle for the ball and win a surprising number of headers.

Such an explanation – Thiago was the problem – ignored that lack of stability at the other end, with a different goalkeeper and centre-back pairing almost every game. Liverpool used a staggering *twenty* different centre-back pairings, and a mind-blowing *thirty* different rearguard trios (goalkeeper/centre-back/centre-back).

Losing van Dijk was huge, obviously; but did not derail the Reds. Thiago returning in the winter did not slow Liverpool down, but equally, he wasn't at his best. Such narratives also ignored ten or twenty other important factors.

They ignored injuries to the two main goalscoring midfielders from open play: Alex Oxlade-Chamberlain and Naby Keïta; the only two who would run ahead of the strikers.

That pair also happen to be elite pressers, too. (As I noted regarding his pressing in May 2021, "Keïta remains the best at the club, but he needed to get an injury specialist to sort him out. He remains a fantastic player, but at this stage cannot be relied upon. I wouldn't write him off, but I wouldn't bank on him either." My view is that you try to limit the churn in the transfer market, and work on getting talented fringe players to challenge for starting berths – as seen at Manchester City in 2021, with İlkay Gündoğan, John Stones and João Cancelo, amongst others whose form completely switched; a year later, the unwanted and apparently hitherto available Bernardo Silva, Aymeric Laporte and Raheem Sterling returned to their roles as key men, having been pegged for exits).

Another elite presser was Diogo Jota, the league's best marksman in terms of shots on target per game, who missed three months. Indeed, in just two games (Everton and Midtjylland), Liverpool sustained *four* serious long-term knee injuries. These two games alone cost Liverpool c.100 appearances (from Virgil van Dijk, Thiago, Jota and Kostas Tsimikas: three *major* players, and one much-needed backup, as Andy Robertson ran himself into the ground to the point where he ploughed a deep furrow into the left-flank of the Anfield turf).

The narrative ignored how Liverpool were not being given penalties (an ongoing trend since a freakish 12 were won in 2013/14), but were conceding them at an unusually high rate (a new trend, which seemed to be ignored; but when they *weren't* being conceded a season later, it was flagged in the media). Despite doing two-thirds of the attacking, the Reds conceded more penalties in the season than they won. That should not be happening, based on all logic, for the third-best team in the league at the time.

The four teams vying with Liverpool for the top four each won between 9-12 league penalties, ranking #1-4. Liverpool ranked joint-7th, level with several other clubs, to mean that every single season had seen Klopp rank lower on penalties won than league position (as did Rafa Benítez), while every single season in the top flight had seen Brendan Rodgers rank higher in penalties won than league finish. (This even continued in 2021/22.)

While that may be merely coincidental in Rodgers' case, there is this very weird pattern that I spotted years ago where not only do British players get favoured in both boxes by referees (based on in-depth studies we've undertaken at *The Tomkins Times* with world-class data analysts), but the teams of British managers seem to fare much better too – it certainly applies to Liverpool: Benítez, lower every year; Rodgers, higher every year (ditto Dalglish and Hodgson); Klopp, lower every year.

In 2020/21, for the second season running a relegated team won more penalties than Liverpool, who had the best *attacking* xG figures in the top division. Again, this makes no logical sense. I also wrote that "no opposition player has been sent off at Anfield for several years now", and that provided another turnaround in 2021/22: Reece James (handball on the goal-line), to go with two red cards for opponents in away league games (and a few more in the other competitions).

The Difference Officiating Can Make

Some huge decisions went against Liverpool in 2021/22 – key ones that may have cost the title – but on the whole it felt like an improvement from some recent seasons. It felt limited to a few outrageously bad calls, rather than repeated moments of madness?

One thing we have shown on *The Tomkins Times* over the past few years is how officials from the north-west give fewer big decisions to the Reds, and that the closer to Liverpool their hometown, the more apparently 'biased' they are; as if, actually, it's a bend-over-backwards bias that is so prevalent in modern society (trying too hard to look unbiased, as the optics are all that counts: you have to appease the masses rather than the specific).

In the spring of 2021, with the help of subscriber *CVT123* (a leading analyst at one of the world's biggest companies), I looked at years of detailed data on referees and decisions for the Big Six clubs dating back over half a decade. (I also studied all Premier League penalty decisions going back almost a full decade.)

The three least-generous refs were all ones when officiating Liverpool matches (i.e. each referee was included six times, one for each Big Six team), and most referees – when it came to their treatment of Liverpool – ranked towards the foot of the table. The only active referee who is even remotely generous to Liverpool is Michael Oliver, whilst the older the refs are (and the more north-west their place of origin), the worse things get on average.

(Note: data was correct up to March 2021, and as such, no further penalties or red cards were awarded in Liverpool's favour in 2020/21. In fairness, Anthony Taylor did award one, but Paul Tierney, as the VAR, overruled it.)

And Liverpool tend to get most of the big decisions that favour them away from Anfield; and of those given at Anfield, most are not at the Kop end, with the Kop kryptonite to referees, who will be scalded by opposing managers and social media for being soft at Anfield, and being influenced by the Kop (things that *may* have been true in the 1970s and 1980s).

Indeed, in April 2022, Frank Lampard, as Everton manager, trotted out the cliché that I've been noting for years: British opposing managers sharing Kop myths, and talking with emotion that contradicts fact. Lampard said: "It [Matip and Anthony Gordon clashing] is a penalty in the second half. I don't think you get them here." It was ironic as, in both 2017/18 and 2020/21, Everton's Dominic Calvert-Lewin was awarded ultra-soft penalties, and you have to go back many more years for Liverpool to get a league penalty in the derby. Lampard was charged by the FA for his comments, especially as he said that Mo Salah would have been given the penalty.

(In a press conference in the spring of 2022, Jürgen Klopp would quote some further research we published on TTT – this time with the help of an Oxford University data analyst – that showed that Salah averaged a free-kick award every 100-120 minutes, season after season, compared to one every 20-40 minutes for many similar types of player. In other words, he was deemed to have been fouled just once circa every 1.3 games, despite being the league's most productive player.)

This overly harsh treatment by north-west refs would explain why, in a season when north-west refs undertook most of their games due to Covid-19, the officiating got even more punishing; along with the loss of the home-team bias that refs generally are proven to show. While we must all be aware of our own biases, we must also be aware of bias overcorrections, which are about appeasing the masses (and image-conscious bosses), and not being honest. We have to correct for our biases, but not *overcorrect* to look virtuous and just.

Outrage on social media leads to a lot of accusations of bias in all areas of life (and sport), and so people veer towards anti-bias virtue-signalling; being biased has become a great sin, and so often the urge is to overcompensate. People will accuse Mike Dean of favouring

Liverpool, yet he remained a nightmare for the Reds in terms of big decision balance (excluding VAR interventions). Dean gives tons of penalties – the most of any referee in recent years – but up to the end of 2020/21 he had given none for Liverpool, and two against (one was outside the box and moved into the box by VAR, but he gave the foul when Fabinho cleanly won the ball). It was only in his final season, 2021/22, that he finally gave Liverpool a penalty, for a blatant handball at Brighton, albeit having already failed to send off (or even book) their keeper, Robert Sánchez, for a remarkable neck-high challenge with hand and knee on Luis Díaz.

In fairness to Dean, the north-west's Paul Tierney should have intervened as the VAR on that occasion, but incredibly, did nothing. Tierney – as referee – had also derailed Liverpool's 2021/22 title bid at Spurs in December, not thinking the outrageous shoulder-barge on Diogo Jota a penalty and not seeing the lunging, two-footed Harry Kane 'tackle' on Andy Robertson as a red card, but somehow seeing Robertson's lesser foul later in the game (also a red) as worse. Pretty much every neutral in the media found the officiating beyond bizarre. Tierney had also made such a huge blunder – albeit made worse by Manchester's Chris Kavanagh on VAR – that Professional Game Match Officials Limited boss Mike Riley called both Frank Lampard and Everton chairman Bill Kenwright on 1st March to apologise for Everton not being awarded a penalty in the 1-0 defeat at home to Man City. With minutes to go, and trailing 1-0, the ball clearly – without question – hit City midfielder Rodri on the forearm, yet it was fudged to say that there was no clear evidence that it struck below the mid-bicep (the t-shirt line, now used to demarcate handball after confusion over shoulders and armpits being deemed offside, as parts of the body that could legally play the ball). This allowed City to maintain a narrow lead over the Reds in the league and win the title by one point, but no apology was forthcoming regarding the title race – assuming that the Toffees would have converted it. (An 80% likelihood for most teams.)

The only north-west referee, out of many, to generally seem fair and balanced towards Liverpool (according to the data and what you'd *expect* to see for a Big Six club that does a lot of attacking) is Mancunian Anthony Taylor, whose terrible decision not to send off Vincent Kompany at the Etihad in January 2019 arguably also cost the Reds a title; but where he was clearly put under a lot of pressure, and where it generally seems a rare aberration (not that he's been perfect since, but no one can expect or demand perfection – just *balance*).

I would put Taylor with Oliver and Andre Marriner as the only three refs who are even vaguely 'fair' towards Liverpool, based on what you'd *expect* to see in the data, in comparison to other Big Six clubs and the balance of attacking/defending.

(The Premier League and the PGMOL *may* be aware of which referees favour which teams when appointing them. It certainly *felt* like they were trying to handicap Liverpool in 2020/21, to the point where favourable refs were replaced at the last moment by unfavourable refs in the run-in. That's not to say it's a *conspiracy*, which makes you sound loopy – just that I wouldn't necessarily trust either the Premier League or the PGMOL, with their rampant self-interests. It's also not right to be playing key games in Manchester with a referee from Manchester – they should not be put in that position, but in April 2022, Taylor was again chosen, ahead of Oliver, to officiate at the Etihad.)

My overall takeaway from studying the data for years is that referees should be from neutral towns and cities, miles away from both teams – to remove any hint of pro-bias or bend-over-backwards-bias. (In Liverpool's case, older refs also seem more likely to be swayed by the myths about the Kop winning Liverpool too many penalties.)

Just to be clear, no one should verbally abuse or threaten officials at any level, but the elite level are incredibly well paid and incredibly powerful – able to influence the outcomes of games. They should be accountable for their decisions. Via a quick google, the website *NationalWorld* suggests: "Collected by *Sportekz* and *Sporting Free*, it is believed that Premier League referees earn £1,500 per match on top of their annual salary. Their salary can range from £48,000 to £200,000, as well as a yearly retainer worth £38,500 to £42,000. It is claimed that both assistant referees and video assistant referees earn a basic salary of £30,000 and another £850 per match. Martin Atkinson, Mike Dean and Michael Oliver are currently the highest paid referees in the Premier League with a whopping £200,000 salary. The likes of Stuart Attwell, Kevin Friend and Paul Tierney earn £70,000 a year, while Craig Pawson and Graham Scott are on £48k per year."

Also, in the fittest, highest-profile league in the world, the referees should should not be a bunch of out-of-shape 50-somethings, with Dean admitting to retiring as he was struggling with his fitness – as you might expect, as the game gets ever faster. Indeed, as the game gets faster, the refs had been getting older, which made zero sense (the retirement age of 45 scrapped a few years ago, and other countries don't have these old, plodding refs who cannot keep up with play).

Soon, Martin Atkinson and Jon Moss, both 51, followed suit in announcing that this would be their last season waddling about in black (aside from anything they get up to in their spare time). Statistically speaking, these two refs were particularly stingy in decisions for Liverpool. (Prior to 2015, Atkinson used to give a reasonable amount of decisions for Liverpool. Then, when Steven Gerrard slated him in his autobiography around the time Jürgen Klopp arrived, the decisions stopped overnight. In his 30-or-so league games afterwards, he gave Liverpool one single big decision.)

Amusingly, both will take jobs at the PGMOL within Select Group One: the top tier of officials. Kevin Friend, 50, also retired. After all this, thankfully Mike Riley will also be stepping down as head of the referees, after allowing standards to slip to such an alarming degree.

Home Discomforts

The simplistic narratives around 2020/21 ignored the vital lack of a home crowd, which turned Liverpool's best-ever home record (four years without defeat, which still applies if you exclude three-quarters of a season in an empty stadium) into the club's worst-ever run, in a season which – for the first ever time across the whole top flight – saw more away wins for teams than home wins. Burnley also suffered their worst ever home run, and Everton and Manchester United had their worst home runs for many decades. Manchester City won the league, and lost a fairly hefty four of 19 games at home. However, adding together the previous three title winners (Liverpool, City and City) saw just two home defeats in 57 league games in those three seasons. So, the lack of crowd was clearly a big factor too. Liverpool's home form flipped back to exceptional as soon as crowds returned.

Simple one-fact narratives ('van Dijk...') didn't even cover the way the Reds' preseason in 2020 – already truncated – was thrown into chaos by last-minute changes to the training camp location due to Covid issues. These narratives did not cover the lack of fitness in the squad as a result, and how, with up to a dozen injuries at a time, rotation was harder; and therefore fatigue in the middle of the campaign became an issue for some players in a more heavily-packed schedule.

Andy Robertson desperately needed cover, but his cover – Kostas Tsimikas – got Covid, and then sustained a serious knee injury; and when the Greek left-back was fit again, Klopp essentially admitted he couldn't really change much of the core of the team, due to the ever-changing centre-back pairings (and there was the issue of compassionate leave for Alisson after the death of his father, in a game lost 1-0 at home to Brighton). The manager could have given more minutes to new signing Tsimikas had it not been two rookie centre-halves, who needed Robertson's know-how alongside them, and a settled midfield ahead of them. Robertson was clearly running on empty, but normal rotation was out, as Klopp strove for stability. And he was proven correct to do so, albeit in a gamble that could have gone either way (as is the case with all judgement calls).

The simple narratives do not include the insane balance of VAR calls that went against the Reds, mainly in the periods when the team was struggling. Seven decisions went in their favour, but a whopping *thirteen* went against. Of these 13, some were as clear as day – but about half were barely believable.

Let's Spend Some Time Together
Let me briefly return to my 2019 book *Mentality Monsters*.

"For well over a decade, I've been talking about what I call Shaun Wright-Phillips Syndrome, where a player is taken out of one comfortable environment (where he has had time to grow and develop, in stages, without any intense pressure) and put into an uncomfortable one – in his case, complete with massive price tag at Chelsea – and he looks a totally different player. I may not be the first to have made this observation, but it's interesting that the influential author Malcolm Gladwell is now focusing on this phenomenon, albeit with a different sport as an example. In a 2018 interview with organisational psychologist Adam Grant, which appeared on both men's podcasts, Gladwell discussed the issue of 'fit' – as in *suitability*, rather than physical fitness."

After discussing examples where 'one man' basketball teams had become a bit less successful and how 'average' players looked good when transferring teams (which I include in that book as part of a longer excerpt), Grant said: "... it makes me think of a study of cardiac surgeons where you track their performance across the day and the question is: how many surgeries do they have to perform with minimally invasive robot technology to the point where they are up the learning curve? Practice has no effect whatsoever in this context, they are as deadly on number 100 and 1,000 as they were on number one. This is weird right? Because we are supposed to learn from experience. And so what [Robert] Huckman and [Gary] Pisano did was break down the data by which hospital they were performing surgery and they said: what is the difference in results and practice between Hospital A and Hospital B? And they found that surgeries were hospital-specific, so that every surgery performed at Hospital A reduced the patient mortality rate by about 1% but then later that afternoon the surgeon would go and perform in Hospital B and it's like they are starting over and have none of the experience – and the reason for different performances is the different team who knows my strengths and weaknesses who have developed a set of effective routines. That kind of suggests that performance, skill and expertise is team-specific and context-specific. You see the same thing in financial services companies."

Grant continued: "… over 75% of airline accidents happen the first time a crew flies together; and the evidence goes so far on this that NASA did a simulation showing that if you a had a crew that was well rested and flying together for the first time they made more errors than a sleep-deprived crew who had just pulled an all-nighter but flown together before."

But the benefits of being a settled team has limits, too.

Grant: "The other challenge which in some ways is bigger, is *too much* shared experience, so in the NBA teams max-out on probability of success around three or four years together and then once they have more than four years of shared experience their odds of winning go down."

In the summer of 2018, when previewing the new season, I wrote on *The Tomkins Times* that: "My guess at Liverpool's best XI this season (if everyone plays as expected), if not necessarily my *preferred* side, would have the following full years spent at the club or full seasons in the first-team setup: Alisson (0), Alexander-Arnold (1), Lovren (4), Van Dijk (0.5), Robertson (1), Fabinho (0), Henderson (7), Keïta (0), Mané (2), Salah (1) and Firmino (3).

"That's an average of just 1.8 seasons at the club. It could be seen as a concern in some ways, in that it's not a lot of time to get bonded and onto each other's wavelengths, but one thing Klopp has done at Liverpool is to quickly integrate players, and to create a unified mentality. Indeed, it's been a defining characteristic: specific new signings slipping seamlessly into the team (while others have a bedding-in period), although my theory on the success of this is that, allied to excellent scouting and analytics – as well as Klopp's ability to know what he wants (and convey that to the player) – there's also not been a great deal of churn at any one single moment in time [in recent seasons]."

To focus on 2020/21, Liverpool had been building up a lot of shared time and experience – starting with the Champions League near-miss, followed by the Champions League success and league title near-miss, followed by the record-breaking title win – but it all came apart with injuries and 'churn'. Liverpool added no first-team players in 2019/20 when starting the league better than any team in history over the first three-quarters of the season. But a year later, there was Diogo Jota, Thiago Alcântara and Kostas Tsimikas arriving (followed by Ozan Kabak and Ben Davies in January), and more tellingly, unexpected excessive game-time for Rhys Williams and Nat Phillips. No fewer than *nine* players made their league debuts for the Reds in the campaign, and that's without handing out end of season starts to kids in dead rubbers (as the season went down to the wire). In the end, perhaps Williams and Phillips proved better than Kabak and Davies (in addition to their height) as they were settled; at the very least, they'd spent 1-2 seasons around the first team, training on defensive unity, if not playing matches. The unprecedented injury crisis made for selection churn, and indeed, the procurement of two new centre-backs, neither of whom (like Steven Caulker in Klopp's first window) were going to have time to settle.

Fans want new signings, and they can certainly add impetus. Plus, no club can keep the same team together forever. But in 2021, when the summer window closed, there was unrest that the Reds had only added Ibrahima Konaté (just as there was an outcry at the lack of transfer activity in 2019, as if all the players necessary had not already been acquired). Often elite, experienced players can hit the ground running – Luis Díaz would do so in February – but how much of it depends on the stability of the situation (and team) they walk into?

Take Thiago. He stroked the ball around beautifully for his first game and a half at the club before his horrible injury, in a settled Liverpool team. He looked instantly at home. But by the time he returned in the winter, he was entering a team that contained Phillips and teenager Curtis Jones, then, soon after, young new recruit Ozan Kabak. Thiago, like Harvey Elliott a year later, lost his match fitness and returned undercooked, as all players do – everyone else has months of match-fitness and sharpness in their legs. The defence in the defeat at home to Fulham contained Rhys Williams, Nathaniel Phillips and Neco Williams. Any one of those three players could have been more comfortably carried in a settled, experienced defence, but once you put several rookies or new buys in together, there's not the shared wavelength; certainly when playing at the elite level.

I would guess that, ideally, you want eight players with sufficient shared experience to be close to a strong unit. Otherwise it's then about individualism, not ingrained training ideas. The return to form in 2021/22 was largely about a return to a settled side, even with the addition of a teenager recalled from loan. As happened with about half of the Klopp-era signings, Konaté was eased in very gradually.

Using a more accurate measuring system that didn't just assign 0 to new players for the entire season, but instead added a month with every month played, it's possible to see the differences between 2021/22 and the difficult season before.

In 2021/22, the Reds started the season with an XI with 3.8 seasons spent at the club, with freshness from Elliott, even if he wasn't exactly new. When Liverpool won 5-0 away at Watford followed by 5-0 away at Manchester United, the averages for years spent as a team were 5.2 and 4.4 respectively. (At a similar point of the season, Arsenal fielded a side that averaged out at just 1.1, due to six new players and some academy kids. They were mid-table. Their better later-season form saw the average years spent at the club rise to 2.7, in part due to the half a year every player had accrued, but of course, that meant half a year of increased understanding. They then imploded, but that's Arsenal for you.)

In 2021/22, Manchester City's average fairly closely mirrored Liverpool's, despite City having bought more players in recent seasons. Between game 22 and 33 their average rose to 4.8 and never dipped below 4.0 with the exception of one game, having been much lower towards the start of the season (2.9) as they threw £100m Jack Grealish into the XI, and Phil Foden ousted Raheem Sterling. Relatively new signing Rúben Dias returned for match 33 after a couple of months out, but City remained high on shared experience. In the same run, Liverpool's average peaked at 5.3 shared years, but there were also two lineups with averages of 3.5 and 3.7 respectively.

But in 2020/21, the season's *average* was 3.6. The early-season lineups were full of bedded-in players, whilst the slump coincided with rookies and new signings, to drag the average back down.

Obviously as the season progresses, every team's average time spent together will increase – barring a Newcastle-like mid-season revamp – along with its average age, unless newer, younger players usurp more senior pros (otherwise, the exact same XI will age by 10 months across a season). Across 2021/22 up to and including game 33, City's team averaged 3.9, Arsenal 2.0, Chelsea 3.2, Man United 3.7, and Spurs' had the greatest shared experience at 4.6 years together on average. Liverpool's at that stage was 4.3 years, a healthy level of team-time togetherness.

Elliott, thrown in for the early games aged 18 in 2021/22, dropped out of the picture after serious injury, but then Díaz lowered the Reds' average age and combined years. A lot was made about how quickly the Colombian settled, but at that stage the XIs were averaging almost five years together. He admitted that Klopp told him to just go out and play his natural game, with work to be done in the summer on more detailed tactical work, but it required that stable platform to seamlessly fit in, along with his abundant qualities, and some familiarity with the style of play – he was joining a team who played a generally similar way to Porto, and he was asked to perform a similar role within it. I find it hard to believe he'd have made the same impact signing a year earlier, in January 2021, with so many players injured, ill or off form, after a truncated preseason; albeit he got into the team in 2022 due to Mané and Salah being away at AFCON. Diogo Jota also started very brightly in 2020 (although he had a bit more time to bed in as a sub), but that was before the early winter injury crisis kicked in, to which he also succumbed.

The Biggest Factor

If I had to pick one single factor – or rather, the biggest contributing factor – to the 2021 slump, then aside from often lacking so many world-class players (whose value often exceeded £300m, which meant the Reds had more financial investment in the treatment room than on the pitch), I'd say that a lack of height (itself due to those injuries) was killing the Reds.

Perhaps this is confirmation bias on my part, as an area I fixate on, but *proper* height in the Premier League is so important than even Pep Guardiola began to buy 'big units', to help protect the nifty little playmakers.

In 2020/21, Liverpool's possession stats had not changed much; open-play xG stats had not changed much; and referees were still not giving Liverpool many penalties. But set-pieces at both ends (and an inability to win headers in the middle of the park) were – to my mind – a driving factor behind the late winter woes, and it was an issue addressed in time to coincide with the fantastic revival of eight wins and two draws from the final ten league games.

The fact that the height came from essentially inexperienced, 2nd-tier-level players backs up my hunch that the height (and a bit of *heart*) mattered.

The slip-ups in the slump just happened to be against the 'smaller' clubs, which incorrectly implied that the Reds just weren't up for it; but these smaller clubs had the tall, bodybuilder players that overpowered Liverpool's technicians in the absence of the Reds' enforcers. Obviously an empty Anfield didn't help, but without the fans' backing, Klopp's men – similarly to the small and unremarkable team he inherited in 2015 (the year I'd started pointing out the need for height) – could be physically bullied.

These teams played aerial percentage football that was Liverpool's Achilles heel (if only there was Achilles' *head;* presumably Achilles had one, albeit not the part of the body that caused him problems). These 'alehouse' units played the kind of football that Joël Matip, Virgil van Dijk and Fabinho (as a midfielder) were brought in to combat.

(Much like Manchester City spending big on Rodri to help make them more solid at set-pieces; there were other defensive midfielders they could have chosen, but it was no accident that the Spaniard is 6'3", and an aerial powerhouse. Their set-piece record improved, and in 2021/22 they had the best set-piece goal difference of any team in the Premier League era; albeit they conceded fewer corners than Liverpool due to their more controlled style of play. As ever, set-piece goals excludes penalties.)

The most simple, startling statistic I can find is the disparity between when Liverpool – overall the shortest team in the league in 2020/21 (and by an even greater margin when looking only at outfield players) – were at their smallest, and when they were at their tallest (which even then, wasn't within an inch of the average of the tallest side: Manchester United).

'Shortest Liverpool' had relegation form, over a run of 13 games. Points per game: 0.8, or 29.2 for the season. Or, the same as relegated Fulham.

'Taller Liverpool' had league-winning form, over a run of 25 games. PPG: 2.3, or 89.7 for the season. Or, better than Manchester City.

It's that simple.

(Even if it's *not* really that simple, as nothing ever is.)

But the stats really are that startling.

The problem was, neither Nat Phillips nor Rhys Williams, who were brought into the side, were particularly special footballers. Phillips was – as shown a season later – a first-choice 2nd-tier player (albeit he's clearly improved a lot in the last 18 months), and Williams was a skinny academy player aged 19, full of potential but short on pace. The following season, 2021/22, saw both out on half-season loans to the Championship; Williams' to Swansea cut short after failing to impress, and Phillips' to Bournemouth a lot more fruitful (while his Cruyff turn in his own packed area in the San Siro in December, during one of only three appearances for the Reds in 2021/22, remained a highlight).

What did Williams and Phillips have? Skill? Pace? Passing skills? Dribbling ability from the back?

No. They had height.

As such, which Premier League player ended 2020/21 as winning the most aerial duels in terms of percentage success rate? Rhys

Williams, 6'5". Which player's inclusion in the team suddenly increased the set-ball threat at the other end? Rhys Williams, 6'5".

Nat Phillips, four years his senior – and two inches shorter – was clearly more *aggressive*, and often contested many less-winnable duels. Even that helped, as he won headers in the top 75 percentile for centre-backs; but Williams, full of potential but as raw as they come, was just bloody tall.

Williams won over 82% of his aerial duels, and he contested almost 40. That is an *elite* figure, and the only player I've seen better it in recent years is Matip, with 90% in 2019/20 (from 46 duels); both players didn't play a lot of games, but contested and won a ton of aerials when they did.

Who ranked 2nd in 2019/20? Virgil van Dijk, at 80%. Who ranked 1st the season before? Virgil van Dijk.

As good – and honest – as Ozan Kabak was, my concern when he arrived was that he stood at just 6'1". With Liverpool he won just 55% of his aerial duels, and whilst Fabinho remains good in the air for a midfielder (in that he's tall for a position where there's a far greater spread of sizes, from 5'5" to 6'5"), he's substandard in the air as a centre-back, not least as 6'2" is a fraction below the average height for the position, and he's not especially strong or aggressive in the air.

Most young players improve in aerial duels as they get more experienced and beef up a bit. Their timing improves, their ability to use their body improves, and they gain power from the gym. They become more confident, more dominant. Almost all skills in football are improvable, to the point where age and injuries diminish potential.

But height seems key. For attacking set-pieces, smaller players can get in front of bigger ones, and sometimes time their jumps better. They can find space. But when defending, being tall means that if that defender matches whatever the smaller attacker does (anticipates the ball, moves in time), then there will only be one winner. Equally, at the other end, taller players still have an advantage. One overlooked aspect is how often the tallest draw the attention, for others to reap the rewards. Often a smaller player will score because both teams' big players are marking or blocking each other.

Williams, in what was then a rare appearance, just happened to be standing right next to Roberto Firmino in December 2020 when the Brazilian headed a remarkable late winner against Spurs. That was the last set-piece goal the Reds would score until Williams returned to the side for the final five league games.

The Reds won all five of those games, and scored their first set-piece goal for five months. Coincidence? They also scored their *2nd, 3rd,*

4th, 5th and 6th set-piece goals since the game after that Spurs fixture back in late 2020.

Again, coincidence?

This was after an admittedly Black Swan run of no set-piece goals for five months, where even a smaller player might score a goal, or one may sail in via luck. There was just one more set-piece goal after Firmino's against Spurs in December: the next game, when Mo Salah headed home in the stunning 7-0 win against Crystal Palace, when all thoughts of a slump would seem unthinkable. This was also Joël Matip's last full game, and Matip – 6'5" – headed the assist, before he got injured again in the next game at West Brom (when Liverpool threw away an early 1-0 lead *after* he limped off, and the rot started).

According to TTT stalwart Andrew Beasley, between Salah's goal against Crystal Palace and Diogo Jota's at Old Trafford, there was a gap of 2,383 minutes and 91 set-piece shots without a goal, across a *shit-ton* (my technical term) of free-kicks and 183 corners. The quality of the balls into the box wasn't necessarily different, as both full-backs played all these games – albeit after Covid and injuries, and with Trent Alexander-Arnold looking sluggish until the final two months of the campaign. The balls were whipped into the danger areas, but Liverpool had no height to contest them. Smaller players can score from set-pieces, as noted, but rarely if the opposition's tallest players have no tall players to mark, so mark them instead.

That five-month drought saw Liverpool field mostly shorter centre-back pairings (which in turn meant a smaller midfield, as that's where one or two of the taller players usually started), and unfortunately that meant an increase in set-piece goals conceded, too. The dip in height correlated directly with the slump in results, albeit height won't have been the *only* factor; it just felt like the main factor.

The Reds started the season as the best team (and were top until all the senior centre-backs fell to injury), and after adding aerial prowess to the defence, ended the season as the best team.

To repeat, surely other factors are at play, including that the stand-in centre-backs were not always specialist centre-backs (and when the average height was lower earlier in the season it was with the then elite-paced Joe Gomez, 6'2", who is very average in the air). Yet from the ten league games where the Reds fielded centre-backs who averaged *below* 6'2"/188cm in height, they took just 0.6 points per game, with just one win: against West Ham away. Centre-back pairings 188cm or taller resulted in title-winning form.

Now, while I admit that this is an area of fascination for me, I'm not cherry-picking the data. For many years I've been talking about the importance of aerial duels in English football. I started focussing on it in detail in 2015, when the Reds were the smallest team, and the worst in the air by some distance. Brendan Rodgers wanted his team to play good possession-based football (albeit the style shifted throughout his tenure), but my argument was that unless you were Barcelona golden-era good (2009-2015), you need height, too; especially in the Premier League, where some clubs will defend with ten men and try to win free-kicks to launch into the box.

It's even more important if your strikers and midfielders are superb *but small*. You wouldn't swap Mo Salah for Ashley Barnes (or Thiago for Moussa Sissoko) because one is a giant bodybuilder and the other is a 5'9" genius, but if over 30% of goals in football are from set-pieces, then you end up essentially gifting results to the opposition if you cannot compete on them. Rodgers tried to add height in Christian Benteke, but it was at the expense of quality. (Benteke was excellent at Aston Villa until he suffered a serious injury that robbed him of some pace, so Liverpool weren't buying the player at his best; and he lacked confidence after the high-profile move.)

Remember, Liverpool's 13 shortest starting XIs in 2020/21 scored *zero* set-piece goals, and conceded five, and had relegation-form results.

You don't need to field a tall *team* per se, but you need four or five tall players to handle the aerial onslaughts. In 2019, Pep Guardiola admitted to City's set-piece struggles prior to beefing up the team (and then adding a set-piece coach, to further help).

Rhys Williams – as tall as Matip, and aged just 19 for much of 2020/21 – started seven Premier League games, and the Reds won six of them. Staggeringly, the Reds scored almost 60% of their set-piece league goals *in those seven games* (and the other 40% came via goals or assists by van Dijk and Matip, earlier in the season). Williams was incredibly raw. The age of 19-20 makes for an absolute neonate for centre-backs, where most players (especially what I call Slow Giants) only start to really look the part at 24/25, when they've gained nous to compensate for a lack of pace.

Williams and Phillips both clearly lack pace, and both lacked experience. Both are indeed Slow Giants, and the last thing you want is to pair a Slow Giant with a Slow Giant, unless you want to defend the edge of your own box in two banks of four. So how did they succeed? It seems that Liverpool had enough quality, just not enough height. Ozan Kabak and Fabinho were quicker than Williams and Phillips, yet it seemed that height was the missing factor. While Phillips proved to be the chaos-monster, Williams stood as the unmarkable object. Phillips' aggression helped, without doubt. He was the one that went looking for the duels, and would head a 50-50 even if the ball was on the ground. But Williams is just a giant, and one who will surely only improve in the air with time spent on the pitch (and in the weights room). I was lucky enough to be at Anfield on the final game of the season, when 10,000 fans were allowed back in after months of crowd-less matches, and I really appreciated his composure and touch, as well as how – despite no great leap and no major aggression – he caused chaos in the Crystal Palace area (and Palace were one of the league's tallest teams, as well as being its oldest. You could count on Roy Hodgson bequeathing a team aged 30 to his successor, time after time).

Incredibly, Roberto Firmino outscored Virgil van Dijk from set-pieces between the summers of 2018 and 2021, albeit van Dijk played only two full seasons in that time. Yet Firmino couldn't score from set-pieces *without* a giant or two to act as distractions. It doesn't even need an elite aerial threat like van Dijk, who has power, leap and timing; it just needs some bloody tall kid, to get in the mix. Being 6'4" or 6'5" makes a huge difference to aerial win percentages, and it makes flick-ons at corners all the more likely.

Years ago I went through all the data and worked out that the best aerial win percentages belong, on average, to the very tallest players (if you group them by height, inch by inch), and their success in aerial duels falls in line with every inch lost in height. Peter Crouch was not a wonderful technical header of the ball – nowhere near as fine as Robbie Fowler or even Diogo Jota – nor could he jump that well. But he was (and presumably still is) 6'7", and thus scored the most headed goals in the modern era. Jota is a far superior header of the ball than Crouch, technically, but obviously is best when finding space (often in open play) to head home, rather than going up against someone half a foot taller. Jota versus Crouch in aerial duels would suit Crouch 90% of the time. Jota's headers are rarely first-ball contacts from set-pieces.

When Firmino headed home the diagonal free-kick against Man United in the 4-2 win at an empty Old Trafford, Williams was initially standing right next to him, taking up the attention of *three* tall United players – despite the fact that Williams had no proven aerial ability in terms of heading at goal (as we saw when unmarked against Palace). Three men on (or near) Williams left one player (Paul Pogba) half-marking Firmino at the far post as he stole a march. Go back five months, to when Firmino scored a header at Spurs, and he found the space because he stood close to Williams, allowing an overload.

Come forward to April 2022, and when Liverpool despatched Benfica from the Champions League with a 3-3 draw (having won 3-1 away), the Reds had just four players forward for a wide free-kick, against the Portuguese team's eight. As happens from such an angle with the offside rule in everyone's thinking, all 12 players were almost in a line, along the edge of the area. Luis Díaz was nearest to the ball (and as such, only really there for a flick-on if needed), and Ibrahima Konaté (6'4"), was in the middle. At the far side, Joël Matip (6'5") made a run. In between, Firmino's height didn't matter, as he side-footed the dipping ball home on the full volley. Yet it was the giants either side of him who allowed him the space.

Against the same opposition, Konaté scored twice, from fairly simple corners: out-swung, onto his head. Then, at Wembley against Manchester City, he did so again. Each time, with all three goals, he was up against 6'0" centre-backs, both with City connections (Nicolás Otamendi and Nathan Aké), while the other centre-back in those teams was only 6'2", and possibly with one eye on van Dijk and/or Matip.

While set-pieces have been a key part of a balanced approach in 2021/22 – Liverpool could cut teams apart in all manner of ways – the end to the previous season saw a simpler style of football, as they sought to battle back into the top four. There was no van Dijk or Matip to bring or ping the ball out from the back, and with no Gomez, the high line was harder to maintain. So, with two slow, rookie defenders, the defence had to sit deeper and the midfield had to drop back too, to protect them. This made playing fast-passing, high-pressing football much harder; as did the pressure of the situation. Instead, set-piece skills at both ends made the difference.

Williams was involved in the set-piece goal against United at Old Trafford – before Firmino's – that broke the Reds' five-month drought. He was the one who was challenged by David de Gea, and not one but two United defenders, which meant space for other players. *Three* United players against Williams, and the ball fell to Mo Salah in space in the box, with the ball rebounding to Phillips, who channeled his inner Messi to dribble and shoot, which Jota deflected home. Williams also helped win the penalty from a corner that was bizarrely overruled (yes, Eric Bailly won the ball, but it was not won cleanly, and the follow-through was extreme).

With the score at 0-0 at Burnley, Williams headed down from a corner and Phillips somehow volleyed over. It was a golden chance. Williams didn't even need to jump. When Mané set up the vital second goal in that game, from a 2nd-phase corner, he lofted the cross directly over Williams' head at the near post, as the Reds' no.46 stood surrounded by several Burnley players; in snuck an unmarked Phillips to finally show that he could be a threat in the opposition box too, after various wild attempts. All this went under the radar, with Phillips and Mané getting the plaudits; yet Williams was taking up the attentions of almost half the home team. *Five* players were stationed to deal with Williams (or that zone), and just one (Ben Mee) had to mark both Phillips and Firmino, as well as being one of the five in a position to challenge Williams (whilst Salah lurked at the back post too; something we'd see a lot in early 2021/22).

And when Williams went off late-on against West Brom, it was the Reds' 6'4" *goalkeeper*, challenging for the ball along with the aggressive Reds' 6'3" heading-monster, who won the game and essentially banished the bevy of Black Swans. There was a height overload at the near post, and it turned Liverpool's fortunes around. Phillips later said it was the only time in his life he'd been happy to lose a header.

While delivery is obviously important, height is absolutely vital at attacking set-pieces – and *sometimes* it seems it can be the goalkeeper on the end of it, too. It's similar to how a quick striker often just needs a half-decent through-ball and he can turn it into a killer pass: a tall player doesn't necessarily need the perfect cross.

(Liverpool score so many headers in open play precisely because the crosses are so good, and Jota, Mané, Firmino and Díaz are all relatively excellent headers of the ball, while Salah can close his eyes and hope. They can find space between defenders for when the cross dips, but this is different to a penalty box containing 20 players.)

When Liverpool broke through against Palace in the vital final game in May 2021, it was Williams, from a corner, heading the ball on to Firmino after getting above the tall Cheikhou Kouyaté; perhaps by accident, but there they were again, the same pair linking up. Kouyaté failed to jump, and tried to foul Williams, to no avail. He did stop Williams from heading at goal, but the ball fell to Firmino. Sadio Mané squeezed the ball home, and Liverpool won the game 2-0.

It's also hard to quantify how much better Thiago did with "bodyguards" in the middle of the park, but he started the season looking sublime in a team containing van Dijk, Fabinho and Henderson, and then had a slump in a diminutive midfield, with issues at centre-back. And as good as Fabinho could be at the back, clearly the midfield had more balance with him in there.

Another issue during the slump was just how bad the Reds' finishing was, but this was also partly linked to height and set-pieces. Remember, Firmino gets a lot of his goals as the free man at set-pieces when taller Liverpool players are being marked. He's the one who finds the space; when the tall teammates aren't there, he'll then be more of a target for tall defenders. A lack of set-piece goals (and penalties) put more pressure on the strikers, and for a while they were weighed down. At the other end, the Reds conceded from set-pieces, and conceded penalties that cost a lot of points.

The law of averages suggested Liverpool's fortunes in front of goal would change, and they did. Sometimes you just have to ride out the storm. The worst season in a decade – up to the Ides of March – turned into one of the best run-ins, and in the absence of up to a dozen players at a time, new heroes were born. Down in 7th place in mid-March, Liverpool finished 3rd, and rather than just allow access to the Champions League, it started another famous run to the final. Much of that was owed to height at set-pieces, and an incredible flying goalkeeper.

Of course, there's still no escaping one thing: that a fit Virgil van Dijk is the best centre-back on the planet, and one of the best to ever play the game.

Imperious Defending: 'Mediocre' van Dijk after Injury Back To His Best

"I arrived quite late in football, but this is why I enjoy my career even more. I will never win as many trophies as Sergio Ramos but this doesn't matter, I am proud of my career."

Virgil van Dijk

In 2021, during the slump, I devised a concept I called 'Imperious Defending' – combining different defensive statistics that could be measured purely as win percentages: aerial duels and ground duels. I wanted to get a sense of what was being lost with the absence not just of Virgil van Dijk but also Joël Matip (and to a lesser extent, Joe Gomez). In the end, it helped to show how slowly van Dijk started upon his return to the side in August 2021, but also, how he returned to his best once fully back in his stride.

There are other ways to judge the defensive qualities of centre-backs, but things like recoveries and clearances are often dependent on who a player represents: just as the keeper with the most saves should usually be in a relegation-threatened team, as they would logically face the most shots.

You can't quantify things like reading of the game particularly easily, but you can quantify who is bloody hard to get the better of once a duel takes place. These are zero-sum encounters. Someone wins, someones loses, and you can work out the percentage success rates;

whereas blocks, interceptions and goal-line clearances are just numbers, totted up more often by weaker teams whose defences are kept busier.

Ergo, if you wanted to look at who are the best blockers of shots (in terms of most blocked), then you have, in order, James Tarkowski of Burnley, Craig Dawson of West Ham, Grant Hanley of Norwich and Conor Coady of Wolves. Two of these were fighting relegation, and the other two in low-block, counterattacking teams. Chelsea's Thiago Silva rates quite highly for blocks, but with half the number of Tarkowski, and half the number of clearances; yet Silva has twice the number of recoveries as the beefy Burnley blockade. Tarkowski did not suggest himself to be ideal to defending a high line, but perfect for a packed box.

So, last year I went back over the data going back to 2011, and combined the percentage success rates of aerial and ground duels, which produced an overall ranking system. As such, it didn't cover the prime years of some other centre-backs, like John Terry, Rio Ferdinand, Daniel Agger, Jamie Carragher and Nemanja Vidić – just catching their later years; and missing others, like Jaap Stam, Sol Campbell and Sami Hyypia, altogether.

All in all, there were 45 centre-backs who played in at least two Premier League seasons and had figures good enough to qualify for the Hall of Fame as duellists, with 26 of those still in action. (Also, there were a minimum number of minutes to be played for a player's season to count, and he had to have contested a minimum number of duels, as explained in more detail below.) In total, the 45 averaged nearly six years of Premier League football.

And there was a clear winner when it came to this *Thou Shalt Not Pass* metric.

Supergaaf!
With 10 years of data churned, checked and digested, a certain Dutchman just happened to rank as the best defender on 'Imperious Defending' metrics; just ahead of Man City's Vincent Kompany. But of course, that Dutchman was cut down in his prime by a flying lunatic, and as such, his 2020/21 did not end up producing enough data.

However, I went back and updated the figures in May 2022, and, in particular, took a more detailed look at Liverpool's key centre-backs: Virgil Van Dijk, Joël Matip and new-buy Ibrahima Konaté, as well as some other defenders of interest, including those who have left Liverpool, and those at the main rivals.

The contrast between the van Dijk returning in the second half of 2021 from Jordan Pickford smashing up his knee, and the van Dijk of the second half of 2021/22 proved startling, and indeed, hugely comforting. The fears that he could be permanently diminished by the reckless goalkeeper proved unfounded.

(*Note:* All data is Premier League games only. Players are excluded if they didn't reach the minimum requirements for minutes played – 400 – or either type of duels contested: 20. I also excluded players who also played as full-backs, as the same players win a lot more aerial duels in that position because they are often contested against 5'7" wingers and not 6'5" centre-forwards. This applies to John Stones, Nathan Aké and Joe Gomez. Andrew Beasley also noted that full-backs' tackling stats can be unreliable when deemed to 'win' the ball when directly conceding throw-ins. My *Imperious Defending Rating* simply mixes the win percentages of aerials and ground duels. It's worth noting that players contest many more aerial duels than ground duels, so the overall metric does slightly favour those who are good in the air.)

De Koning!

In the first 14 games of 2021/22, Virgil van Dijk didn't even take his customary place in the top ten defenders for percentage of aerial duels won. Slightly leaden and lacking full fitness, it was a struggle at times. To leap when not quite fit is a bit like sprinting when not quite fit: the power isn't the same.

But then from games 15-35, he ranked no.1 in the league on that metric. The King was back; long live the King.

The ranges for my *Imperious Defending Hall of Fame* proved fairly broad. The worst scorers of the 45 central defenders who at least made the cut were Daley Blind, 60.8, just ahead of Toby Alderweireld, 59.4. Mid-ranking, and just below the top 20, were Jamie Carragher at 69.1 (clearly on the wane in 2011-2013) and Dejan Lovren, just below at 68.8 (which also included one season at Southampton, where his figures were unremarkable).

Fifteen players in the Hall of Fame have a score above 70, but only five have a score of over 73. I would say that two of the top five are surprising – for one, a later dip in form creates the recency bias that makes the earlier commanding performances easier to overlook.

Joël Matip ranks 5th, with 73.3.

Kurt Zouma, outfoxed only by the RSPCA and purely a 'stopper' compared to Matip and others, ranks 4th with 74.1.

Liverpool's footballer of the year in 2011/12 and set-piece scoring machine in 2013/14 (an incredible seven league goals), Martin Škrtel ranks 3rd, at 74.6.

Then comes the man many considered the best centre-back of his generation – at least until Virgil van Dijk came along. More than two points clear of Škrtel is Vincent Kompany, in 2nd place, at 76.6.

Yet even Kompany has to bow to the Dutch master's 77.2.

To show how much van Dijk's injury carried over into the first part of 2021/22, his *Imperious Defending Rating* sat at just 70.1 after the first 14 games, to the start of December, when the Reds sat 3rd in the table. By that stage, Liverpool had conceded two or three goals in four of the league games, as well as twice in the Champions League group stages (albeit van Dijk was rested against AC Milan).

Now, 70.1, if that was his *career* average, would place van Dijk 15th in the Hall of Fame; or basically, a Gary Cahill or Phil Jones: a very solid stopper, and just ahead of Ryan Shawcross, a very basic stopper. That's the level he was performing at.

However, from games 15-35, van Dijk blew the bloody doors off the art of defending. In that 20-game sample his *Imperious Defending Rating* was 83.7; also known as 'frankly ridiculous'. Averaged out across the whole season (with three games to play at the time I ran the numbers), it still ranks as the Dutchman's best season in English football, at 77.8.

(To be fair to Škrtel, his entire 2011/12 was even better, at 84.4, albeit in a team that defended far more deeply. I'll get onto Škrtel's nosedive in form later.)

One interesting thing is that van Dijk doesn't really tackle anymore. He made 68 in one season with Southampton, but averaged around 30 with Liverpool; in part as he has less to do. In 2021/22, after 35 games, it was just 18, with an exceptional 15 won. It's well noted that Alex Ferguson offloaded Jaap Stam when the defender's tackling statistics fell, but the manager later realised it was more that Stam was reading the game better. Still, a drop in quantity in any statistic *could* also show signs of concern. Yet the main thing is that the success rate remains high, and very few goals were conceded in that 20-game run – suggesting that van Dijk remained a massive presence.

In the *Imperious Defending Rating* Hall of Fame he now averages 77.2 overall, up slightly from 77.1 when I first created it in 2021. But perhaps most astonishingly, his rating each year reads as follows: 77.9, 77.5, 75.3, 77.5, 77.0 and 77.8. The consistency is incredible, especially as it spans two clubs and one super-serious injury. Compare the scores of the eight seasons Vincent Kompany qualified for, as the player who, overall, ranks 2nd to van Dijk: 82.6, 78.3, 77.6, 66.4, 80.9, 75.6, 74.7 and 76.5, which shows far more volatility.

Kompany, three years into his time in England at the starting point of the study in 2011, ended strongly, but started imperiously. In between he had one very mediocre season: 2014/15, when Manchester City finished a fairly distant 2nd to Chelsea, went out of the Champions League at the round of 16, and never made it past the 4th round of the domestic cups.

Halfway through 2021/22, Antonio Rüdiger appeared the most improved defender, after some low-scoring years (61.8, 58.3, 64.9) up until 2020. His score was over 80 in the first half of the season, but when it became clear that his future lay elsewhere and Chelsea began defending poorly as a team, it fell to an average of 75.0, down from his 2020/21 score of 78.9.

After that amazing start (albeit he'd been in England since 2008, just like Kompany) Martin Škrtel deteriorated quite markedly, year on year. By the end he was timid and mid-table: 84.4; 76.3; 72.8; 72.3; 69.2, which shows a clear downward trend over his final five seasons at the club. Again, no one gets close to van Dijk for consistency.

Joël Matip still ranks #5 in the Hall of Fame, out of the best 45 defenders since 2011, and clearly his game is not about winning tackles. If 'goes on mazy runs and crazy adventures' was added as a metric, he'd rank top. While not as consistent in this side of the game as his main partner, Matip is another player who has improved over the years, from a skinny, tall and talented but error-prone new arrival to a stronger, more confident quiet leader on the pitch.

What's surprising is that Man City's big-name, 'leader' centre-backs (Aymeric Laporte, Rúben Dias) rank as fairly mediocre as Imperious Defenders. Clearly they're excellent on the ball, and good readers of the game, but it seems that City 'defend' by keeping the ball at the other end, or keeping it so well at the back that they don't slip up much. They actually play with an even higher line than Liverpool, which means fewer aerial situations to deal with.

Almost the worst centre-back in the Premier League this season in terms of Imperious Defending? One Ozan Kabak. He ranks one place from bottom of 50+ qualifying centre-backs this season, just ahead of Leeds' Robin Koch. Playing in open sides, who are being overwhelmed, obviously can make life difficult, but it does at least provide a lot of involvement. Kabak's Liverpool figures were not great last season, particularly in the air. But after a slow start he did end with an almost-respectable 58.8% of his headers won, albeit still well below the standards required. Kabak's ground-duel rate was very good for the

Reds, at 84.2%, but the sample size, in the end, was only nine games. His overall Imperious Defending score at Liverpool was 67.9, which would put him in the top 30 for the Hall of Fame if his sample size was big enough. At 6'1", however, he couldn't cope with the aerial side of the game, especially at such a young age.

Alas, with the extended sample size of his time at Norwich (albeit still only 11 games), he would sink badly. Of 49 aerial duels he won just 22, at 44.9%; and his ground duels, of which there were far fewer, were good but not as good as with the Reds (71.4%). The overall score was 50.8, with the greater number of aerial duels keeping the figure lower. What's interesting is that he arrived from Germany with excellent aerial statistics, but the Premier League is a different beast when it comes to that side of the game. Being just 6'1", to me, is never enough, unless you can also defend like Franco Baresi.

By contrast, Konaté's first eight league games for Liverpool would have put him at all-star level on the *Imperious Defending Rating* (73.6, or the 5th-best score, just edging above Joël Matip's six-year average); but again, the sample size was too small. By the time he'd played his ninth game, his rating fell to an average of just below 70. That said, his best performances came in the Champions League (and he had a sensational final, which Liverpool unluckily lost); and his Premier League stats were way ahead of the man he essentially replaced, Ozan Kabak.

Nat Phillips' contribution to the end of 2020/21 was exceptional in many ways, but he wasn't a standout in the *Imperious Defending Ratings,* albeit the 66.1 would have ranked about 30th in the Hall of Fame, were his sample size to have been bigger. He actually ranked a little behind Kabak, who was better on ground duels. However, the key difference-maker was Rhys Williams.

In his few games, his score of 81.8 would rank him as the most unbeatable centre-back in the Hall of Fame. Obviously this was unsustainable. But it was, all the same, an incredible cameo. He won 30 of his 38 headers, and all six of his ground duels. He was brought in to a job, and while there were lots of things he could not do that van Dijk and Matip could, he was, for those vital games, a one-man wall.

Going forward, it will be interesting to see how Ibrahima Konaté fares. An all-round talent, he began the season using his gigantic physique carefully, and maybe didn't contest aerials as aggressively as he needed to. This is common for younger defenders, especially mild-mannered ones. In time, a sense of authority can build, and aggression becomes more natural, even if the player is never going to be snarling bully. The fact the Konaté edged out Matip in the run-in after the latter's most consistent season is partly to do with his greater pace (to help cover for Trent Alexander-Arnold), but it shows the quality the young Frenchman has. It also proved a way of getting the team's average age down, with so many players aged 30-or-so; something that the transfer and contract inertia of Covid allowed to happen (along with the fact that all the players were still performing to such a high standard). Dropping Matip seemed unthinkable; but Konaté usurped him.

One key to elite squad building is not to buy squad players (albeit one or two 'fillers' can help), but buy players who can, in time, make the existing first-XI stars exceptional substitutes. Mediocre squad players often never get the chance to understand how the team plays, never get to feel important; whereas if your subs' bench includes Matip, Roberto Firmino, James Milner, Joe Gomez and maybe even Jordan Henderson, then the knowhow is all there, waiting to be called upon; ditto gradually-integrated youngsters like Harvey Elliott and Curtis Jones. As the Premier League finally moves to five substitutes in 2022/23, the Reds' best-ever squad could be key for another title race, another assault on the Champions League.

Another Trophy: When A Cup Final Coincided With War In Europe

Football (and life) had been extremely strange for two full years, but it got stranger still, to be playing a game – days after the ending of the UK's Covid restrictions, pandemic seemingly finally in full retreat after 24 months – against a club whose owner (allegedly) gained his obscene wealth via ties (allegedly) to the very Russian despot (allegedly) who (allegedly) had (allegedly) just taken it upon himself to attack Ukraine, whilst (allegedly) (allegedly) (allegedly) getting his nuclear arsenal on standby.

(Roman Abramovich is also quite litigious. Allegedly.)

Nuke-less, unlike his leader, Abramovich's arsenal came at the cost of £1.6billion, owed to the club as a mark of his 'overspending' since acquiring the club in 2003. (With football-specific inflation, in terms of what he got in terms of player acquisition, you could easily double that – maybe *quadruple* it – given that he helped drive up the price of transfers; indeed, all those early c.£30m purchases equate to around £200m in 2022 money.)

On the eve of the match, Abramovich, on the run from the UK government's impending sanctions, tried to hand over "stewardship" and "care" to the club's charity's trustees, like a man handing over a ticking time-bomb to unwitting bystanders as its seconds ticked down to zero. The trustees of the charity – most of whom had nothing to do with the running of the club, and some of whom were not even businesspeople (such as Emma Hayes, the women's team manager, and Sebastian Coe, the athletics shill) – were obviously not so keen, but in order to protect the club and his assets, he used its charity as a metaphorical human shield; so not only did he hand over the device, he crouched behind them in anticipation of its detonation. All the while, the man he knew, who became president, launched literal explosives at the people of Kiev.

This meant that tied up with the League Cup final – not one of the *major* trophies, but a big Wembley occasion between two heavyweight rivals – came the whole debate about sportswashing and dubious foreign ownership. It occurred on a weekend when Liverpool were relying on Everton – partly bankrolled by über-oligarch and even more of a Putin acolyte, Alisher Usmanov (such as his company paying £30m *just for the privilege of a mere option* on naming rights to the new stadium, to show the kind of largesse at work) – to take down Man City in the Premier League; following just a month or so after the farce of the Chinese Communist Party and Russia making a mockery of clean sport at the Olympics. By late February 2022, there were troops invading a European country for the first time since 1945. Within days, Abramovich had Chelsea up for sale, and Everton hastily severed links with Usmanov, who was then sanctioned by the UK government. (The amount of money Everton were going to receive via Usmanov seemed integral to their financial model for their new £500m stadium.)

For oligarchs, it was the week when the shit hit the fan.

TTT Subscriber Ian Bryan, in the Czech Republic at the time, noted on the site just before the game that, "I have just come back from an incredibly emotional 60,000+ demonstration on Wenceslas Square in Prague. I just pray that Liverpool FC and the fans put on a huge show of support for Ukraine. This match will likely be beamed into Russian living rooms as they have stations which show English games and Chelsea have big support for obvious reasons. Some things really are more important than football."

Yet even in the worst of times, football can offer something to cling to. *Most* things are more important than football. But we do the football all the same, until doing it *itself* becomes a matter of life and death; until it arrives at the stadium door, via plague or ordinances or violence, or an ageing infrastructure on the brink of collapse or disaster.

(Since the turn of 2020 alone, we've had three of the four horsemen of the apocalypse; the last horseman – 'wild beasts' – perhaps saddled up a few months later, to don riot gear and tear-gas fans at the Stade de France.)

At any moment, somewhere in the world innumerable people will be dying in poverty and in agony and of disease, and so taking the chance to enjoy freedom – *while still yours* – is not something to feel guilty about. Still, thoughts were rightly with the people of Ukraine, suffering such barbarism.

(I'm no political expert, but once a leader rides a horse bare-chested and, in one sense, *barebacked*, all bets are off. Let's face it, as much as I loathed her, no one ever accused Margaret Thatcher of *that*. Disclaimer: the author accepts no responsibility for the evocation of mental images that can 'never be unseen', and any subsequent therapy is to be endured at the reader's own cost.)

Liverpool were due to go into the game with just Roberto Firmino injured, and Joe Gomez, Harvey Elliott, Curtis Jones and other fine players unable to make the matchday 20. The bench was, yet again, about as strong as it gets; albeit not packed with expensive stars. However, the situation soon changed for one of the youngsters. Thiago Alcântara – winner of just about everything, multiple times – ended up in tears after injuring himself in the warm-up, and so Elliott then made the bench. Elliott later got onto the pitch, and scored his penalty in the shootout; becoming the Reds' youngest-ever finalist, while James Milner proved the club's oldest-ever to play at Wembley. In addition, 31 other players represented the club during the cup run, many of them teenagers.

On the bench, of the outfield players, only Naby Keïta cost £50m or more (not adjusted for inflation) – or half a Romelu Lukaku, who sat warming Chelsea's bench. Of course, with inflation, Kepa Arrizabalaga cost almost £100m (£97.5m), and he would get onto the pitch in unusual circumstances, and prove the game's decisive player. Alisson Becker – on the Reds' bench in order to weaken the team (to give a chance to the rookie no.2 out of loyalty) – is a £90m player in 2022 money.

Including the home-grown Reece James, the five subs Chelsea used cost £318m adjusted for inflation (just over £250m unadjusted, as many of them were fairly recent acquisitions and prices haven't risen massively since pre-pandemic days). Timo Werner, £50m before inflation (£53m), joined Jorginho, up to £57m before inflation (£68m). Starter Kai Havertz cost £81m in 2022 money. Lukaku, bought in 2022 money (given that it was part of the 2021/22 season), therefore still cost £99.5m. In the end, the 17 players Liverpool used cost a total of £570m in 2022 money, and Chelsea's 16 cost £680m.

When Liverpool spend over £40m on a player, they are usually relying on them to be in the XI when fit, or perhaps first choice from the bench. Adjusted to 2022 money, four of Chelsea's subs averaged £80m apiece, with three of them not shoo-ins to Thomas Tuchel's team; indeed, often left out when fit in recent times. The Blues had cut their cloth a little tighter to FFP's demands since 2010, after Chelsea and their Russian owner blew the transfer landscape apart in the mid-2000s, but the spending, curtailed even more by a brief transfer ban a few years ago, certainly ramped up again when Covid-19 meant financial rules were slackened. *SwissRamble*'s Kieron O'Connor noted that in only two seasons out of 19 had Abramovich not invested substantial money into the club's kitty, to cover shortfalls.

A Great 0-0!
The game itself proved a thrilling, end-to-end 0-0 draw, with the Reds often lacking a little midfield control due to the absence of their Spanish maestro, but having the upper hand in that area, for periods at least, due to outnumbering the indefatigable N'golo Kanté and Mateo Kovačić. The normal-time xG had the Reds "winning" 2.41 to 1.84 according to Opta, but that could obviously (roughly) round down/up to a 2-2 draw. (Interestingly, Liverpool also won the shootout on post-shot xG, which is based not on shot location, as everyone shoots from the same 12-yard spot, but shot *placement*.)

Liverpool looked leggy later on, with Diogo Jota on as a sub after just one training session following injury (and his season never really recovered), and Elliott having started just one game after five months out. Incredibly, Mo Salah was playing his 5th period of extra-time *in just 31 days*, four of them in the African heat. As deep as the Reds' bench looked, it didn't have the pace, power or expense of Chelsea's. For all their faults since joining Chelsea, Werner and Lukaku are not the kind of fresh substitutes any tiring defence would want to face. Their pace is a nightmare for defenders, and it took the introduction of Ibrahima Konaté – whose giant frame means he can be slow off the mark but rapid once into his long sprinter's stride – to stem the threat, after the excellent Joël Matip gave way in extra-time.

Indeed, Matip looked to have won the game in normal time, with a far-post header, in a goal reminiscent of the Community Shield draw with Man City in 2019. This time, it was belatedly deemed offside by VAR in that Virgil Van Dijk, who didn't touch the ball, apparently interfered in blocking a Chelsea player (even though he was the one being held; with a new tactic at high-line set-pieces to push Liverpool players either into offside positions, or at the other end, push them so they step back and play a forward offside).

The inconsistency of the decision-making remains the main bugbear on offsides, as players can make offside decoy runs to influence the play, to allow an onside player to profit. That is seeking to gain an advantage, and Liverpool concede goals via that tactic. The only exemptions for offside players being ignored should be for players who are not near the play, and who are not running forward; anyone coming back from an offside position with an arm up in acknowledgement should be deemed as 'not interfering', but anyone who chases forward, towards the ball, or to create space, even if they then stop, is disrupting a defence. (Of course, this is football, and the PGMOL.) It's a lottery to know if officials feel someone is interfering or not, when anyone forcing a defensive line to move is clearly affecting the play.

Several TTT subscribers were at Wembley for the Reds' first domestic cup final since 2016. Mick and Jennifer Thomas bumped into another (unnamed) subscriber, which is interesting for a niche site. Allen Baynes, present at Wembley 57 years earlier for the Reds' first domestic cup success (as one of 28 finals attended), also attended the occasion when Ukrainian flags were seen amongst both sets of supporters. Allen shared his experiences in an article for the site, which included, "As you might predict, one end was pretty full before the kick-off, the other had large areas of red empty seats; one end had numerous home-made banners, the other end had plastic flags. How different the two clubs' supporters are. Their lot didn't understand that during the minute's applause for Ukraine, our rendition of *You'll Never Walk Alone* was for the people of Ukraine, and so they booed.

"As per normal, the national anthem got short shrift from the Reds' end, just as the cheerleader before the 1965 final did. Kopites have never needed, nor would allow, a conductor. We are not English, we are Scouse. It was great to meet many not-born Scousers before, during and after the game. I met a lovely nurse from Norwich, clearly signed-up to the pre-match Scouse mentality. I do think that Scouse should be redesignated not as a place of birth but an attitude to life."

The Reds' booing of the national anthem would become front-page news a few months later.

'Just' 3,459 miles away, subscriber *Criynwa2* took her place at New York's distinctive 11th Street Bar, home to the LFCNY supporters group. So popular have the Reds become that other bars now take the overspill, but the "11th" – a capacity of 125 set by the Fire Department – remains the group's official home. Kick off in the US was 11:30am. The bar opened at 10am for club members who had a 30-minute window to get in before the general public. Her experience hinted at the lingering societal impact of Covid-19.

"It's a long, narrow bar with an open room at the back," she explained to me. "LFCNY committee members arrived between 9am and 10am to help check vaccination cards, membership cards, etc. I am on the committee [since 2006] but my colleagues took care of most of this on Sunday. Since we knew the bar would be packed, we planned our annual party to occur on the same day. This means basically pizza for the whole bar after the match and a charity auction and raffle. This year the funds went to the LFC Foundation. We raised $3,000 between the 11th Street Bar and the Grafton, an affiliated bar nearby in the East Village, that also held a raffle.

"Since we knew we had to arrive early to get our spots at the 'Kop end' of the bar – in the front – my friend brought bagels and cream cheese and fruit salad, and I brought croissant, *pain au chocolat* and cheese bread for the bar staff and attendees.

"I have been attending matches at our home bar since 2005, so I pretty much know all the regulars and since I handled the memberships for years, I know quite a few of the ones who can't come as often, as well. They certainly know me because I start the singing and I curse at the referees a lot. It's really a friendly, lovely crowd, in general. LFCNY is, they tell me, the oldest supporters group in North America and it was lovely that some of the founding members were there too. It was utterly fantastic to see so many friends who came out to share this experience together, that I hadn't been able to watch matches with for some time."

Across the other side of the world, Navin Ramachandran awoke at 4am, ready for the kickoff an hour and a half later.

He explained to me that, "The Auckland Branch of the Official Liverpool Supports Club of New Zealand had organised for a private event at a local pub, The Paddington, to show the game live. It had to be a private event as New Zealand liquor laws don't allow pubs to be open to the public at that time of the day. And given it was a private event, numbers had to be restricted to 100 fully-vaccinated people due to the Covid regulations and the current rampant outbreak in the community. Never mind all that, there is a trophy to be won by the

Reds! Tickets for the event were NZ$20 and it included a coffee and bacon and eggs on toast for breakfast."

It felt strange to think of Covid surging in New Zealand on the very week it had become *almost* an afterthought in England, although for two years, Australasia had done its best to limit any spread at all, so once it did arrive it would do some damage, but at a time when vaccines were in play.

Navin continued, "I was at the pub at 5am queueing outside waiting for the doors to open at 5.15am. Once opened, there was a quick check of everyone's vaccine passport before they were allowed in. The atmosphere felt quietly confident but not overly confident. The excitement and noise level increased as it neared kick-off. A loud cheer at kick-off and we settled into watching the game and cheering on the team – 120 minutes of joy, despair, anger and a whole lot or other emotions fill the pub. Although most of us had the choice of watching the game at home on our own, we chose to come together like this and revel in the comradeship, despite the threat of Covid, as it adds to the enjoyment of the game and the special feelings and love we share for the Reds. Plus it can give a sense of normality to life albeit for a short while as we forget the pandemic surge affecting our communities."

Keepers Kepa and Kelleher as Kickers
The game, after an exciting but goalless period of extra-time, eventually went to penalties. There followed a procession of expertly-taken kicks, with all outfield players for both teams successfully scoring: 10-10 the score, no misses.

The shootout became all the more interesting by the last-minute extra-time introduction of Kepa Arrizabalaga, and his approach to facing the Reds' spot-kicks: jump up and down; refuse to take his designated place until forced to by the ref; dance along the line; stand to one side of the goal; bash the crossbar; point to where the taker should place it; and essentially every trick in the book bar Bruce Grobbelaar's wobbly legs.

Nothing worked.

Even allowing for the change of goalkeeper, Liverpool's placement suggests success in the shootout was merited – unless, of course, Edouard Mendy had proved more intimidating, and the takers duly rendered more nervous. If the standard conversion rate of a penalty is around 78-80%, then an expected goals figure would be the same; Liverpool's 81% (8.9 expected goals from 11 shots) showed an improvement on the norm, in terms of shot placement. A difference of 8.9 to 7.0 meant Chelsea's expected return was a 64% success rate –

albeit a keeper has to dive early to reach the corners, and if he dives (or is sent) the wrong way, the goal gapes, and it doesn't matter if the placement is technically "bad" (as the keeper is not *there*) as it rolls into a empty net. For his part, having starred in penalty shootouts on the way to the final, Caoimhín Kelleher could do no better than get close to a couple of low efforts towards the corners.

Kepa, as a taker, then reduced Chelsea's xG average by a huge chunk, as a penalty heading out of the stadium has never, in the history of football, resulted in a goal; ergo, 0.0 xG, and 0% success. In the end, Liverpool scored 100% of theirs, and Chelsea "only" 91%.

The highlights were Fabinho gently *Panenka*ing after Kepa's mind games, followed by van Dijk putting his into the top corner with the Chelsea keeper literally standing on that side of the goal; the Dutchman's glare afterwards a work of art in its freezing stillness and contempt. Then Kepa told young Harvey Elliott, aged 18, to put his penalty to the right, and Elliott duly obliged, as the keeper dived to his left. The only nervous moment came when Konaté side-footed a saveable shot – taken as the last outfield player – that just about had the power to press back the keeper's fingers and hit the net.

(Incidentally, a quick bit of Photoshop measuring I undertook of a still image taken from the spider-cam directly behind Virgil van Dijk as he struck his penalty suggests the gap to the other side of Kepa's goal was roughly 2.4 times the gap to the side the keeper was covering, as measured from the edges of his boots on the goal-line to the inside of the posts; or nearly 14ft, of the 24ft goal width left exposed, with less than 6ft to the other side of his stance of feet spread out at just over 4ft (I supposed van Dijk could have tried to nutmeg him, as about the only possible improvement on what he chose). Yet even with less than 6ft to cover to his right, Kepa still couldn't stop the shot. Or, in other words, if the keeper was defending a *phonebox*, van Dijk would still have scored.

With all 20 outfield players successful, it came down to the two custodians, and Kelleher curled his expertly into the top corner, while Kepa blasted his high into the night sky.

(Voyager 1, the spacecraft launched in the late 1970s, is currently 15 billion miles from Earth, well into interstellar space, as the furthest man-made object in the universe – but given its velocity, NASA noted that they expect Kepa's kick to overtake it by 2037.)

The skinny lad from Cork, clad head to toe in yellow, leapt with joy, as his teammates made the time-honoured sprint from halfway to join him. It wasn't quite Istanbul, 2005, but it was a moment made all the more special after two years of Covid, mass injuries and empty stadia, with no proper celebrations for the 2020 league title, beyond pyrotechnics at an eerily empty Anfield. As most of the players still remained at the club a year and a half later, this could then serve as a proxy for that denial.

In New Zealand, Navin felt the strain. "Down to penalties – I checked my heart rate. It was a steady 125 throughout the penalty shootout – that's almost as good as going for a run!"

My own heart-rate, at home in front of the TV, suggested I was sprinting the final stages of a marathon, as I paced up and down my lounge.

"At the end of the shootout," he continued, "the pub erupted into song with *You'll Never Walk Alone* playing loudly over the speakers and everyone in the pub signing along. Loud cheers followed during the prize presentation before it came time to head home for those of us working from home, or to the office for the lucky minority able to work in the office."

In New York, *Criynwa2* noted, "When Matip scored the later disallowed goal, the decibel level went through the roof. It was such a tense match and we were all chatting about what we were seeing. It was lovely not to be able to hear the commentators due to the chatter and singing in the bar! People stayed around for the raffle/auction and pizza so we had plenty of time to discuss the match and, to me, that's one of the reasons to watch together – for the opportunity to share thoughts and observations on the performance and the teams and how you're feeling about the victory."

Meanwhile, in Singapore, Wayne Cheong – Liverpool fan, forum host and prolific podcaster – had been hospitalised with Covid-19 in the week leading up to the cup final; suffering some complications, having overcome cancer a few years earlier. A regular correspondent and sharer of my work, in the previous 18 months I'd agreed to interview him for, and then speak to him about, this book on his podcast, but writing the book ended up being pushed back, and thus, so too the podcast appearance.

The day before the final, when he should have been gearing up for the big match, instead marked his funeral; he had died four days earlier, on the Tuesday, leaving a wife, Rose, and two school-aged children.

Riotous Against Historical Rivals

Nine Goals In 180 Minutes

While 2021/22 brought 'only' two trophies for Liverpool, it delivered moments that will live long in the memory. This includes some absolute *hammerings* of historical rivals.

Indeed, a lot of the impetus – if not *momentum* ("the most fragile flower on the planet," as Jürgen Klopp noted so eloquently a year later) – came from the 4-2 win at Old Trafford near the end of the difficult 2020/21 campaign.

Winning at Old Trafford still remained a difficult task for the Reds, albeit helped by a scarcely believable three penalties in 2013/14, a few years after the famous 4-1 win in the 2009 title race. (One that sadly petered out with a bizarre 4-4 draw at home to Arsenal and Andrey Arshavin, who scored almost 20% of his Gunners' goals that night: the other 27 goals he scored came in 143 games.)

Then in 2021, two wins at Old Trafford came along in short succession, with an incredible *nine* goals scored. (Before another four were added at Anfield.)

A 4-2 win arrived in May, after the original game had been dramatically postponed due to rioting by the United fans. (Their protests, centred around their owners and the proposed European Super League seemed to conveniently coincide with playing Liverpool. Nearly 18 months on, and maybe some of their fans would be desperate for the ESL, as the only way to see top European football.) No fans were inside the stadium to see the rescheduled match, and so none could walk out in disgust, even if the result was in the balance until Mo Salah's 90th-minute game-killer. But there were 75,000 there for the 5-0 drubbing five months later; or rather, there were 75,000 there until *half-time*, at which point, seeing their side trailing 4-0, the attendance appeared to halve before the second period got underway.

Liverpool still had another thrashing of United in store, this time for a new manager to endure.

Indeed, add the other historical foe, Everton, and the aggregate becomes an even more stark 17-3, due to wins of 4-2, 5-0, 4-1, 4-0, in a run of four games in eleven months. One game later, Liverpool defeated Everton again, but 'only' 2-0, to make for an aggregate of 19-3, five wins from five, in eleven months. The first three results – 4-2, 5-0 and 4-1 – came in a period of just six months.

I originally wrote two full chapters on these two rival clubs, looking at all the things they did wrong since 2016 in contrast to what

Liverpool did right. In the end, I thought I'd save most of that for elsewhere, and focus more on the brilliance of Liverpool's football in these encounters, as tribute to a kind of high-water mark of on-field success, even if it was underpinned by the smartness of the Reds' operation; while both Manchester United and Everton made operational decisions with all the sagacity and foresight of the now-deceased bungee jumper who measured out 69 metres of elastic cord for a 70-metre drop above concrete.

Ole's No Longer at the Wheel

Though he wouldn't last much longer, Manchester United started the game on October 24th at Old Trafford relatively well.

By that I mean, *at least they had an attack*.

But by half-time the stadium would be emptying, Liverpool 4-0 up and the Spanish-style *olés* from the crowd mixed up with songs about the Norwegian manager, and how 'Ole's at the wheel' (which, according to a quick google, was a song that had "become synonymous with the optimism which initially accompanied Solskjaer's appointment." At this point, only Liverpool fans were singing it.)

Soon after half-time it was 5-0, and United had Paul Pogba sent off. The visitors stopped attacking: conserving energy and trying to avoid more spiteful challenges. As such, to use cricket parlance, they 'declared' after 49 minutes. And so, just the 5-0 then.

The first goal came when Alisson, pressed by a manic and non-organised United attack, passed to Virgil van Dijk, who laid it to Andy Robertson. The Liverpool left-back was still 20 yards within his own half, but suddenly Aaron Wan-Bissaka was haring towards him. By the time Robertson had flicked it to Diogo Jota, who had been closed down by Victor Lindelöf in the position Wan-Bissaka vacated, it just took a simple ball infield to Roberto Firmino and the whole of the United half opened up, with three Reds (in ecru) against two struggling defenders. The ball through to Salah looked offside, but he'd just remained on as Luke Shaw stepped clumsily out. Salah turned and fed the onrushing Naby Keïta, albeit after delaying for a beat, that could have proved costly – the through-ball was initially on *in front* of Shaw, but Salah let Shaw run back and slipped it the other side, behind him, and Keïta stroked coolly home after taking a good first touch. Tellingly, Robertson was by then up alongside the no.8, and Wan-Bissaka was jogging back, 30 yards from goal. (For a player whose defending and athleticism were supposed to be his strong suits, this was scandalous; and as it was after just four-and-a-half minutes, fatigue could be no excuse.)

After 13 minutes, Wan-Bissaka was again closing down Robertson and leaving a gap in behind. His lofted pass, meant for Jota, bounced over the Portuguese, and comically, Shaw and Harry Maguire collided going for the same ball. (Obviously this phrase exists *despite* there only ever being one ball in play. It's up there in its needlessness with 'in a foot race', as if there are swimming or cycling races in football, too.)

Keïta picked up the loose ball, fed Alexander-Arnold, and his low, zipped-in cross was smashed home from close range by Jota, who just about beat James Milner to the open goal. Jota had also scored in May (as had Salah), back when Roberto Firmino added the other two goals, either side of half-time (which seemed to be a particularly prolific period in the two Old Trafford games: four of the goals – two each match – scored between minutes 45 and 50, including added time).

The movement and interplay for Liverpool's third, on 38 minutes, was exceptional, albeit Salah's shot from 19 yards hitting Harry Maguire could have been the end of the opportunity. But again Keïta was sharp, squaring the loose ball to the Egyptian, who had shown incredible tenacity and acceleration to burst past Shaw, who tried to hold him, and Maguire, who was much nearer to goal. The ball fizzed into the net from an expertly executed first-time finish, only possible for a player absolutely in the zone. The Reds then went 4-0 up on the stroke of half-time, despite only playing with 10 men, with Keïta off the pitch receiving treatment. The move again originated down the left, with Robertson, Jota and Firmino linking on the wing, and then remarkably, linking again on the edge of the United area. Jota squared the ball to Salah, and his first-time finish – essentially giving David de Gea 'the eyes' to go near post instead of far – was again peak flow.

Perhaps Pogba felt humiliated at coming on at half-time with his team 4-0 down, and then being ambushed by Jordan Henderson on the press after 49 minutes, to the point where the French World Cup-winner was soon aiming his studs at Naby Keïta's knee. In his few minutes on the pitch, he gifted Liverpool a goal, albeit it still required a lot of work to capitalise on his error. Not only did he get robbed by Henderson, but the Liverpool captain curled a sumptuous pass with the outside of his foot that dissected the entire United defence. Salah ran through, took a great first touch with his right foot, then a poor one with his left, that made de Gea think the ball was his; yet it just allowed the Liverpool man to prod home his hat-trick after a further burst of acceleration.

Henderson's tackle on Pogba was interesting in that it's part of a very Kloppian philosophy: win the ball fairly and cleanly. The captain could have cleaned out Pogba with a lunge – just as Pogba would soon do on

Keïta, but went for the braver option: the side-footed block-tackle, which leaves a player open to a lunge in reply. Henderson could have fouled Pogba (while Firmino also pressed from the other side), and got a yellow card; even a red, had he been snarling and thoughtless, in the way that Pogba soon was, and with it, a three-game ban. But the beauty is that, having won the challenge, Henderson was upright, the ball at his feet, the United half open ahead of him. Even a clean sliding tackle – an obvious option in a derby – would have sent the ball to the covering Scott McTominay, with the Liverpool man left on the floor.

While they press frantically and frenetically, Liverpool try to nick, nab and pickpocket their way into possession. They get 'in the face' quickly, but don't want to foul. A foul only halts your own attack. It slows the game down, and you risk further punishment from the referee, as well as potentially injury yourself. At times it can be frustrating when Liverpool players don't go flying into challenges, and a block-tackle proves insufficient, but that player will then chase back, as will others. None of which is to say that the team *never* puts in a bad tackle, but it's about catching the opponents off-guard, not trying blood-and-thunder tackles that often only give them the ball back via the loose rebound or the referee's whistle.

As with fans shouting "shoot!" when a player has the ball 35 yards from goal, this smarter, modern way is not always something a crowd appreciates. They still get roused by a thumping tackle. And thumping tackles, if done well, can still have their place. But Liverpool receive the fewest yellow and red cards, season after season to win the Fair Play award, because they don't make many *reckless* tackles.

Ralf Rangnick and Liverpool, Anfield April 2022

However, before moving onto the football, a brief aside. In another life, Ralf Rangnick may have become Liverpool manager in 2010 or early 2011.

Back in 2010 I was asked by John W Henry – who had taken to contacting me for unofficial advice – as to who I thought should replace Roy Hodgson (seeing as I felt he needed replacing). Admitting that it was not my area of expertise (my knowledge of European football is not particularly remarkable, but I do feel that I know when Liverpool definitely have the wrong man in the dugout), I spoke to a leading football scout, who soon went on to become a director of football at a major European club. He recommended four managers, and I passed on the list to the Reds' new owner, albeit I never heard what he thought of the list, just as I never expected to (it's not like I was 'in the loop'; none of it may have been acted upon, for all I know).

One manager soon won the Champions League, unexpectedly, and another of the names was that of Ralf Rangnick. This was just before Rangnick's health scare at Schalke, after which he became more of a super-smart overseer at the Red Bull stable of clubs in the next dozen years, with just two of that decade spent managing.

At the time, I had also been asking John Henry to speak to Kenny Dalglish, in part at the behest of the legend's family, given that the 'King' felt frozen out at the Academy by Hodgson. I certainly felt Dalglish should be listened to, albeit I wasn't expecting him to be appointed caretaker manager, even if I made it clear that he would surely lift the club out of its funk, which grew worse by the week. As such, it was a great relief after the ongoing car-crash of Hodgson's tenure.

Looking back, Rangnick had helped shape the modern German game and influenced Jürgen Klopp, but perhaps in 2010 Liverpool were not ready for his revolutionary approach; he was a little too unknown in England, perhaps, for fans to get behind, had he arrived at that point. Rangnick may not have been the right person to sort out the mess of a squad that FSG inherited that October, with a mixture of players signed by various managers, including a few ageing mediocrities brought to the club by the ageing mediocrity managing since the summer of 2010, who liked older players who defended deep in two banks of four: hardly the modern German way.

Amusingly, *Sky Sports* noted before the fixture at Anfield in 2022 that Rangnick had lost only one of his last nine games against Klopp, but the two had not met since 2011, given Rangnick's time as a sporting director in the intervening 11 years, with both his seasons managing in the Bundesliga since then occurring when Klopp was in England; an utterly meaningless statistic without any context, given the different direction of travel as managers: Klopp having won every trophy imaginable since 2012, and Rangnick, rarely in the dugout since, having won none.

That said, the year after Rangnick was recommended to me, he won the cup with Schalke, where he'd been runner-up in the Bundesliga half a dozen years earlier. The years in between two stints at Schalke were spent at Hoffenheim (where he left within weeks of a young Roberto Firmino signing). At Schalke the second time, he briefly worked with Joël Matip, before giving up his role at the club.

There could be no doubting his expertise, and his ability in 2010 – as well as being cutting-edge at the time (as well as Klopp, he also influenced Thomas Tuchel, Julian Nagelsmann and Ralph Hasenhüttl)

– but his hands-on coaching had been light since illness in 2011, and that made it a slightly strange appointment for Manchester United.

And while Klopp clearly learnt from the technocratic and erudite Rangnick, the latter lacks the personality that makes the former so formidable.

In the buildup to his first trip to Anfield, the BBC ran the headline: *Manchester United will not repeat Liverpool's 30-year title wait – Ralf Rangnick.* The manager had said: "I suppose this will not happen [to United] because it is pretty obvious what needs to change."

He stopped short of saying *Everything*.

The piece noted that Rangnick played a role in the careers of six current Liverpool players: Firmino at Hoffenheim and Matip at Schalke (albeit as noted earlier in this section, he barely managed either of them), in addition to Sadio Mané, Naby Keïta, Ibrahima Konaté and Takumi Minamino, who were all signed while Rangnick was director of football at the Red Bull group of clubs. Again, he *managed* none of the four players, but clearly helped with their recruitment.

"It is not complicated. It is not rocket science," Rangnick said, before his tenure ended and his planned two-year stint as a consultant dissolved. "Liverpool finished eighth in the season Jürgen arrived. Then it took two transfer windows. They brought in the right players and got rid of the right players. That is why they are where they are."

It's worth pointing out that Liverpool were 10th when Klopp arrived a quarter of the way into 2015/16, and despite 'only' making it up to 8th in the remainder of the season (so, an improvement), the Reds, with a mixed squad and a ton of injuries, also reached the League Cup final and the Europa League final, to mean a lot more games than the squad – perennial cup failures under Brendan Rodgers – was used to. There were also clear signs that, even with limited players, Klopp could get a series of huge results in his first seven months. It's not just Rangnick, but various other pundits (and managers) who mistakenly paint Klopp's start as a slow one.

The Reds thrashed Man City at the Etihad, 4-1 in the League, then 3-0 at Anfield. They beat Man United 2-0 in Europe, and then got a draw at Old Trafford to progress; then drew in Dortmund against Klopp's old team, before turning around a 2-0 and 3-1 deficit in the return leg to win 4-3 with an incredible late salvo. Villarreal – to pop up again six years later – were beaten 3-0 in the semi-final. The Reds were unbeaten in two games against a strong Spurs' side, and beat José Mourinho's Chelsea, the reigning champions, 3-1 at Stamford Bridge (again, Mourinho was sacked); Chelsea being another team who failed to beat Liverpool that season. Everton were humbled 4-0 at Anfield, and in the process, Liverpool's in-form young striker, Divock Origi, had his leg broken by a horrific tackle by Ramiro Funes Mori. Aston Villa were beaten 6-0 at Villa Park, and Southampton 6-1 at St Mary's. There were some duff displays, but more than enough big wins to think it was more than a mere slow-burn. Then, in his first full season he delivered Champions League qualification for only the second time since 2009, all without the kind of transfer spending possible at richer clubs.

So, the idea that Klopp struggled in his first season in English football is clearly shown to be incorrect. Obviously it needed transfers to take the club to the next level, as there were so many average players at the club with limited ceilings, while some of the better ones (such as Daniel Sturridge, Joe Gomez, Danny Ings) were struggling with serious injuries. The only period of regression (Covid-era aside) came in October 2017, when I found myself having to defend Klopp to other Liverpool fans who couldn't see the progress; but the team was soon back on track again. Progress is never linear, and little in life is achieved without setbacks, and even regressions. You just have to have the sense to know if it's a blip, or a catastrophe.

April 19th 2022, and Liverpool went into the Anfield match one point behind leaders Manchester City with seven games remaining. The Reds had just risen to be the #1 ranked team in the world again on the Elo Index (and would go further ahead after beating United, ranked 10th, partly due to their the lingering benefits of their 2020/21 form), but it was also clear that the season could end with just the League Cup for Klopp's men. Talk of the 'quadruple' had become a tiresome refrain, but as Virgil van Dijk pointed out, it's never been done as it's nigh-on impossible. It was not as if the Reds had a healthy lead in the league; they were behind Man City (at one point, 14 adrift). That said, they would go above City with a win over United – but then having played a game more. That was achieved, but from that point, Man City stopped dropping points, except against Liverpool, when both dropped two to the other, and at West Ham (at a time when Liverpool had drawn with Spurs).

In *Red Letters: Two Fervent Liverpool FC Supporters Correspond through the Epic Season That Wouldn't End,* American sports journalist Michael MacCambridge and *The Anfield Wrap* icon Neil Atkinson – both Liverpool fans – published the letters they exchanged during the incredible 2019/20 season. Atkinson noted, as Covid threatened the conclusion of that campaign: "A lifetime-defining season, a season that in many ways ends all seasons, could well be dead by the last week of

March. How strange. So much of football for me has always come down to this truism:

"Have something to play for third week of April.

"That's it. That's the key to a happy life, to a good campaign. Just have something to play for third week of April. Have the journey, the process. And then if you still have something to play for mid-May then really we are blessed."

Back in that unforgettable season, the whole of football was mothballed from March to June, but *normally* it's a truism. That April, no one had anything to play for; for the time being, anyway.

I always noted how Rafa Benítez took almost every one of his seasons into early May, with something to play for – and often something major; even the disappointing 2009/10 saw a Europa League semi-final at the end of April result in elimination on the away goals rule (subsequently banished), and that came after his team had to travel – arduously – by bus and train to Spain due to Eyjafjallajökull erupting in Iceland. Four of his six seasons saw European semi-finals, three of them in the Champions League. To me, that became the benchmark for modern Liverpool, in the age of richer clubs and financially-doped rivals; but obviously Klopp has since managed to take things even further, with four European *finals*, three of them in the Champions League.

"We have to be angry in a good way," Klopp said, in his pre-match conference, with Rangnick's United in town. "Greedy, all these kind of things, like you are if you have won nothing and would be with nil points and it's the most important three points in your life."

Ian *Dowdy* Dowdell, on the way to Anfield for the game, was enjoying his pre-match routine: "First stop is Chiquito's for what is normally a swift refreshment stop. Of course, with Covid restrictions eased we're again allowed to 'stroke the gecko' – it's not a euphemism but literally a model gecko that you stroke for luck! But it was busier than I've seen it in years, leading to more concerns about the timing.

"Once fed and watered, we headed for our normal car park and to the ground. As we strolled along, strangely everywhere seemed too quiet and we half-jokingly wondered if we'd got the kick-off time wrong! Jake and Aaron [his sons] went to their Kop seats while Marcus [his friend] and I headed to ours in the Main Stand Upper. By that stage, we knew we were fine for time after all and made our seats in time for a catch-up with the usual crowd around us and to soak up the atmosphere, which was building nicely. The nerves were also still building too because, despite the form, it's still United! A quick swap of messages with TTTer Tash [in Barcelona] and 'here we go'!"

It proved to be another remarkable game. Surprisingly, United kept possession with precision, finding time and space, no Liverpool players getting even close to them. Who saw that coming? Aaron Wan-Bissaka, to Jadon Sancho, to Bruno Fernandes, to Nemanja Matić, then back again. It was a long, unbroken spell of possession.

Except, *it was their half-time warm-up*. And the Kop chanted the multi-faceted "olé!" with glee at every touch. Harry Maguire, on the floor to stretch his hamstrings (presumably made of cement), like an angry ogre, punched the ball to his team-mates; one way to guarantee finding them, in contrast to his woeful distribution on the night. Fernandes tried to get the passing going again, but Marcus Rashford, aware of the Kop's mockery, put his foot on the ball, to stop the fun.

"It's embarrassing, it's disappointing, maybe even humiliating," Klopp's counterpart Rangnick said after the final whistle, albeit describing the whole night, rather than the half-time rondos.

Subscriber *DeetotheGee* noted on the site: "I thought it was nice of Man Utd to turn up and be the Washington Generals for us. You can't be the Harlem Globetrotters without them."

United were without Ronaldo, whose son had tragically died the day before, during childbirth; a horror touchingly marked by the Kop with a minute's applause in the 7th minute, along with singing *You'll Never Walk Alone*.

(Man United fans later sang about the *Sun* newspaper being right, and that Liverpool fans were murderers – which is a reminder that certain sections within any group of people will be arseholes, and others in crowds can be corralled along too. Days earlier at Wembley, some Man City fans had sung throughout the minute's silence for the 33rd anniversary of Hillsborough. Perhaps improvement may come after both Manchester clubs promised to speak with fans to address the issue, albeit in City's case it was one of their own fans asking for his club to support initiatives to educate fans about the tragedy. A month later, Tottenham's Supporters' Trust, responding to their own fans' songs about Liverpool fans 'signing on', said "Poverty and joblessness are not fair game for banter.")

As well as Ronaldo, 37, being absent, they had the injury-prone Cavani, 35, missing. Anthony Martial was being paid to play for Sevilla (albeit they too soon stopped playing him), and Mason Greenwood was on enforced leave undergoing investigation for rape and other serious charges. Meanwhile, £73m signing Sancho only made the bench.

But Phil Jones started.

Paul Pogba also started, and as soon as Liverpool scored – a wonderful breakaway goal (with a massive overload on the right) slotted home by Luis Díaz after just five minutes, from Mo Salah's low-slung cross – the Frenchman limped off; lasting about as long as he had in the Old Trafford game, and his Man United career, in turn, was over. Within 15 minutes, Phil Jones was blowing like a middle-aged pub footballer asked to sub in to a Premier League match.

What an omnishambles. Within 24 hours, United's chief scout, Jim Lawlor (16 years in the role), and Marcel Bout, the head of global scouting (for seven years), had both announced that they would be leaving. Matt Judge, in charge of contract negotiations, soon followed. When Rangnick had arrived, several of United's highest-rated coaches, expected to stay on, jumped ship. Rangnick himself failed to take up the two-year consulting role, once the season ended.

Earlier in the season it was Ole Gunnar-Solskjær who bit the bullet soon after losing to Liverpool, just had José Mourinho in 2018. As United drifted towards a 6th-placed finish, Rangnick, as interim manager, couldn't really be sacked; and the issues all predated his arrival. Instead, the scouting staff fell on their swords. In the summer, several big-name players walked out as free agents.

In 2022, Paul Hirst of the *Times* wrote about new executive vice-chairman Richard Arnold: "Senior figures at United admit that handing control of the club to a man whose expertise is in commercial matters may not go down well with some supporters. In 2012, when he was commercial director, Arnold summed up the marketing appeal of the club by saying that United had '25 George Clooneys' in their squad."

Clooney was 51 at the time, and now aged 61, could probably have made more appearances than Phil Jones in the past decade, and still turn quicker than Harry Maguire.

And of course, Klopp was turned off by United in 2014 when Arnold's predecessor Ed Woodward likened the club to Disneyland.

Pogba – their most insidious purchase until the return of Ronaldo – had a good view on the bench for Liverpool's second: one of the all-time great Anfield goals. Having just scored a remarkable final-third interplay goal at Wembley to go 3-0 up against Man City – real dreamland stuff – this was an even more sumptuous move, with 25 passes and only Virgil van Dijk failing to register a touch. There was a sublime diagonal by the imperious Thiago, flicks and nudges by players on the left and the right, a Cruyff turn, all uninterrupted until the ball reached Matip in the midfield area (where he had played at times for Schalke in Rangnick's era).

The beauty of Liverpool's passing, when done right, is the pace on the ball, especially to players with their back to goal. You can argue that in bygone eras these would be considered overhit to feet, but now, on perfect pitches with elite techniques, the best players can handle that. Slower passing means slower moves, and also, more chance for an opposing team to get goal-side, as well as more time to slide in and intercept. That said, it takes confidence and flow to pass this quickly, this firmly.

Matip zipped it into Díaz, and the Colombian controlled the ball and laid it back, with four United players creating an eerily perfect square around him: two behind him (one to his left, one to his right), closing to try and nip the ball, and two in front of him (one to his left, one to his right), trying to intercept the pass back to Matip. Then, with those four players around Díaz, Matip absolutely *slammed* a low pass into Sadio Mané's feet. Mané moved towards the ball, but in one movement turned it around the proverbial corner; not even looking as he contorted his body to play a pass that would dislocate the groin and explode the kneecaps of some mere mortals. (Poor Phil Jones had to go off at half-time, perhaps in shock.) It had just enough elevation to sail over Harry Maguire's outsized head, to land on a sixpence for the inrushing Mo Salah, without an open-play goal in months, to race in and smash the ball past David de Gea for the fourth time in 2021/22. Any more on Mané's pass and it would have been 'keeper's ball'; any less, and it wouldn't have fallen into Salah's path. Any lower and it would hit the player nicknamed 'slabhead'; any higher and it would have drifted towards the Anfield Road stand, likely to bounce and roll out of play. All this at the end of a sublime passing move. The finish itself was nothing special: a simple and clinical side-foot after one-touch control; but it was one of *the* great Liverpool goals, in a season of great Liverpool goals.

The second half was drifting a bit, with Liverpool following the recent pattern of great first-halves followed by trying to rest in possession after the break, but getting a bit sloppy. Then Andrew Robertson burst forward, and suddenly Liverpool were swarming into acres of space; a four vs. four, albeit the Reds were momentarily in a straight line across the pitch, with United holding a generally good defensive line (in line with Liverpool's breaking players) … except for Maguire, five yards behind the others. When Robertson played it to Díaz, Mané was in the middle, unmarked as Maguire backed away to an excessive degree. At no point did Mané try to get within those five yards Maguire had given him; the United captain looking at the Liverpool striker at the start of the break, but then focusing only on the ball for the next 40 yards of back-pedalling. By the time the United defender neared his own six-yard box, Mané was nearing the penalty spot, where he swept home a first-time finish from Díaz's low cross; Maguire turning just in time to see the space he'd left the Senegalese, and able to watch the ball sail past him into the net. It was an object lesson in how to find space: there was absolutely no need for Mané, even though quicker, to try and chase beyond Maguire, given the excessive distance the lumbering defender allowed himself. The England stalwart, terrified of any striker's pace, constantly backs away to the safety of the six-yard box, and so Mané didn't then need to try and make an explosive near-post dart in that narrowing area of the pitch, as players converged; he just needed to hang back, unmarked. By the time the Reds reached the box, two further United players had entered the picture: Fernandes had jogged back but never got within 10 yards of Mané, and Matić had been drawn out to Robertson and Díaz on the flank.

By this stage of the season, the Reds ranked top for league goals scored after the 75th minute, with 18, and top for fewest conceded in the final stages, with just two.

"People might say I'm obsessed with the counter-press," Klopp said in a subsequent press conference. "The counter-press [against United] was absolutely, completely, different level."

Meanwhile, the most famous media pundit for the defeated club mixed anger and admiration when noting, "Thiago was laughing when he came off, he was laughing at Manchester United all game. I don't normally swear on *The Gary Neville Podcast* but he took the piss out of Manchester United tonight."

He wasn't wrong. Thiago's numbers were: 95% Pass accuracy (105/110); 6/6 Accurate long passes; three chances created; 3/3 dribbles completed; 7/9 duels won; 3/4 tackles won; two interceptions; 1/1 laughing when he came off.

The rout was completed in the 85th minute – a 19th late league goal – when Maguire played a woeful pass out to the flank to substitute Hannibal Mejbri (six stone in weight, five of them consisting of hair). Robertson shrugged him aside, and substitute Diogo Jota – not at his best since an early-spring injury and now struggling to get a start due to Díaz's impact – escaped the teenage midfielder to slide a beautiful pass into Salah's path, to remind people of his quality. The aesthetics were then a little dented by the deflection on Salah's shot off the sliding Wan-Bissaka as the ball looped over de Gea, but it was the Egyptian's goal, and the score was 4-0. A chance a few minutes later for Salah to make it 5-0, *again*, with a hat-trick against United, *again*, went begging due to a loose touch in a one-on-one, with Wan-Bissaka able to get back and block this time without the ball ending up in the back of the net. Salah smiled ruefully, as you can when you're 4-0 up against your arch rivals.

Dowdy was impressed, when sharing his experiences of the match. "From the start of the game we were clearly on the front foot. We carved them open early and got ahead with a lovely cross and finish. An explosion of joy and, internally at least, a sigh of relief.

"As I mentioned on TTT yesterday afternoon, the minute's applause for Ronaldo's tragedy was excellent; a chance to show our class as fans and a club. Rivalry rightly put aside temporarily, some things are just more important. It was actually a beautiful moment, with a rendition of *You'll Never Walk Alone* to boot, and reminded me of a game years ago when Norwich keeper Brian Gunn made his first appearance back at Anfield after his own similar tragedy. It's what sportsmanship is all about in my mind. A good friend – a United fan – texted me at half-time to say what a quality gesture it was. Shame about some of the United fans' chants afterwards but that's sadly par for the course with most visiting teams."

Gavin Maxwell, an expat TTT subscriber whose sister-in-law (a well-known television actress) had recently died (and for which he sought advice about the unpublished book she'd left behind, and how it might be released posthumously), ended his off-topic email with a quick reflection on the game, that I asked if I could share with readers, given the different experience it represented. "A mighty result tonight! What a team. The beauty of living in California is that we get all the footie early in the morning at the weekends, and midweek games like this, beautifully at lunchtime. And every single Premier League game televised – it's remarkable.

"When I was back over [in England] for the funeral it was really odd that the first game begins at noon on a Saturday, rather than last game finishing at noon on a Saturday as it does with us, so you can get out into the sunshine and enjoy the rest of the day!"

Meanwhile, TTT Subscriber Robert Ducker started his day in Malta, and still made it to the match. Once home, he shared his experiences with me.

"Over the past decade or so, I made it a point to watch Liverpool at Anfield at least twice a year, until Covid-19 put an abrupt end to my plan. Little did I know that our win against Chelsea in April 2019 would be my last game for almost three years. Yet that is how it turned out to be. At the start of this year, I asked my dad if he could get hold of any tickets – any game but the United game. I just could not bear to watch Liverpool vs. United live, having gone through the experience twice before. The first one was a bore draw in 2005, the second one, we dominated for most of the match until Wayne Rooney managed to score from their only shot on target in 2016. I was sitting close to the away fans on that day, and it was one of the worst experiences of my football life. I told myself, never again against this shower.

"Yet, the only tickets I could get my hands on were for the United game. I thought we would either batter them, as we are so much better than them, or lose to some lucky goal out of nowhere. You can never call a Liverpool vs. United game and the closer the game got, the more nervous I was getting. Imagine for a moment losing to this poor United team, ending our quadruple hopes. I think winning the quadruple is close to impossible, but rest assured that they would use it as a stick to beat us with. It would be their trophy for the season. Just like what happened when we lost to Watford in our nearly flawless title-winning season.

"Easter Monday came by, and it was time to go. I picked up my dad at around 8.30am to make the c.3,000-kilometre journey to Manchester, before catching a train to Liverpool Lime Street. A journey that takes approximately nine-to-10 hours, and meant some quality time with the old man. We discussed the improvement we have seen over the past years since we first started to make this trip. We witnessed some great games against Everton (3-2 in 1999, 4-0 in 2006), Man City (3-2 in 2014, 3-0 in 2016) but also some poor ones, like the dull 0-0 against Swansea (2011) and the 3-0 loss to West Ham (2015). We didn't just make the effort when things were going well for us.

"On the day of the game, we went for a stroll around the city centre. Lots of Liverpool fans around, and the expectation seemed high. We got ready, had a quick pub meal and a couple of beers, and then proceeded to catch the 917 (I think) bus to Anfield. Dad was in the Upper Main Stand, whilst I was in the Lower, close to the Kop. Not a great spot to watch the game, but at least close enough to the singing and far enough from *that* lot. The guy behind me was a loud one, which was great. I thought the atmosphere was excellent from start to finish, the best in a while. The absolute best for me in terms of support was the Liverpool vs. Man City game in 2014 when Anfield was bouncing, but this was close.

"The one thing you could clearly see live is how fast and well-drilled we are. Our passing was accurate, players were making runs opening passing lanes. The Kop sang *Poetry in Motion* at one stage because that was just it. Every player knew his job, what he had to do and how to make life easier for his team-mates. Thiago's movement, his control of the ball was out of this world. Nobody could get close to him. Yet he was running his socks off and winning back the ball.

"After the match I met dad in front of the big screen outside Anfield, and we walked to the bus all smiles. We laughed at our pessimism before the match, the Thiago masterclass and how he was supposed to be our problem last year. The question we kept asking ourselves was how did we become so good? We are challenging a stated-sponsored football team that can afford to pay £100million for someone to sit on the bench and model for Gucci. Then they go and spend another fortune on a striker and pay him half a million a week the following year. That's probably why we are so glad that Jürgen is a Red."

Around this time I asked subscriber Allen Baynes to pen a few words about the title races of old: "There is no doubt about it, league title run-ins were different when we had black-and-white TV! Of course, even when we got colour TV there was no internet/Sky/Twitter/ LFCTV, not even *Match of the Day* in 1964 etc. You followed the run-in by going to the match or buying the *Echo* or a daily paper. I remember, as a 13-year-old, only knowing that Everton had recently won the League because I was born and was living off County Road, also I knew that Wolves had a good name but there wasn't the same media information or hype that sucked you in, wound you up and then pissed you off. Simpler times.

"Also, as a thirteen-year-old, you thought that you knew everything because you read the occasional *Charles Buchan's Football Monthly*, (that's one for the auld fellas!). You in fact got most of your information from your elderly relatives or, best of all, listening to your dad's mates when they came back to your house after a few/many bevvies. It was from these weekly education sessions that you understood about football, what was current and most of all the story of the Reds and in particular the revered Mr William Beveridge Liddell, our very own King Billy.

"So, when I started going to the match with my mates from Kirkby (from the start of the 1963/64 season) – we moved there when I was 10 – I started to take more notice of the league tables and particularly at this time, as we seemed always, or nearly always, to be winning. Of course, when you go to the match on a regular basis you get sucked into the match-going culture and you find yourself listening to all that goes with supporting your team. The players, the songs and chants, the abuse and praise that are heaped on players: who is good, who is respected and who is hated.

"I have to say, as someone who went to every home game in the Boys' Pen, I remember very little of the detail of the games, after all I was 13 years old, and it was nearly 60 years ago! I do remember a wondrous goal from Alfie Arrowsmith against Derby, however, there are no video clips to prove, or disprove my assertion that it was the most wondrous goal that has ever graced Anfield. Trust me it was brilliant, but with Alfie you never knew if he really meant it. (Thanks to *LFCHistory* guys Arnie Baldursson and Gudmundur Magnusson for confirming that Alfie scored in the 88th minute of that game on January 4th 1964 in their excellent book: *Liverpool the Complete Record*.)

"So, there I was, 13, a regular in the Pen, with a gang of mates from Kirkby and suddenly we were about to win the league for the first time since 1947. It all seemed like that this was the normal thing, a bit like starting to watch the Reds in the 1980s. The enormity of it was only realised by listening to my dad's mates and the way they had started to worship the Saint, the as yet un-knighted Sir Roger and big Rowdy, but most of all the messiah, the great Bill Shankly. It was clearly a big deal: we were now almost on a par with the Toffees – imagine only being almost on a par with them?

"The league was duly won after a seven-match winning streak that culminated on a warm April day with a cracking 5-0 thrashing of the Arsenal. You will have probably seen the BBC *Panorama* report of the game and the interest in the culture around our club and the city which had suddenly become the centre of the world music scene and, as we later christened it, the Mecca of modern nightlife. As Scousers we are never knowingly understated. If you haven't seen the *Panorama* programme it is a must see, it gets very close to showing what watching the Reds at this auspicious time was like, albeit without bruised ribs and jeans with wet legs – use your imagination! The Kop and the adjoining Boys' Pen were the most exciting places on earth to watch the match. It was noisy, full of humour, a swirling, swaying, tumbling, roaring stew of humanity. A pan of Scouse with everything and everyone thrown in, and it was fantastic to be part of it. It is also heartening to see that most of those ingredients were to be found in and around Wembley on Saturday. How lucky to be a Red!"

Trounced

After the game Opta Joe tweeted: "Manchester United have lost 0-9 on aggregate in their Premier League meetings with Liverpool this season. In their league history, they've only suffered a combined heavier defeat once – 0-11 vs Sunderland in 1892-93. Trounced."

It was also the first time since 1896 that Liverpool had scored nine in a season against United, back then known as Newton Heath. In more recent times, in the Premier League era since pass-numbers were recorded (2003) only four players have had more than 100 in games against Manchester United, and three were Reds: Jordan Henderson (121) in the 5-0 in October 2021, and 108 each by Thiago and Virgil Van Dijk in the 4-0 six months later. (The other, Rodri, scraped in with 100 from November 2021, and clearly, all occurred in one season.)

BBC Chief football writer Phil McNulty: "Two league games this season, a 9-0 'aggregate' in Liverpool's favour. A chastening example of what happens when a club with a structure that has recruited brilliantly comes up against a monstrosity compiled via a lack of structure and a recruitment strategy seemingly based on the logic of plucking names out of a hat."

A bubbly Andy Robertson told BBC *5Live*: "It was a really enjoyable night … If you can't have fun at this period of the season with what we're doing then you're in the wrong profession. We're fighting for all trophies, trying to play cup finals every single week it feels like. We all play with a smile on our face but we're determined inside. You have to enjoy games like tonight – if none of us are smiling after this we have a bigger problem. We have to keep doing what we're doing and keep winning games."

Gary Lineker succinctly summed it all up: "That was an absolute demolition job. @LFC were utterly joyous to watch. @ManUtd were utterly joyless to watch."

Rafa Left Blue in the Derby

Rafa Benítez's hopes of getting one over on his old club – upsetting his true love, while locked in a new, loveless marriage of convenience – didn't last long (just as his tenure didn't last much longer). The game, at Goodison, was almost up after 20 minutes. Having got to know Rafa quite well during his time at Liverpool, I fully understood why he'd take the job (all those years later, with a good deal of time in between), but to me it felt like he was on a hiding to nothing, with zero leeway to be granted as soon as any game was lost.

With nine minutes gone, Liverpool won the ball on halfway, Andy Robertson intercepting and playing a swift forward pass. Diogo Jota pinged one back to Jordan Henderson, and the captain, first-time, lofted a ball to Sadio Mané, that flew a fraction too high; Mané only able to head it out wide, albeit when retaining possession. He then laid in the underlapping left-back, and something much-needed happened for the Scot, in a way that hadn't in several recent games.

For some reason, when Roberson was hitting the byline in that stage of the season, his pull-backs were actually angled too obtusely: *behind* the onrushing Liverpool players, and often to the opposition on the edge of the box. Teams then could break, with five or six Reds ahead of the ball (as Brighton had done when drawing at Anfield, with Robertson making the same error several times right in front of where I was sitting). Fortunately, despite the ball missing the intended target of Mané, this time there were eight Everton players in the box – all of them nine yards or closer to their goal, as he pulled the ball back. That left a spare nine yards towards the edge of the box, manned by not a single player from either side. Bizarrely, there didn't appear to be another Everton player within 40 yards of their own goal: the area, 20 yards outside the box, patrolled by Thiago and Henderson. Mané and Mo Salah both made moves back towards the ball that appeared to be going to no one, but coming onto it, in acres of space and starting his run deeper than the D of the box, was Henderson, who curled a first-time low shot into the corner. (Even Jordan's arms appear to be longer than his namesake and fellow ex-Mackem in the Everton goal.)

The second came when Joël Matip headed away in his own box, and Henderson controlled the ball on his chest. His ball forward was intercepted, but Thiago won it back, and Henderson resumed control, hitting a lovely grass-cutting pass 40 yards along the inside-right channel, where Mo Salah was able to sprint free, take a touch, and then curl a beauty past Pickford, as the angle (like the keeper's arms) was narrowing slightly. As at Old Trafford a few weeks earlier, the game wasn't even 20 minutes old, and the Reds led 2-0.

To make things interesting, Demarai Gray pulled one back on 38 minutes with a thumping drive in off the far post, but that was as good as it got on the night for the Toffees. They thought they had a chance to equalise in the 65th minute, with a corner; mere seconds later, they were 3-1 down. Robertson headed the danger clear at the near post, and Gray turned to play the ball back to Seamus Coleman. The defender took his eye off the ball, and suddenly Salah was behind the entire Everton defence, and he hadn't quite crossed halfway. He raced through and hit a slow but accurate shot into the far corner. With ten minutes to go, Jota Cruyff-turned Allan in the box, approached Pickford at a narrow angle and just absolutely leathered it past him with utter disdain. Cue a mass exodus at Goodison Park.

Benítez lasted another six weeks, when Frank Lampard replaced him. At the time Benítez was sacked, Everton, though sinking, were still relatively safe from relegation.

Lampard vs Klopp

There seems a strange sense of entitlement to Frank Lampard's career as a manager. In July 2020, in a 5-3 victory over Lampard's Chelsea on the evening that Liverpool were due to receive the Premier League trophy, the Blues' boss responded to what he perceived as a slight from the Liverpool bench to snipe: "One title you've won and you're fucking giving it the big 'un. Fuck off!"

Even in the heat of the battle, this seems an incredibly strange thing to say. Did Lampard think his *playing* trophies counted in this particular debate? Once you become a manager, then your playing days are not part of the equation.

As it stood, Lampard had been a manager for a couple of years, *and won nothing*. Liverpool had just won the Premier League in 2020, having also won the Champions League and the World Club Cup. Did Lampard think being losing playoff finalists with Derby County was such an achievement that it made winning the Premier League, the Champions League and the World Club Cup inconsequential? And if the barb was directed in part at Jürgen Klopp, there was his promotion (along with some of his staff members) with lowly Mainz, his back-to-back titles with cash-strapped Borussia Dortmund, and a domestic cup win thrown in, along with reaching a Champions League final. This was a manager who, by that stage, had contested three of the latter (a fourth would follow in 2022), as well as a Europa League final. As players, Lampard was miles ahead of Klopp, as Klopp would duly admit; as a *manager*, Lampard is not fit to lace his boots, or to chalk his tactics board.

After the Reds beat Everton 2-0 in April 2022, Jonathan Liew wrote of the visitors in the *Guardian*, "…There was grappling and timewasting, bawling and brawling, diving and pratfalling. Richarlison seemed to spend most of the game lying on the ground like a cow preparing for a rainstorm. Jordan Pickford deliberated over his goal-kicks as if he was choosing a mortgage." Indeed, a highlight of the game (and the season?) was Alisson exaggeratedly falling on the ball in injury time, to mock Pickford's antics.

Ken Early wrote in the *Irish Times*, "Everton, Lampard claimed, were not in a position to go 'toe to toe', instead they had to be 'smart'. But sitting back and trying to defend your own box for 90 minutes against Liverpool at Anfield is not 'smart'. It's dumb. Everton finished with 17 per cent of possession – the second-lowest figure since Premier League records began. There are many words you could use to describe the plan that produced this outcome but 'smart' is not one of them.

"The smart teams of today don't play ultradefensive against superior opposition, as they often did in the years when José Mourinho and Frank Lampard were European football's leading power couple. The smart teams now go after the opposition. The smart teams chase the opposition. They express their humility by working harder than the opposition, by running more, by using all their energy to force the game in directions the opposition do not want.

"Everton did not do any of this. Everton sat back and let Liverpool have the ball and tried to waste time and frustrate and every so often send Anthony Gordon haring after a long pass like a Scouse Caniggia. This might have worked against Brendan Rodgers' Liverpool, who were a collection of gifted individuals, making it up as they went along. Against Klopp's Liverpool – the modern superteam, fitter, stronger, more talented, more experienced, better organised, and better led than any Liverpool side of the past – it's like playing a game of Russian roulette where you are the only player."

Football365's John Nicholson also took issue with the Everton manager: "My Lampard antipathy is rooted in the fact that this was a job that he ought never to have been given and was not qualified in any way to do and was only given because he's Frank Lampard, ex-top footballer. Same goes for the Chelsea job. While that sort of over-promotion of someone because they're a famous name is less common in football now than it once was, the fact it still happens needs calling out.

"Anyone who had Frank's short nearly four-year managerial CV who wasn't Frank Lampard would never have been anywhere near that job. Firstly, because managing Derby County and Chelsea is not a grounding to pull Everton out of a spiral of decline; fighting relegation is a skill and you need some experience to draw and great man-management to motivate the players to do it."

"… More annoyingly still, his appointment fits into broader societal trends where the over-privileged constantly fail upwards, fecking up one job after another only to be given another high-ranking, highly paid job, only to do it all over again ad infinitum, meanwhile opportunity is denied to other more talented people, blocked by this underperforming elite.

"What has Lampard actually done for the club? Taken them from 16th to 18th, that's what."

In fairness to Lampard, he then became a hero for taking them back to 16th.

If you look at Klopp's record, he started at a similar level to Lampard, managing in the 2nd tier, albeit with the German club the poorest in that division, in contrast to lavish-spending Derby County (whose largesse came back to bite them in 2021/22 when, docked 21 points for various historical financial and administration breaches, they were relegated to the third tier). Klopp did seven years at the tiny club, taking them to the top flight for the first time in their history. Lampard did a year at Derby, then got the Chelsea job.

Lampard's Everton signings after his late arrival in the January transfer window also suggest an arrogance. Battling relegation – or at least, close enough for it to be a concern – he plumped for two extravagant, big-name, highly-paid recent flops, who arrived on the back of little or no football, but still to be paid over £100,000-a-week for their efforts (or lack thereof). Donny van de Beek walked in as joint top-earner, and Dele Alli wasn't far behind. Much further behind, however, were the few Everton players who were battling to keep the team in the Premier League (as well as various ones who didn't appear to be trying). These felt like luxury signings, rather than dedicated and talented grafters who'd drag the team up the league by the scruff of its neck. Neither added anything of note to the survival efforts.

Indeed, Everton had copied Manchester United in the previous five years in snapping up relatively big names and seeing them fail in a multitude of ways.

Schadenfreude

United and Everton fans deliriously mocked Liverpool's failure to land the quadruple, but 2021/22 saw Liverpool beat both sides in ways almost never seen before. United ended the season 6th with the 2nd-biggest £XI in the league, and Everton, with the 7th-highest £XI, finished 16th. United and Everton won nothing and played absolutely awful football for most of the season; Liverpool won two trophies, came close to two more, and scored 147 goals.

It's not *necessary* that any schadenfreude be involved in sport, although individual fans will take their own levels of pleasure from the misfortunes of a club whose fans enjoyed two decades of ascendency and nose-rubbing. A little enjoyment of rivals' failings is natural, especially in a dog-eat-dog world, but making it your *focus* feels unhealthy.

Still, if anyone who supports United or Everton wants to laugh at the Reds over 2021/22, then it feels akin to The Cheeky Girls mocking the Beatles because *Penny Lane / Strawberry Fields Forever* – arguably the greatest double-A-side in history – only went to no.2 in the UK charts after four years of nothing but no.1 hits for the Scouse legends; the very same chart position reached by *Cheeky Song (Touch My Bum)*.

Dickheads and Lost Boys, Old Dogs and Egotists, Smart Buys and Starmen

Success in the transfer market isn't just about buying the right players; it's also about avoiding the *wrong* ones. This chapter addresses the need to avoid bad eggs, but also, how players lose their way, while others remain seemingly evergreen, at least on an individual level.

One theme I keep addressing when assessing the ongoing success of Jürgen Klopp is his strict rule on 'no dickheads'; none will be signed, no matter how talented – a personal maxim for him and his coaches beginning in his Mainz days, as he continues to seek unity as a way of a team exceeding the sum of its parts, and which endures while working on a smaller budget than rivals. Two years on from my last book, *Perched*, it's amazing how many other clubs, in that time, have continued to sign dickheads, disruptors, egotists and fading forces; while Liverpool continued to do the exact opposite.

Dating back to his earliest days as a manager, Klopp used strict questionnaires to discover what really made a player tick, asking a prospective signing about how hard he'd be prepared to run; if he was the kind of player who didn't like to train too hard – happy to coast and reserve energy – but would promise to give his all during matches; if he'd be happy scoring a couple of goals without doing the hard graft, either for the team or in preparation.

Anyone who wasn't prepared to work insanely hard all week in training *as well* as giving their all 90 minutes each game for the team found themselves instantly dismissed.

While most clubs would now say that they have a 'no dickhead' policy, few seem to stick to it. I've detailed in my previous two books the Liverpool players who, in the years before Klopp arrived, would have failed the test. Two that Klopp inherited – Mario Balotelli (just not a serious trainer and a general distraction) and Lazar Marković (not a dedicated trainer) – were never even considered by the German.

The 'dickhead' – in football parlance – may just be a bad or lazy trainer. Or, he may be a bad teammate – a selfish player. He need not be a bad *person*, albeit that can obviously be an issue too (team harmony isn't helped by sleeping with a teammate's wife, for example). He could be a lovely bloke, but a pain in the arse; a time-drain on the management and coaching staff. Sometimes, he's just a Lost Boy: taken from a safe environment, and suffering under the spotlight, or bereft of direction and motivation; someone potentially recoverable, but where it may take time and effort (and that's okay if you have the time to make the effort). While you can get a bargain if you can rekindle their spirit and desire, you can also get a white elephant who drains resources and saps team spirit; especially if he's paid based on past glories, rather than current effort.

With every passing season, 'no dickheads' is a rule that makes more sense to me, as I observe what makes some teams tick and others implode, as Liverpool continue to sign model professionals – and many big-spending rivals rack up high-profile signings who rock the boat, and upset the apple cart, and piss in the pool; or various other metaphors that show how negative effects can spread. The whole concept of the bad apple – why it's so disastrous – is that *it rots the rest*; the full phrase being that "one bad apple can spoil the barrel". Another metaphor is that the weakest link breaks the chain, and so you don't want weak links in terms of attitude. While scouting players and managing a football team is about much more than this one rule, it remains vitally important.

It has even spread to dickhead family members and dickhead agents, all of whom need to be avoided. Hangers-on need to be scraped off like unwanted barnacles. A united team and a united squad requires a sublimation of the ego – what I call the *egosystem* – to make for a whole that pulls in the same direction. Again, it's no coincidence that modern Liverpool don't sign superstars, and that players *become* superstars at Liverpool; and if they leave, certainly after shining under the management of Jürgen Klopp, they often return to being mere mortals.

Part of this is having a wage structure that allows no one individual to be out on his own.

It's about focusing on their football to the exclusion of other excessive energy-drains and distractions.

It's about players *wanting to be here*.

All of these require strong leadership, from the manager, the coaching staff and the analytics and scouting staff who make the big decisions. The stronger the leadership, the easier it is to keep everyone in line; but strong and *unfair* leadership can prove disastrous, too. Again, it's one thing assembling a squad without bad apples, and another to get them to play great football, and remain committed and enthused over the longer term.

When reading this chapter, think about whether or not Liverpool would have made some of the decisions discussed. Remember, these are players often earning more money than those who play for Klopp, and in some cases, at least twice as much. Later on, I'll discuss the positive impacts of some of Liverpool's record-breaking squad, as well as the difficult decision of when to phase out great servants.

Dele Alli's Brother

In mid-January, before Dele Alli moved to Everton for a fee that ranged from £0 to £40m, Jonathan Northcroft wrote about the player's strange decline in the *Sunday Times*.

"[Mauricio] Pochettino voiced fears about the pitfalls the player faced as early as in 2017, in his book *Brave New World*. 'Dele is experiencing a new situation. Praise can create confusion,' Pochettino wrote. The Argentine also observed that Dele 'needs to be surrounded by the right people' and in the agency world they wonder whether his representative is the best-placed person to gee him up and push him on. Dele's previous agent was the experienced Rob Segal, who has a reputation for being able to challenge his clients, but since 2017 he has been managed by his best friend and adoptive brother, Harry Hickford, who is part of a group of mates with whom he enjoys socialising.

"Another lives with him, and anyone who has met Dele will attest to a laidback, fairly shy, polite and gentle nature."

So, he's not some nasty lunatic, but the warning signs had been there since 2017, with the alarming change of agent and the best recent-years Spurs' manager's warning; and 2016/17 marked the player's peak, with 2017/18 seeing a halving of his league goals, from 18 to nine. Between 2020 and 2022, he scored just once – for Spurs and in his first five months at Everton. Indeed, he didn't even start a league game for the Toffees until the final game of the season: a 5-1 defeat at Arsenal, where he departed after 67 minutes with the score 4-1. Maybe his talent will shine through again, but it needs hard work and dedication.

Relating to another sport, but with parallels of the pitfalls, in May 2022, Owen Slot in the *Times* wrote about how one of Britain's greatest-ever boxers saw his career derailed on the back of family interference.

"Some would argue that it was Hamed's family who removed him. The great soap opera of 'Prince Naseem' was the family takeover; the

Hamed brothers took over the management from Frank Warren and took Naseem away from the [Brendan] Ingle gym and overseas.

"'They ruined him,' is how Warren reflects on it now. 'I mean, if Naz played for Man United, does that mean they could manage Man Utd?'"

[As an aside, here, could they have done much worse than the *actual* managers United chose?]

"Maybe this is a side of the story still to be told because one of the few Hamed siblings left in Sheffield is Ali, four years Naseem's younger, now a personal trainer, who is trying to sell a TV documentary about how boxing's millions detonated an everyday Asian working-class family.

"'Unfortunately the family has eroded,' is how he puts it. He alleges that the considerable estate left behind by their late parents, which is a consequence of Naseem's success, is now being scrapped over by the kids.

"This is a family that always appeared so tight. "That is what it looked like,' he says, 'but internally, it was an absolute free-for-all with the younger ones not having the maturity or the intelligence to be able to grasp the millions on the table.'"

Too much too young, as the two-toned poet Terence Edward Hall put it in 1979. Occasionally a family member or friend can offer a wise guiding hand, but too often it now seems to be about spreading out the wealth within an entourage at the expense of proper guidance and long-term career planning. Friends and family do not tend to offer dispassionate advice, especially in an age where 'home truths' are no longer fashionable, and there's a culture of just telling people how brilliant they are; that they are *perfect,* just as they are. That's an invitation to stagnate.

(The French midfielder Adrien Rabiot's mother, Veronique, who acts as his agent, is famously overprotective, to the point where dealing with her, and her son, sounds difficult in the extreme; even if family difficulties led to the decision to 'helicopter parent' his career. Chaos seems to follow the player, wherever he goes.)

After moving clubs, and with a lot to prove after two years of decline, Dele Alli arrived at his first training session in a £300,000 Rolls-Royce. While people may not want to be judged by the cars they drive – and clearly it does not sum up everything about a person – the choice of a vehicle is a conscious decision, that *displays* something.

Zlatan Ibrahimović wrote of his time with Pep Guardiola in 2009/10: "At Barça, players were banned from driving their sports cars to training. I thought this was ridiculous – it was no one's business what car I drive – so in April, before a match with Almeria, I drove my Ferrari Enzo to work. It caused a scene."

Yet as great as an individual player Ibrahimović was, he did not fit in at Barcelona, the best *team* he played for. Barcelona got better without him. He got better without them, too, but no team he played for got close to the Barça team he was essentially booted out of. And even then, you could argue that if anyone had the right to drive a Ferrari Enzo to work it was *Zlatan*. But did it help anyone? Did it help him? Did it help Barcelona?

Who won?

The more ostentatious the car, the greater the sense of attention it will draw; unless perhaps a beaten-up old Volkswagen, in which case, attention is drawn by a different kind of shock. People may be outraged at a footballer driving a £300,000 car (playing for a club whose stadium is situated in an area where the average house price is one-third that amount); and then a kind of backlash arises, where people say, "why can't they drive a £300,000 car if they want?" and find reasons why the criticism might be sinister. But none of that really matters.

The *issue* is: on the first day of training, when properly meeting many teammates for the first time, what signal are you going to send? It feels like peacocking, and yet does that bond and unify? While Everton and Spurs are both traditionally big clubs, the latter remained part of the Big Six, and the former – last a mighty force in the 1980s – were fighting relegation, albeit still a few points and places above the drop-zone. So Alli was taking a step down, as his career drifted. After four Spurs managers had questioned his attitude or disliked his work ethic, a sense of responsibility had to fall upon the player himself.

Writing for *Caught Offside* in April 2022, Alli's ex-agent, Rob Segal, noted: "From Everton's point-of-view, there are players who went there in the winter, who were free transfers, but are on big contracts. Dele is a player who, since being at Goodison Park, just has not delivered, so I would be surprised if any of the top clubs are considering him even if Everton does end up going down. Dele didn't go in there as an £80m player – he was a free transfer. To add insult to injury, to turn up on his first day in a Rolls-Royce was really rubbing it in the fans' faces, well documented and ill-advised…"

While José Mourinho has clearly lost a lot of his ability to relate to, and inspire, players who obviously get ever younger in relation to himself (and has become a manager out of time, in terms of elite levels – the Europa Conference League, full of mid-table clubs, is now more his speed), he clearly also knows when a player doesn't train properly.

"I told Dele very directly that he doesn't train well," he said when in charge at Spurs. "He's not a good trainer. I'm not saying he's a disaster but I'm not saying he's Harry Kane. Harry Kane trains well."

The spiky Portuguese also said, "… He's not a good trainer, we need to find the right motivation for the guy." It is a message that Mourinho repeats again, albeit with more force – caught by Amazon TV cameras for its 2020 *All Or Nothing* documentary – in Tottenham's pre-match team meeting when he says to Alli in front of his teammates: "I understood already that you are a fucking lazy guy in training."

"I asked him if he was Dele or Dele's brother?" Mourinho also famously said.

Meanwhile, as Everton battled relegation, Dominic Calvert-Lewin appeared in various photoshoots, wearing 'outlandish' clothes, including a schoolgirl's uniform. While each player has a right to do whatever he wants privately, the *public* image – when fighting for a football team – ideally needs to reflect a sense of dedication. Of course, had Calvert-Lewin done so a year earlier, when playing such good football, it might have been different; at that stage he could have played in the Premier League in a tutu and tiara if scoring goals, bullying defenders and tearing past opponents.

Calvert-Lewin ended up battling some dark thoughts, and as such he deserves some sympathy: "One thing I learned this season is that everyone in whatever walk of life is fighting battles you know nothing about, and there is no shame in finding someone to talk to and being open and honest with yourself about how you really feel. To all the young kings suppressing emotion I advise you to talk, to a friend, family member or someone that will listen, talking saved my life."

Yet the more high-profile you make yourself, the more you will invite certain pressures. Fame can obviously, and frequently, be destructive; and greater the fame, the crazier people seem to get.

Unlike other high-profile pursuits, footballers can't really take time off to coast and pursue other interests. A film star can embark on a music career, or vice versa, but they are not part of a fixed team, where constant unity is essential; they can take a sabbatical, mix things up. Beyond often simply needing to look good, peak physical conditioning is not essential. Elite players are contracted to play football with the long-term stability of deals up to six-years in length (unless the club tries to sell them, but of course, cannot without their permission), and in return there needs to be total devotion to the cause.

Football fans are not like other cultural consumers, in that they pay a lot of money week after week; not for one great concert a year, or a two-hour film, but for a commitment of ten months each season. Most people don't care if their favourite singer is out partying or doing enough cocaine to kill a hippopotamus; but most football fans want their players to be serious about what they do (especially now that exceptional fitness is required to excel, and the cost of watching is so much greater than in the more amateurish days of yore). And while 'optics' is often a terrible concept – how something looks is not always how something *is* – there ideally needs to be a projection of professionalism and dedication. Indeed, there should *be* professionalism and dedication. And while some extracurricular pursuits are healthy, especially to escape the pressure-cooker environment of being constantly surveilled and judged, there will always be questions asked if a player draws attention to himself with anything other than performances. Even doing virtuous things can backfire.

For example, it would be totally wrong to say that Marcus Rashford is a 'dickhead' because he led extremely worthwhile movements to help underprivileged children. But at the same time, any off-field activity that raises a player's profile also raises the focus on them *on the pitch*; and while it may be wrong to say that it *causes* a dip in form, being high-profile drags into the orbit all manner of external factors. Rashford was awarded the MBE, which seemed well deserved – but it took him to a higher profile level that his mere playing talent had not yet merited. The more you draw attention to yourself, the more you'd better be sure that you're performing at an elite level. (Such as: Paul Gascoigne and Robbie Fowler bleaching their hair shocking blonde in the mid-'90s – it helped that they played to elite levels, which was not a luxury Øyvind Leonhardsen and István Kozma could afford.)

If a player would rather focus on social issues, or fashion, or a music career, then that is every individual's choice and their right. It is their life, after all. But it cannot be at the expense of the football; if it becomes more important, then the football career will wither. These days, you cannot be a casual footballer; especially when earning north of £200,000 a week. By all means, play part-time in non-league for the love of the game if other issues have become more important. (Doing so would arguably be a net-good for humanity.) Of course, then the cachet of being at a huge club is lost; the fame will dwindle, as will the influence. One of the things fans expect, when players are being paid that much money, is commitment to the club and to their profession. And as soon as it *looks* like that's not the case, there can be trouble; even if the trouble is not entirely fair. At the very least, it makes life harder by inviting criticism that can be hard to shift, and which becomes a vicious cycle.

After all, Liverpool did not lose the 1996 FA Cup final *because* of the cream suits, nor did David James' Armani photoshoots cause him to drop simple crosses. But it all added to a sense of diminished *seriousness*, as Manchester United, arguably no more talented, hoovered up titles. The Reds – seen also in cream or ecru – were dubbed the 'Spice Boys' because they had a bit too much public fun while failing to meet on-field expectations. They were a great team to watch (I acquired my season ticket at the start of that time) and had bags of ability, but they did not focus as much on their game (and on things like nutrition) as that United team, who stole a march in terms of professionalism. Had the 'Spice Boys' won the trophies expected of them, then the cream suits and Armani shoots would have been moot, and no one would have been calling them the Spice Boys. They'd have called them legends, winners, immortals.

"I said to (assistant) Brian Kidd, '1-0'. Because of that," Alex Ferguson once said, apparently thinking that the designer suits played a role. "It was ridiculous. Absolutely ridiculous. Blue shirt, red and white tie and white suit. And a blue flower. Who designed that? They say it was Armani. I bet his sales went down."

By early April 2022, Everton had fallen from five points clear of the relegation zone when sacking Rafa Benítez in January, with two games in hand, to one point clear, with no games in hand (on Burnley, their closest rivals). Speaking on the eve of Everton's throwing away of two Mike Dean-awarded penalties to lose 3-2 at Burnley, ex-West Ham striker Carlton Cole said, "Right now, Dominic Calvert-Lewin can't be seen doing this! You've got to time it … It's all about Everton staying in the league, not striking a pose like Madonna!"

Everton survived, by the skin of their teeth; but it was a travesty that they were even in a relegation battle, as the 7th-most expensive team in the division, with a big wage bill and massive spending in the past half-decade. Their players let them down for an entire season, escaping relegation despite not even hitting 40 points.

Carlton Cole rightly noted that players need to have interests outside the sport, but the *timing* was terrible. And a day later it was a game where Calvert-Lewin was slated for a lack of work-rate by irate Everton fans. You could ask, why couldn't Calvert-Lewin do his attention-grabbing fashion shoots in the summer, when players are given an extended holiday? Sometimes we all have to do things to help ourselves; or to at least not make life even harder.

In 2018, Gary Neville and Roy Keane slated Jesse Lingard for launching a fashion label in the buildup to a huge game against Liverpool. Speaking as a pundit on Sky Sports, Keane said: "If that was a good, strong dressing room that wouldn't be tolerated. That's why I worry about the United dressing room.

"For a young player, still learning his trade, he could be the nicest kid in the world, I don't know him. But you're coming out with all that nonsense. I think football should be your number one priority. People say you should have other stuff outside of football but I don't think you should. Don't hide behind your cars or tattoos or girlfriends, you can do that when you retire!"

(This was, in a similar way, something Gérard Houllier successfully instilled in a young, slightly wayward Jamie Carragher: you can do all the socialising you want when you're finished. Over 700 appearances later, Carragher could hang up his boots and lead the life he wanted, with no regrets about not reaching his potential. A successful playing career then helped him transition into a successful punditry career.)

Back in 2018, Neville added: "Earlier this week, you talk about players and characters. I am actually a big fan of Jesse Lingard and I have no problem with him launching a clothes range, but don't launch it before Liverpool away, one of the biggest games of the season. Not this week, concentrate on Liverpool. Do it before Fulham. I am not having a go at his character because players should have other careers, should do other things. But you see that little thing and I thought 'not this week' it's Liverpool. Concentrate on Liverpool, no distractions. No disruptions."

Lingard scored, but United got smashed 3-1 after 33 shots from Liverpool, in a game that cost José Mourinho his job. Lingard, meanwhile, scored just three Premier League goals for United between that game at the end of December 2018 and May 2022. Again, the fashion brand didn't necessarily cause this, but it doesn't help with *perceptions*. And perceptions are what fans often work from. If enough fans think a player is underperforming because of the publicity given to outside distractions, *that matters*. They cut him less slack, and perhaps start to react differently to him at a game, or online. Again, it draws the attention towards the player, and there's less chance to hide and go under the radar during runs of bad form. Perhaps teammates who are working hard, and being paid less, also start to feel resentful.

In an article on the *Athletic* about Watford's relegation, the writer notes, "[Claudio] Ranieri's first game couldn't have gone worse. The 5-0 defeat to Liverpool was disarray personified. Ben Foster's fascination with his *YouTube* channel also led to a club rebuke after he gave away tickets to UFC fighter and Liverpool fan Paddy Pimblett in a home area. It was dealt with internally but is known to have angered several club officials, who understood the 39-year-old's desire to prepare for retirement but questioned whether his hobby should be carried out on club time, and often in private training ground areas. Whether someone should have ensured the parameters were more clearly adhered to is up for debate."

(Incidentally, as an aside, the article also offers an insight into the 'joys' Roy Hodgson brought them, with little note made in most places about how his points per game ratio was the worst of the three permanent bosses in the season. "They won at Aston Villa (1-0) and drew at Old Trafford (0-0) but why couldn't Watford pick up results at home? Hodgson's abrasive responses when questioned about it didn't endear himself to fans. Yes, he was being honest, but the relationship never really recovered from that point, even with the glimmer of hope afforded by March's 2-1 win at Southampton. The intended bounce ended up being a thud instead." Indeed, when relegation was confirmed at his old club Crystal Palace, on May 7th, he applauded the home fans but ignored the fans of the team he was actually managing. This is classic Hodgson: not such a nice guy if it happens to be your club he's dragging down. His final home game was a 5-1 defeat to Leicester, and he retired, again, after a defeat at Chelsea.)

In the old days, the problem would be hangers-on who took players down the pub, out to nightclubs, or to mingle with a bevy of beauties whose nocturnal activities sapped the stars' energy; George Best obviously remains the poster-boy for wasted talent. Maybe he had a great time. I'm *guessing* that he did, funnily enough – but it also ate away at the thing that created his fame: his footballing brilliance, and as his powers prematurely waned, he drank himself into oblivion. Nowadays, it often seems to be all about social media influence, and fashion, and perhaps music too. These are (mostly) not players staggering around blind-drunk and getting into punch-ups in seedy boozers – they generally look after themselves and behave much better – but their focus is on their own brand, and any extensions of that, like actual fashion brands. It's become so much about *image* that you have to wonder if focus is being lost – even by 5% – with their football. A drop of 5% in the marginal gains-world of ultra-fast and competitive Premier League football could be huge.

Fashion, in particular, seems to be playing a bigger role in football. Jack Grealish, who hardly set the world alight at Man City (and who would surely have failed the Reds' 'dickhead' test due to various off-pitch incidents, including various drunken stupors between the ages of 19 and 25), was reported to be in line for an expensive sponsorship contract with Gucci.

Meanwhile, in France, the Paris Saint-Germain players continued to be accused of being more interested in Paris Fashion Week than donning the kit and giving it their all for 90 minutes.

PSG

To me, PSG represent almost everything that's wrong with modern football: financial doping and sportswashing to obliterate the competition and make the league a near closed-shop; but unlike Manchester City, not especially serious about their football either.

There is a culture of disposability of managers, worship of individuals, and a fight for power and control within UEFA, in the drive for fame rather than hard-earned status; and above all else, to boost the reputation of Qatar. Even the Parisian fans have grown sick of the circus, where procuring superstars and being seen as a fashion hotbed – as the club desires – outweighs the ability to win trophies outside of France. Domestically, they operate at three times the budget of their nearest rivals, and even then they can't quite win the league every year. In Europe they've been flaky, and in previous books I've detailed my distaste for aspects of Neymar's attitude; noting how Brazil won their only Copa America in his career *the time when he wasn't there* – Roberto Firmino leading the line instead.

It got so bad in Paris in the spring of 2022 that Neymar and the new crown jewel Lionel Messi were booed for an entire game – their names jeered even before kickoff – days after crashing out of the Champions League. (And later, when they won the French title for the 8th time in ten years, the fans left early, still angered by their European collapse. According to the BBC, "The club's ultras, annoyed by the club's Champions League exit to Real Madrid, started to leave the stadium 15 minutes before the final whistle rather than celebrate with the players. The ground was empty 10 minutes after full-time and the players did not do a lap of honour afterwards.")

Adam White for *Get French Football News* wrote after they threw away a big advantage against Real Madrid: "Worryingly for PSG, their ingrained culture has become the problem. They were defeated by their own inner demons and self-destructive streak. Their pathological inability to rise to the occasion continues to bite, regardless of who the manager is. Changing that culture of defeatism and mental fragility is getting harder by the year with each crushing defeat.

"They need to act decisively, and soon. This was the clearest sign yet that their top-heavy recruitment strategy, which focuses on attack and neglects defence, is self-defeating. PSG cannot be in a position where an off-day from one man can so quickly lead to an all-consuming defensive collapse.

"… Endemic entitlement within the squad needs to be eradicated. Placing more faith in academy products who have a hardwired connection to the city and the club would be an obvious route. It's something many Champions League-winning teams have done and it adds an intangible edge that PSG lack. The quality is there. Bundesliga stars, and recently sold academy graduates, Christopher Nkunku and Moussa Diaby prove it – although that argument is counterbalanced by the haughty attitudes of fellow alumni Adrien Rabiot and [Presnel] Kimpembe."

The summer of 2022 was all about PSG paying a fortune – in signing on fee (to stay at the club) and wages – to keep Kylian Mbappé for just three more years, and offering the player power to make decisions about the running of the club, which included him (apparently) instantly sacking the sporting director Leonardo and lining up Luis Campos. This is player power taken to a whole new level. The striker had been set to join Real Madrid, and the decision to stay in France sparked a bitter battle of words between key people at the two leagues, with questions about how PSG could afford it, and why Mbappé would stay in what the French call a 'farmer's league'.

Sean Ingle, wrote in the *Guardian* about the madness of "PSG being able to stump up a €200m-plus package for the world's best player – despite making a €224m loss last year."

(This followed previous huge losses, too.)

Ingle continued, "There are no good guys here, only a gnawing unease that the laws of economic gravity are being defied to the further detriment of the game we love. As *La Liga* put it in an unprecedented attack, the transfer showed that state-owned clubs, such as the Qatar-run PSG, 'do not respect and do not want to respect the rules of a sector as important as football' and that 'sporting integrity' was at stake.

"… cynics will hope the rules are more robust than the previous incarnation, which proved easier to circumvent than the Maginot Line – with PSG and Manchester City among those found guilty. There are also well-founded fears that state-run clubs are creating inflationary pressures in the transfer market, while PSG's chief executive Nasser al-Khelaifi's enormous influence across Uefa and the European Club Association is also impossible to ignore.

"To my mind, though, the reaction to Mbappé's new deal goes beyond the understandable squeamishness about sovereign wealth funds running clubs. It is also about how easy it is for the teams to entrench their advantage and ruin leagues. Would anyone bet against PSG, who have won eight of the past 10 *Ligue 1* titles, winning next year? And the year after that? Or Bayern Munich, who have won 10 Bundesliga titles in a row, another procession?

"Of course there are exceptions – look at Manchester United. But while English football is certainly more unpredictable, as was seen again on a dramatic final day, Manchester City have still won four Premier League titles in five years and just eight clubs have finished in the top three in the past 25 years. Eight! – the same number as in the first five years of the Premier League between 1992/93 and 1996/97, when Norwich, Blackburn and Aston Villa all challenged for the title.

"… In the US, where salary caps, luxury taxes and drafts for college players ensure that the major leagues are kept spicy and dicey, the difference is stark. Major League Baseball has had eight World Series winners in the past decade and five further teams finishing as runners-up. In other words, 13 of the MLB's 30 teams have fought for the sport's biggest prize in the past 10 years.

"In the NHL, meanwhile, 14 of the league's 32 clubs have played in a Stanley Cup final since 2012. In the NFL, the figure is 13 out of 32, with some teams able to go from also-rans to Super Bowl contenders within a couple of years.

"Curiously though, that lack of football's competitive balance has not dented the game's popularity. One explanation, based on detailed analysis of the data by the economists Dr Babatunde Buraimo and Dr Rob Simmons, is that TV audiences are far less interested in watching competitive matches than they once were – and instead they want the big names, regardless of the opposition."

As such, PSG are surely perfect for the modern young fan, then, if that's what's craved: big names, and to support the *superstars*, not teams. Most people older than 30 surely still prefer football as it was conceived: played by teams, with unity, spirit, skill and desire, led by a manager, not a mannequin. You can still enjoy football without trophies, of course (that's part of the point of this book, after all), but if you hoover up all the best talent, and invest several times more money than your rivals can, and do so in the name of sportswashing, then to be a mere bunch of show-ponies adored by immature people seems distasteful.

Signing an ageing Lionel Messi in 2021 was a vanity move. Having already bagged free-transfers on mega-wages – including £300,000 a week for ex-Red Gini Wijnaldum, and big-names Sergio Ramos and Gianluigi Donnarumma (as well as spending almost £60m on Achraf

Hakimi) – it seemed that PSG leapt on the sudden availability of Messi via Barcelona's awful financial management over recent seasons.

Except, Messi didn't really want to be there; he was almost kidnapped. It felt a bit like Michael Owen, stuck in Spain in 2005, desperately wanting Liverpool to match Newcastle United's £16m bid, a year after the Reds had lost him to Real Madrid for just £8m (due to his entering the final year of his contract). Liverpool would go as high as £10m in 2005, but not break their transfer record a year after Owen had left for less than half his market value. Owen ended up at Newcastle, never really wanting to be there. It didn't go well.

These sudden vanity purchases can be seen elsewhere in the past two years. In the summer of 2020, there was the priceless – or should that be *costly?* – farce of James Rodriguez at Everton. Signed seemingly to 'win' the transfer window, he arrived at a club he didn't even want to play for – he later admitted that he only wanted to play for the manager – to earn more per week than any of the Liverpool side who'd just been crowned champions (on the back of also winning the Champions League 12 months earlier).

Rodriguez at Everton also sums up almost everything that's wrong with modern football: the transfer as form of dick-swinging, where the transfer itself is to be fetishised, as a show of wealth and power and PR, and ignoring the possibility of the harms outweighing the benefits – the player, whose move is overseen by super-agents, who is only there for the money, and who gets an unhealthy excess of it compared to the honest pros and current best performers who work for the team and the club; the player who initially wows his teammates in training, only for them to soon consider him 'invisible', as if they feel they are playing games with 10 men when he's barely strolling about a few months later; the player who has a great first month and then goes missing when the temperature drops below 20°C; the player who just takes a game off, as … well, he can't be arsed every week, right?; the player disappearing on a private jet *before the end of the season*; the player as status symbol, not squad member and team player.

A year later, this particular player was *given away*, to get his £250,000-a-week wages off the books as the club panicked to meet even relaxed post-Covid FFP standards after years of vanity purchasing. Aged 30, he spent the past year in the Qatari league, which just about sums him up.

When these big names unexpectedly appear on the transfer market, it's interesting to watch clubs suddenly throw their plans out the window to make sure they get them.

Given that his goalscoring and creativity output had remained sky-high in Spain, Messi is a unique case, but it shows, as I keep reiterating, that players are often products of their environments, and elevated or diminished by those around them. Sometimes others are helping to hoist them up, while shared understandings are lost in an instant when placed alongside ten new teammates.

The *egosystem* represents the sum attitude of a squad, and how they interact on and off the pitch. It is an ecosystem, but where egos play a huge role. A perfect egosystem will be one where everyone is pulling in the same direction (without needing to hold hands and sing *Kumbaya*), and where the egos – which will still be at play (as these are highly motivated and competitive human beings) – are kept within acceptable bounds. The aim is to win games, and to win trophies; not to be more famous, more followed on social media, and win more individual trophies. At least, to be a proper football club, that *should* be the aim.

A simple but enlightening issue with Messi is that he's taken well over 100 penalties in his career, at a success rate that's marginally below average; at the time of writing, he has missed 30 of his 131. Over such a large sample, perhaps anyone will revert closer to the mean; he has scored 77%, and the current success rate for penalties is now up to around 80% (albeit keepers are now slightly more hindered by being forced to stay on their line, which has seen the conversion rate creep up a little).

However, compare it to Liverpool's penalty-takers in the past five years (excluding shootouts), nearing to the end of 2021/22: Mohamed Salah had taken 25, scoring 22 (88%); in the same period, James Milner had taken 10, scoring nine (90%). Fabinho, with a near-perfect record from Monaco, had scored all four of his Liverpool penalties. Roberto Firmino missed two of his four, and so he doesn't really get to take them any more. Sadio Mané's goalscoring figures would also be boosted towards the top of the scoring charts if he was the one who took the penalties, but his attempts have yet to convince. (He also missed one for Senegal in the first half of the AFCON final in February 2022, but scored in the shootout to beat Salah's Egypt; and scored in the shootout that eliminated Egypt from the World Cup qualifier a month later, only to then miss once back in a Liverpool shirt in the FA Cup final shootout.)

Someone, somewhere along the way, should have taken the ball off Messi. If you are merely an average penalty taker, why are you taking them? Salah is the main man at Liverpool, and all penalty takers should have the leeway to relax by not thinking they'll lose the duties if they miss a single spot-kick. But if they start to miss too many, or their record is mediocre, they should lose the privilege. In a world of marginal gains, this is consistent marginal losses.

It should not be about how many goals Messi or Salah score, as even bad penalty takers can boost their tallies (take ten, miss five, and that's still five more goals to you than the other strikers), but about having the best person for the job in possession of the task.

There's something similarly wasteful about Cristiano Ronaldo's free-kicks. Between the start of 2017 and April 2022, he scored *one* league free-kick, coming as one of his 69 attempts (in all competitions) at Juventus, after a barren final season at Real Madrid from dead-balls. When he finally netted one late in the season at home to Norwich in 2022, he had gone nearly two years, and almost 60 attempts in league football, without success.

In 2021, an article on *Business Insider* during the delayed Euro 2020 noted: "The Juventus forward's two misses mean he has now taken 28 direct free-kicks at the European championships since making his tournament debut in 2004 – at least four times more than any other player during the same period – and has scored none. At World Cups, Ronaldo has also taken a total of 23 direct free kicks, scoring just one.

"… Between 2009 and 2018, the Portuguese star scored 33 free kick goals in 444 attempts for Real Madrid – which equates to a conversion record of 7.3%. For Juventus, that conversion rate has plummeted to just 1.4%, with Ronaldo having scored just once in 72 attempts across the last three seasons."

The article also suggests that, "the rolling average conversion rate for free-kick takers in the English Premier League is 9.2%," albeit that sounds high.

Again, the superstar reputation means that Ronaldo *demands* the ball, and then wastes what, over a longer period of time, will amount to several 'lost' goals for the team. (And my constant point is: who is quantifying all the *lost* goals?)

Perhaps it could be argued that these superstars become more confident overall by adding penalty and free-kick goals to their tallies – a scored penalty might get them out of a slump (and as such, would make some sense if a game is already essentially won) – but it still feels too much about them and not the team. The best penalty taker should take the penalty, unless there's a sentimental reason with the result not in the balance. Direct free-kicks are obviously much less likely to lead to goals, but why keep wasting situations due to the superstar taking them no longer being up to the task? Most fans are utterly deluded when they say "I could have scored that", but equally, most fans might have at least a *chance* of bettering Ronaldo's record on free-kicks during the run when he failed to score from well over 50 in a row (and far more if you include his wasted attempts for Portugal). Even one deflecting in from an aimless toe-punt by a middle-aged man would be an improvement.

Again, bringing Ronaldo back to Old Trafford was an *impulsive* buy by United, that seemed to undermine what they were actually trying to do. As soon as he rejoined, I felt it likely a mistake for all concerned (as I made clear in my writing). The craziest part – similar to the free-kicks – was how it seemed no one dare say to him "you're 37, sit this one out". If a player is too iconic and powerful to take orders, then there's trouble. If a player is more iconic and powerful than the manager, then discipline will be lost. If he has to play every minute of every game, despite fading physically, the team will suffer. For that level of laziness (or energy conservation, he might argue), you'd expect a couple of goals per game. After all, how many goals are not scored because of runs not made, or attempts to win the ball back in the final third? If pressing is what Jürgen Klopp calls football's best no.10, then how many chances are not created because the strikers let the opposition waltz out with the ball? Ronaldo can jump and spin whilst making a strange noise (like someone squeezing a tiny cat) when he scores a goal, and social media will light up, but what's the point if United are now actually a far worse team?

Contrast this with Liverpool. Dan Kennett, early pioneer of data analysis on TTT, said of the Reds on the *Anfield Index Under Pressure Podcast*, "167 shots from pressing this season. 32.5xG created, which gives 19.5% xG per shot. League average shot quality is just under 10%, and ours has been 12.3%. Shots from pressing are 37% more valuable! Pressing is still the best playmaker you can ever have!"

Ergo, how many shots 'died' at United because they were never fully conceived, due to Ronaldo's lack of movement? (Obviously Erik ten Hag should improve United as a team, but he will need to find ways to compensate for Ronaldo's negative traits.)

While his transfer fee was modest (albeit still expensive for someone of his age), in 2021/22 Ronaldo picked up the same weekly wage as Mo Salah, Diogo Jota, Sadio Mané and Luis Díaz *combined*.

If there's one thing Alex Ferguson knew it was never to let a player get more powerful than he himself; when they started getting close, they were out the door. Yet, weirdly, Ferguson seemed to play a role in Ronaldo returning to United in 2021, to play for a middling manager with sentimental value to the fans, but no great clout in the dugout. (Remember, Ferguson also chose the ill-equipped David Moyes as his successor. This was a titan of the game whose time had passed – going out with an unconvincing league title and leaving a squad that had issues – but whose influence remained outsized.)

Even then, United had been on a much better trajectory before the return of the Portuguese megastar, based on a more youthful approach, and the offloading of big-name players including Alexis Sánchez, brought in – just like Ronaldo a few years later – in a panic, on wages far exceeding the existing squad and failing to deliver. Ronaldo's laziness in his younger years could be offset by his explosiveness, and the willingness of hard-working others (Wayne Rooney, Carlos Tevez, Park Ji-sung) to pick up his slack. Instead, with the ageing no.7 they played game after game with him doing virtually no closing down, in a team where young starlet Mason Greenwood also strolled about; which (before his far more serious issues arose) seemed unforgivable for a young striker in modern elite football. Also, neither passed to the other, in a battle of the egos. Marcus Rashford also seemed incapable or unwilling to press, and in midfield, Paul Pogba was never noted for his work-rate. How was this supposed to fit together? Egotistical older players and self-important youngsters, leaving all the hard to work to each other? The reason Fred and Scott McTominay had to play so much appeared to be that they were the only ones prepared to run. (It also seemed weird to me at the time that United boasted about scouting over 800 right-backs before plumping for Aaron Wan-Bissaka, apparently without realising that full-backs *attack* these days, even in mid-table sides, let alone ones supposed to be pushing for the biggest honours. Even he looked lazy and sluggish as Liverpool waltzed in time and again to blast five goals at Old Trafford. The lack of joined-up thinking at so many big clubs seems staggering.)

Some time ago I wrote an article entitled "The Toxic Rot of the Ageing Superstar". The issue is that the superstar demands the ball; and everyone feels that they have to give him the ball, all of the time. Yet he cannot do what he used to do, nor do his teammates – to him, in his warped mind – feel up to his standards. Frustration surges, and he starts moaning. Yet the manager is often too scared to leave the superstar out; and if he does, then the attention it draws then becomes toxic in itself.

Play Ronaldo: you lose the running, the equality, the team spirit, the youthful zest.

Don't play him: you get a circus.

As noted earlier, Ronaldo's son died in childbirth in April 2022, but that doesn't alter the fact that up to that point he'd always been an immensely egotistical player, whose waning powers were likely to cause problems. A supreme athlete who has looked after his body (in part due to doing less running in games), he hasn't ever really focused on *humility*.

When, in late April 2022, Ronaldo scored to secure a home draw against Chelsea in a game they needed to win, the internet was flooded with hot-takes about how bad the team would be without him.

The *Manchester Evening News* noted, "As you can see from the messages displayed in the tweets above, some United fans have sarcastically joked that Ronaldo has been the problem behind United's woes this season. Throughout the campaign, it has been suggested that his return to the club last summer has been the catalyst for their demise. However, his tally of 23 goals this season suggests otherwise."

This came with United fans saying they'd be relegated without his goals.

Yet this simply fails to understand how football works; the power of the team, and that team goals scored does not include goals *not even created*. You can build a team around the strengths of one individual, to the detriment of the other ten. Remember, this is the player who ranked as Europe's "laziest" before he joined, and after he joined. No matter how many goals Ronaldo scored, the question was: has his return to United *improved the team?* Statistically, the opposite seems glaringly obvious.

United's points per game since Ronaldo's second United debut fell dramatically from that of their 2020/21 total plus the three games of 2021/22, before he returned to a hero's welcome. In the 41 games prior to his second debut, United had accrued 81 points from 41 league games, at 1.96 points per game. The next 35 games resulted in just 1.46 points per game, which was inferior to that of 8th-placed Wolverhampton Wanderers, who were one place below United in the actual table going into the run-in. United had fallen from 1st place on his return after three games, return down to 7th, with the form of an 8th/9th-place team. The man who was supposed to take them from 2nd-place (albeit in a season without ever really troubling Man City) to title challengers instead steered them off course. Even when Ronaldo became more prolific as the season wore on, perhaps adjusting more to new teammates (none of whom were there when he first left in 2009), the *results* were still bad.

With just one game to play – having been astonishingly hammered 4-0 at Brighton (notable for a bad foul by Ronaldo, and a 30-yard free-kick sent 30 yards over the bar) – Man United had guaranteed posting their worst points tally in the Premier League era (58, with 64 the previous worst; they then lost the final game 1-0 at Crystal Palace). Yet obviously they already had *seven* of those points from three games before Ronaldo signed, and were top, after finishing 2nd. So, only 51 points in 35 since Ronaldo returned. The points per game since his return had dropped to below 1.5.

Now, it would be overly simplistic to put *all* of any downturn down to one individual or one decision, but in this case, that individual was so *overwhelming* – overbearing, even – that it also cannot be ignored. United won their first two league games on the adrenaline rush of his return (one against a clueless, rudderless Newcastle), but then won only one of the next eight, once he was playing regularly. Though he did score goals, they won just three of their eight Champions League games, exiting at the round of 16 to an Atlético Madrid side Liverpool had beaten home and away, and failed to beat Young Boys home and away in the group stages. (Let's be clear: a limited but hitherto semi-succeeding manager failed *only after* Ronaldo arrived, and his replacement, Ralf Rangnick, also failed. Ole was doing okay at the wheel before the mega-move for 'CR7'.) The trouble with buying a player who comes with his own circus is that, before long, they'll send in the clowns.

By the winter, Ronaldo was 'outed' as doing the least running and pressing of any Premier League striker. In early games where points were dropped he berated teammates and stormed off without applauding the fans; something he did several more times throughout the campaign. He produced several petulant offences that would have got lesser names sent off, including kicking the ball twice into the groin of a prone Curtis Jones, as Liverpool humiliated United at Old Trafford. In April, he smacked a phone out of a young Everton fan's hand when storming off the pitch. Injured for the game against Man City, Ronaldo hopped on a plane to Portugal rather than support his teammates.

Back in December, during an insipid team display at Newcastle, a despairing, high-pitched Gary Neville said of United on Sky, "They've not done one single thing right as a team, and not one single player can go in and say they've done their jobs, or even done themselves justice. There were no positives. Nothing. They're whinging at each other! They're a bunch of whingebags! A bunch of whingebags! Watch them on that pitch, honestly, arms in the air, complaining about everything! Honestly, they're absolutely shocking out there in that first half. They got the last manager the sack! Ralf Rangnick is not going to get the sack, he's only had a few weeks with them, but honestly, they'll get a lot of managers the sack, that lot, if they carry on like that." (Exclamation marks courtesy of Sky Sports' transcription, albeit you can almost hear Neville's voice screeching away.)

He added, "Something isn't right in there. I don't know what it is, but there is definitely whinging going on – they are all at each other and not helping each other."

It seems that this attitude arrived – or certainly exploded – with Ronaldo, the worst culprit of the whinge wars. It didn't appear as apparent at the club in previous seasons, albeit there were other issues, and there was a bit of moaning. Were he less influential, his behaviour would not be so contagious. That's the kicker with the frustrated ageing superstar: too big to drop, too iconic to be censured.

An additional problem was that it totally undermined United's fresh-spark superstar, Bruno Fernandes. A compatriot of Ronaldo, no one could be more aware of the megastardom of the returning no.7. Fernandes started the season with a hat-trick … and then Ronaldo returned, and into the older man's shadow the younger man fell.

On the BBC, after United capitulated 3-1 at Arsenal days after losing 4-0 at Anfield, Phil McNulty noted: "Fernandes and Ronaldo have played in the same team 33 times for United but only combined for three goals. Fernandes assisted Ronaldo against Young Boys in September, Spurs in October and Atalanta in November. There have been no Ronaldo assists for his compatriot.

"In his first season at United, from when he signed in January, he made 22 appearances and managed 12 goals and eight assists in all competitions. Last season he made 58 appearances with 28 goals, including 13 penalties and 18 assists.

"This term, he has made 42 appearances with only nine goals and 13 assists – after starting with an opening-weekend hat-trick in the 5-1 win against Leeds United."

Ronaldo's arrival clearly affected Fernandes, with the established, exceptional penalty taker soon missing against Aston Villa in September 2021, with a sense of 'Ronaldo should be taking this' – presumably due to his status, not his success rate compared to his compatriot's – clearly in the air. In the Arsenal game in April 2022, Fernandes missed again, with Ronaldo looming in the background.

Having made some good points, I feel that McNulty then missed the mark entirely with: "Ronaldo, on the scoresheet again at Emirates Stadium, is portrayed by some as a 'problem' for United (and therefore ten Hag) because of his status and ego, but plenty of clubs would love a goalscoring problem like him."

This, after an article detailing where it had gone wrong for Fernandes; with no hint that the problem could be the arrival of his compatriot. Given that the buck-toothed Portuguese had scored 28 goals and created 18 assists the previous season, and started the new season with an opening-day hat-trick, then why wasn't the question, *whose goals was Ronaldo taking?* Rangnick himself said that no striker of his would have to press hard if he scored 25 goals and got 15 assists, which was taken by people to refer to Ronaldo, but that's what Fernandes *exceeded* in 2020/21; by contrast, Ronaldo had 16 league goals (23 in all competitions) but just three assists. In essence, they had replicated one Portuguese player's goals whilst removing the work-rate and assist-making of the other. They had added a penalty-box predator to the team, but where the team stopped functioning. And now there's a doubling, or even a squaring, of the whingeing.

People still don't grasp how much adding a player can simultaneously subtract. At Chelsea, a similar transfer – the big-wages arrival and what it did to others in the egosystem – indirectly cost them the chance to retain key players, as well as seeing the team regress overall. The signing of Romelu Lukaku was supposed to propel them to the title; instead, there was one game where he had seven touches of the ball, an all-time league low record for someone playing a whole game. (That said, Allan of Everton managed just one successful pass in the game at Anfield later in the season, and that was from the kickoff. But he played "only" 73 minutes.) As of the start of May, Lukaku had scored just five league goals (adding three more in the dead-rubber run-in, before disappearing again in the FA Cup final), and barely created anything. Like Andriy Shevchenko and Fernando Torres, he was a mega-expensive signing who didn't necessarily suit the team; a vanity purchase, like the yachts the then-owner famously collected.

Lukaku's arrival indirectly cost them Antonio Rüdiger, their best defender, and one of the elite centre-backs in the division. Even before Chelsea lost the ability to renew contracts, after the war in Ukraine saw their owner sanctioned, the German had yet to sign a new deal because the bar had been raised by this new guy.

As the *Athletic* reported, "Chelsea's first contract offer was made last August [2021] but the proposal was seen as something of an insult with Rüdiger already one of the lowest-paid senior players on around £90,000-a-week.

"It did not help matters that Romelu Lukaku was given a base wage of about £340,000-a-week when he joined from Inter Milan."

Again, noses put out of joint; the egosystem crushed. Rüdiger had been their best player in the first half of the season. In June 2022 he officially joined Real Madrid (and Lukaku was *loaned* back to Inter – ouch!).

Back at United, it's not even like Ronaldo created chances others were missing; his expected assist rate (xA) after 34 games was a measly

2.7 for the season, so a fraction below his actual output of three; and averaged just 0.13 per game. Fernandes xA the season before was a whopping 11.0, at a rate of one every three games, compared to Ronaldo's one every ten games.

In 2021/22, Mo Salah's expected assist rate was 0.35, with all Liverpool's attackers (including squad attackers) well ahead of Ronaldo's 0.13 for creating, bar Sadio Mané – just ahead at 0.15; but Mané was dribbling lots out wide, and chasing back, and when playing as the centre-forward, linking play and scoring open-play goals.

Plus, Mané wasn't replacing anyone who was more productive. (Also, he earned a mere fifth of what United were paying Ronaldo, and whose arrival in 2016 sparked team improvement, not regression.) In 2020/21, Fernandes had 0.77 xG/xA per 90 minutes (expected goals plus expected assists). In 2021/22, it had fallen to 0.54, and of course, he *started* the season with great numbers – goals and assists in those opening games. United were finally a smoothly running machine, even if only a BMW and not a Ferrari. His shots per 90 minutes then fell by over 20%. Indeed, Ronaldo used to get double-digit assist numbers with Real Madrid, then close to that level with Juventus, but those numbers had been falling in recent years, along with the goals – even if he still scored a reasonable amount.

When you add a 'goal machine' (which Ronaldo still is, to some degree), it's utterly pointless if that individual scores 20 or even 30 goals, and the team falls four or five places in the league table. In all 38 games in 2021/22, United scored 57 goals, but seven of those were in the three games before Ronaldo made his second debut. In 2020/21, they scored 73 league goals, at 1.92 per game; a season later, after Ronaldo's second coming, they had scored just 50 at 1.43 per game. It's almost identical to the drop in points per game mentioned earlier: 1.96 to 1.46. Ronaldo, who hit few goals late in the season when chances of the top four had all but gone, could have scored *fifty* goals, but if that was because he was the only player taking shots – never passing, never moving from the penalty spot, never creating anything for anyone else, and everyone directed (or compelled) to pass to him – and they lost every game 3-2 or 4-2, it would have been utterly self-defeating.

It felt, to me, like United had no tactical plan when buying Ronaldo for a second time – it was panic, mixed with marketability, with perhaps some sentimentality. And even if he just needed six months to settle back in to English football, how will he fare when he turns 38 *next* season? Again, the idea of signing him was for instant impact. They got it: a nosedive.

This is not squad building, but vanity shopping. Indeed, one of the reasons United made Ronaldo their highest-paid player (more than twice what Liverpool paid anyone) was to stop him going to Manchester City; albeit it's hard to see how he'd have fitted in there. (Although at least all the other City players work hard, and might have carried some water for him, as they did for Sergio Agüero – before the Argentine, after being left out of the side in the early Pep Guardiola months, at least started to put in some kind of out-of-possession work, at the insistence of the manager.)

Lionel Messi going to PSG felt very similar: starry-eyed opportunism on the French club's part, with no thought to any second-order effects. How will the team play, with a manager who demands pressing – when, on a whim, bringing in the game's other great modern superstar, who, at 34, had been doing less and less work off the ball over the years? (A presser in his youth under Guardiola, Messi now walked about the pitch.)

How would someone – a talented and dedicated worker – like Wijnaldum feel, having been gazumped in his move to Barcelona, only to suddenly be made peripheral with the need to shoehorn another attacker into the team? With Neymar, Kylian Mbappé, Julian Draxler, Ángel Di María and Mauro Icardi, the ex-Liverpool midfielder could not balance the top-heavy team with the arrival of Messi. By the time the French champions exited the Champions League at the round of 16, Wijnaldum had been on the bench for half the league games, and made just three starts in Europe. As someone who looked absolutely fuming to be left out of Liverpool games (see his angry reaction that drove him on as a half-time sub against Barcelona, where he helped the game to explode towards that 4-0 scoreline), he got the pay-rise he wanted (and more), only to be surrounded by prima donnas who were strolling about on the field, as he watched from the bench. He got a league winners' medal (again, as a bit-part player), but watched from afar as Liverpool had a far more exciting season. He ended the season on holiday while Holland played games without him, and was voted the biggest flop in *Ligue 1* for the season.

PSG have more 'marketable' stars than Liverpool, and will win domestic trophies, but he joined an absolute madhouse. He seemed to have his heart set on a move to Barcelona, a far more romantic ideal, before they ran out of money (and then, belatedly, scrabbled around to find some via loans and, of course, offloading Messi and various others). Under Xavi, Barça, after a terrible start to the season with Wijnaldum's old Netherlands boss Ronald Koeman, seemed to have rediscovered their identity, and Wijnaldum would presumably have been happier there.

As with Philippe Coutinho, Wijnaldum got the big-money move, only to become an afterthought, unappreciated and unloved.

Indeed, it was reported in May 2022 that Coutinho had agreed to take a huge wage cut from his eye-watering £480,000-a-week wages to fit into Aston Villa's structure, where he could only expect £125,000 a week, at the top.

"I don't think you can underestimate football happiness – and in any walk of life, in any job, in any role," Steven Gerrard said when asked to explain why Coutinho agreed to join Villa on a permanent deal for such a colossal drop in earnings. To me, it sounds like Gerrard has learnt a lesson from Klopp. It's one of the truest things in football.

"If you get out of bed every morning and you're playing for an ambitious club where there's a journey where everyone's pushing towards it and moving it, and you're a big part of that, and you're made to feel welcome and you're essential and people want to build around you, I think that's very important," Gerrard added.

One of the issues that almost drove Barcelona to bankruptcy was their wage structure; and how Messi, despite 'deserving' to be the best-paid player in the world, distorted the rest of the squad's wages. According to a report in the *Financial Times*, Messi's wages tripled during Josep Maria Bartomeu's presidency, and the no.10 earned more than £500m between 2017-21.

The issue was, in paying Messi fortunes, everyone else could ask for mini-fortunes. This is where people fail to grasp the second and third order effects of a wage bill, and how just paying anyone 'what he wants' distorts everything asked for by new players, junior players, squad players and kids signing their first deals. In Catalonia, if Messi were to get a 50% rise, and others, already paid a mere fraction, asked for a 30% rise, then Messi would be talking about tens of millions – but everyone else, as those mere fractions, would still be talking about excessive millions. Multiply that by a whole squad, and it's chaos. Any other business would have gone bankrupt. Indeed, Barcelona should have; just as Chelsea *would* have, once Roman Abramovich's wealth was sanctioned and the usual cost would be going into administration.

Liverpool's Wage-Bill Wisdom

This, I assume, is why no Liverpool player signed during the Klopp era has arrived on more money than the highest earner already in the squad. The closest yet seen is Thiago, coming in on £200,000-a-week, to be on a par with Mo Salah and just behind Virgil van Dijk, on

£220,000-a-week. (All that said, Liverpool's wage bill is also clever in how incentivised it is: the better you do, the more you earn, and estimates of wages can vary. As such, coasting on £250,000-a-week, as James Rodriguez did at Everton, is not an option.)

Most *serious* players want to join a world-famous club, to play under the world's best all-round manager, and to compete for trophies: as such, the Reds don't have to try and bribe overpaid superstars to choose them; they will only pick those who are happy to join the collective effort, and as such, who do not expect to be paid a king's ransom.

Van Dijk arrived on less than £100,000-a-week, despite the big transfer fee. Both Diogo Jota and Luis Díaz are similarly at the £80-90k-a-week mark. The aim at Liverpool is to prove yourself *at Liverpool*, then the next deal can take you towards the top of the pile. And even then, the top earner cannot be out in a financial world of his own, lest it set him up as the lone superstar, and lest it disrupt the payment structure below. To pay someone else twice what the second-top earner gets, let alone then rest of the squad, could create division.

The smoothness of Liverpool's wage negotiations was somewhat disrupted by Covid-19 and the loss of over £100m in income almost overnight, with negotiating new deals for established stars clearly suspended until the situation was clearer (and Covid issues returned in 2021/22, albeit with postponed games rather than lost income). That delay allowed several key players to drift towards the final year of their contracts, as of the summer of 2022. Many of these were also approaching their 30s, or already in their early 30s, so that further complicated matters.

The problems in giving Mo Salah what he and his agent felt he deserved highlighted the drawback of the club's policy, yet it was the policy that underpinned the success, including that of Salah, who arrived as a Premier League misfit. Salah's agent (and – warning bells – close friend), Ramy Abbas Issa, veered into 'dickhead' territory after Klopp, in a press conference, stated in reference to the negotiations to keep the player at Liverpool, "We cannot do much more, that's how it is. But I don't think it's about that. It's Mo's decision pretty much. The club did what the club can do. That's how it is." Issa responded on Twitter by posting seven 'crying with laughter' emojis.

Negotiating via Twitter is never a good idea; indeed, it's plain crass. Agents should be in the background, being smart and unseen. After the aggravation the club had with Mino Raiola, who called Klopp a "piece of shit" after he refused to accommodate his client, Mario

Balotelli, Liverpool simply refused to negotiate with him. Raiola, a deeply unhealthy looking man, died aged 54 in May 2022.

Matt Dickinson of the *Times* spent two hours with key Raiola client Paul Pogba in 2019, and found the player likeable but immature, and almost childlike. "Pogba is not the only superstar with a big team around him believing they are protecting him," Dickinson noted when the midfield left United on a free transfer three years later (with a £4m 'loyalty' bonus), "helpfully steering a career and maximising his commercial interests. But it always does raise questions about how much this can infantilise athletes and whether it stops them taking responsibility."

Pogba, who had sat mute and childlike while his advisors argued over what the interview could cover, "… had his fantasies – and had lived a few – but what about control, focus and maturity? When we talked about what he might put out on social media, he was told that it was not even his for the next couple of days because a sponsor had paid to take it over. Pogba shrugged."

The manager's job is to get everyone to give up their ego and sublimate it for the team. But everyone on the *outside* who is telling the player something different essentially weakens the egosystem. They are often the problem: agents, advisors and acolytes, damaging the bond like a 'friend' who always tells his or her best mates – who date steady, reliable and unremarkable people – that they 'deserve better' when, in truth, no one *deserves* anything special. To expect as much is entitlement.

Raiola publicly stated that Pogba should be played in different positions, as he put his oar in, time and again. There are often various advisors who think their client deserves more money, more game-time, more of a central role. Yet it's the manager's job to pick the team, and not to pander to pressure. Increasingly it feels like there are teams 'outside' the team; teams around players, pulling them all in different directions. No one wants to see players be exploited (hence why they started to have agents), but it can seem counterproductive. The more agents, advisors and personal assistants a player has, the more money is needed to be creamed off the top. It becomes a voracious machine in need of constant feeding. Their advice becomes tainted.

In June 2022, Charlotte Duncker of the *Times* reviewed *The Pogmentary*, a new five-part … ah god knows, *whatever* the fuck it is.

"It explains Pogba's first departure from United to Juventus in 2012. Raiola says in the series: 'Respect is something you give, before you get it back. Mr [Alex] Ferguson thought the family of Paul were exaggerating by saying it and [that] he should have been happy to sign.

I told him that for this money [United were offering] my chihuahua would not walk on the grass of the training centre. The break was not about money, it was about no respect, no appreciation, no trust.'

"This sense of disrespect reoccurs when United's latest contract offer to Pogba – worth about £290,000 a week – was made last summer.

"On a FaceTime call to Raiola while driving on holiday in Miami, Pogba appears genuinely shocked he is not being offered more. 'Paul, you're in a very special situation. You have no idea,' Raiola says. 'Yes, they really want you to stay, but for me the offer doesn't reflect that. I said, 'They can't make this kind of offer and if they really want you to stay and they want to build something with you then this time they have to do something different. They have to put money on the table.'

"Pogba responds: 'How can you tell a player you want him and offer him nothing?'

"United's answer may well have been that their lack of success, and Pogba's inconsistent form, meant he had not earned a bigger increase on his previous salary. But the player's inner circle remain convinced that with Pogba, people should be paying for more than just his talent – there is a commercial premium for his brand.

"Or, as [his new lead agent, Rafaela] Pimenta puts it: 'Pogba is something that we built.'"

So there you have it – a massively failing, overpaid player, who wants to be richly rewarded for being a *brand*. He is not a footballer – a human being – but something someone built; someone living in some alternate reality, devoid of contact with the real world. This is a rot at the very heart of the game; people like Pogba can make all the money they want, but with that approach, it won't be *through playing a team sport*. Get your money from Pepsi and Adidas and selling your 'PP' clothing range; don't expect it from a serious football club, unless your own attitude improves pronto. It seems that it hasn't occurred to the coddled Pogba and his entire entourage that they spent years enabling mediocrity; ruining his playing career, and blaming everything on Manchester United, where only part of the blame lay with that lame-ass club of recent years. Imagine having to deal with this *circus*, as a manager?

A strong manager is required to keep everyone in check; a weak or undermined manager will give in to demands, reminiscent of a parent acquiescing to the emotional blackmailing of a child, having never enforced boundaries. Indeed, Klopp's emotional intelligence, as well as his intimidating physical stature – and his standing in the game, having won everything – makes him fairly unique. He'll do tough love; he'll also do tears and bear-hugs. He's smart, funny, honest and demanding. He'll give high-fives, and also scream in someone's face. No other manager ticks as many boxes, and it makes him uniquely placed to make big decisions, and to keep a squad in check. At Manchester City, it's more Pep Guardiola's absolute power, and the financial heft of the club, that keeps everyone in their place; albeit regarding 'places' he will deploy players in their 'wrong' positions (but where it mostly works), and leave them out altogether, in part because of his authority – his ongoing success breeds the respect required, with players knowing that it's his way or the highway. They knuckle down and press hard, or they don't play. For Klopp it's similar, but with less money to spend, he ekes out more from what he has at his disposal with superior 'human' skills.

Yet it helps to not bring in 'difficult' players (and their difficult entourages) to start with.

Like Dele Alli, Pogba was a teenage sensation, and perhaps both are somehow hampered by a failure to properly mature; caught in the increasingly harsh media glare, albeit one to which they contribute via their various personal platforms, which sees their fame contrast with their on-field output. Ahead of the rest at 19, their love of the game, and work-rate, seemed to diminish over the following years. It cannot be easy for youngsters who find stardom, especially when inevitably surrounded by immature acolytes. (Plenty of footballers have spoken about how many friends they had when first famous, and how those people all quickly disappeared when their careers hit the skids.)

It was different for Salah, who was incredibly humble when he arrived at Liverpool, having come up the hard way; suffering the brickbats of already being a Premier League flop, albeit without any big fanfare upon his move to Chelsea. Clearly Liverpool were prepared to make Salah their highest paid player as he entered the final two years of his contract. But there was a lot of talk in the media about Salah's 'market value', in terms of wages. Clubs with wayward wage structures or petrodollar doping can afford more; Liverpool operate within their means, and that means *everyone gets paid well*, and no one gets paid excessively. The tighter the wage spread – the smaller the gap between lowest and highest earner – the tighter the squad bond, as long as no one is picking up their £100,000-a-week pay-packet when taking the piss, or the best player is earning the least money.

For the first half of 2021/22, before the gruelling trip to AFCON (four periods of extra-time, only to lose in the final), and two more periods of extra-time (League Cup final, World Cup qualifier knockout), Salah was the world's outstanding player. By April 2022 he looked exhausted, as well he might. In the autumn he was unplayable, scoring two of the finest solo goals you'll ever see, as part of a prolific run. He created a ton of goals, too. As such, in late April he was deservedly crowned the Football Writers' Footballer of the Year for the second time in four years; with twice as many goal involvements (goals and assists) than anyone else in the league. In the end, a last-game goal – which when he scored it could, to him, have been the title-winner (before he discovered that Man City now led) – meant he grabbed a share of the golden boot, having been leading the charts all season, and was also the top-assister (not that these individual awards should count for much – the aim has to be to be the best team, not the best individual).

He was massively outperforming Ronaldo, on over £500,000 a week, and Messi, on over £600,000 a week. Yet Liverpool could not afford such figures. The 'going rate' is skewed by all manner of issues. If the going rate for 2022/23 is going to be £1.3m per week (Mbappé's wage plus spreading out the re-signing fee over his contract), then that is because PSG are not financed in a normal way.

As noted, is Gini Wijnaldum happier on £300,000 a week to sit on PSG's bench? Did Coutinho love being jeered at Barcelona when on higher wages? The only wage structure Salah and his agent should have been looking at was Liverpool's. He should be the top dog at Liverpool, albeit that also requires him retaining his qualities into his early 30s.

People will often accept lower wages in life, in order to occupy a higher place in their local egosystem. Studies show that most people will take less money if others around them are also getting less money; however, people will refuse a 50% increase in wages – turning down the chance to be significantly better off – if everyone else in their office will get a 100% increase.

As Will Storr notes in his superb 2021 book *Status Game*, comparisons and hierarchies are often more important than net financial gains. As such, it all depended on whether or not Salah and his agent were looking at the right financial ecosystem: Liverpool's, or the global one, skewed by all manner of factors that could be undone at a moment's notice (such as the sugar daddy being sanctioned, with assets frozen; see Chelsea).

A good agent is not there to get the best financial outcome for his client, but to *do the best by him*. And that is multifaceted.

It's about integrity, acceptance, fulfilment, human relationships and fun, as much as the cold hard loot. A serious musician would surely prefer £50,000 to guest on a Radiohead or Kanye West album than

£100,000 to play the kazoo for Kajagoogoo. You'd sack your agent if he chose the latter.

As such, at the start of July 2022, Salah signed a new three-year deal with the Reds, worth a reported £350,000 a week (including incentives), which seemed ideally balanced between what he's 'worth' (arguably £500,000 a week) and what the next-best players at the club earn (£220,000 a week). In addition, three years for a player aged 30 seemed sensible, with £350,000 a week a lot of money for someone who, by that stage, would be 33; at which point, if he still delivered, a new deal could be brokered. It felt like win-win-win for Salah, Ramy Abbas Issa and Liverpool Football Club.

Footballers also have so many aspects to their 'worth', from image rights to marketing deals to social media clout. They have millions of fans who support *them* and not the club that they play for; only following that club whilst they are there, only to move on when they do. It's a far more complicated world, where even mediocre players live in mansions and many seem to be spoon-fed and to even have someone to wipe their backsides. There's a certain glassiness seen in many star players' eyes, a faraway look, a sense of disengagement; aware, as they must be, that their every word, look, gesture or action is captured, either by the broadcasters or the people, wherever they go, filming them on their phones, looking to read their lips. They become performative creatures rather than connected human beings. The pressure must be immense, and it's probably not healthy.

And, of course, they are commodities, to be valued, rewarded and traded. Messi to PSG undermined their project in other ways. Perhaps in some ways even worse than Ronaldo returning to United, there's the demotivating sense that your best player *really doesn't want to be there*. It's one thing a mere squad player wanting to be somewhere else; different when it's the most famous player in the world. Ronaldo could not have seemed happier to be back at United, trapped in some dream of the past.

Messi, cosseted at Barcelona for two decades (and for most of that time, a genuine world-beater), had to move out of his comfort zone, into a team that had not been built up around him. By the spring, with as many league goals in the season for PSG as the barely-seen Taki Minamino had for Liverpool (two each, albeit the Japanese international had more goals in all competitions than the greatest player of his generation – nine to eight – in far fewer minutes, and he did not take the penalties), Messi's every touch, along with those of Neymar, was booed by the Paris crowd in a league game against Bordeaux days after the team's capitulation against Real Madrid in the

Champions League. (It's also an indication of how winning virtually everything will not satisfy a fanbase, once acclimatised to winning virtually everything, and the one elusive crown becomes the only thing that matters.)

I've criticised Neymar at length in previous books, but his bizarre Netflix documentary series, *The Perfect Chaos*, summed up the nonsense and PR fluff of modern superstar football, along with how pressure and obsessive family involvement can derail a career. Those levels of fame are so toxic. (As are the *constant* TV hagiographies about these stars.)

Neymar wanted to leave Barcelona to escape Messi's shadow, when everything was perfect for him in Spain – other than not quite being the main man. The team and the league both better than where he moved to. Then he couldn't even buy his way out of Paris when he realised he'd made a mistake. (Do *any* footballers know the phrase "the grass isn't always greener on the other side"? And if so, do they think it just relates to the quality of turf at different stadia?)

Now 30, Neymar's elite years have instead been spent in a farmer's league, at a club whose fans hate him. The hype and fame from the age of 17 cannot be easy to live with, and often cocoons players in a mental timewarp, freezing them as adolescents, as they find themselves surrounded by coddling, enabling entourages, often including obsessively pushy parents who love their children but know nothing about *what's required* (and this seems an increasing problem in football). The shallowness and sniping of social media only makes the problem worse, as players crave 'reach', competing to be the most famous, not necessarily *the best*.

Not all of the players discussed here are classic 'dickheads', and many were exceptional at points in their career; others for over a decade. But the issue is: what's the player's future likely to be? And: why would you ever want to pay for his past?

Which brings us onto another issue associated with age and the passing of time, and the role of team cohesion. Europe is suddenly full of prolific older strikers, but there's generally a common thread that links them together.

The Trend For Ageing Goalscorers

For an article written during the summer of 2021 I decided to look at the previous season's top scorers across Europe, and the trend for ageing strikers proving evergreen. I'll reference some of that article here, and update it for 2022, with new observations.

It's fairly self-evident that explosive wingers are the earliest to 'melt', although players like John Barnes (enforced by injury) and Ryan Giggs went on to become ball-hugging central midfielders. Dribbling success tends to peak in the early-to-mid 20s.

Then there's the 'miles in the legs' conundrum, and whether über-fit footballers who play constantly from the age of 17 (such as Gini Wijnaldum) are more or less likely to go on until they are 35 or 36; if they are somehow ultra-durable, or if the constant football takes a toll.

(In the case of James Milner – now MBE – his longevity is obviously helped by starting fewer than ten league games in 2021/22, even though he has made between 35 and 47 appearances in each season throughout his time with the Reds – now most are from the bench.)

Another variable is specific body type: the endomorphic Wayne Rooney looked increasingly washed-up as he approached 30 (which people foresaw many years earlier), whereas the initially injury-prone Giggs' ectomorphic leanness possibly helped him to go on in the Premier League until he was 40, as did the similarly strong-but-wiry Teddy Sheringham, who was also 40 when West Ham lost to Liverpool in the 2006 FA Cup Final. In 2005, when he signed for Liverpool, I suggested that Peter Crouch could play Premier League football into his late 30s, and he bowed out at 38 in 2019, albeit he quit the game as Burnley were just using him as a 6'7" target ('a head on a stick') rather than the all-round footballer he once was.

In 2021, I noted that there were a staggering number of examples of elite goalscoring ratios for strikers in major leagues aged 33-39. (Of course, as noted earlier, the aim is to win games and win trophies, not top-scorer awards, but it's interesting to look at what helped these players remain prolific.)

Bob Paisley famously said that he let players lose their legs on someone else's pitch, and he often released stars aged 29 or 30; but times have changed. Equally, Kenny Dalglish was 32 when Paisley retired, and there was no sign of the 'King' being sold or phased out (1982/83 turned out to be Kenny's last big-scoring season, albeit he played two further full seasons under Joe Fagan – 1983/84 being the club's first treble campaign – before taking charge himself in 1985, and then phasing himself out – and then, briefly, back in again to help land the 1986 title and FA Cup in his mid-30s).

Paisley's mantra was not a hard-and-fast rule. Dalglish was always faster in mind than body. But as Bill Shankly found with an ageing side in 1970, sentiment cannot cloud the need to overhaul a squad if Father Time had taken its toll; something Paisley, at his side, had to be observing. The trick is discerning which players are melting, or which ones are just off form; and, of course, what someone who is still scoring goals might be costing in other areas of play.

My hunch has always been that you start to worry about players aged 29, except keepers and centrally-placed defensive players (thus including holding midfielders), who do less running and often use their experience to snuff out danger before needing to sprint. As such, anywhere up to mid-30s seems reasonable. (The same used to be true of playmakers and no.10s, like Dalglish, Dennis Bergkamp and Gianfranco Zola, but they've largely gone out of fashion; finding pockets of space and providing canny assists is still valuable, but the modern teams need more energy, with pressing, as noted, often a more effective 'playmaker'.)

A quick scan of the goalscoring charts around Europe's major leagues from 2020/21 suggested that there might be an extension to the life of the goalscorer.

Incredibly, five of the top 10 goalscorers in *La Liga* in 2020/21 were aged 33 or 34: Luis Suárez, Lionel Messi, Karim Benzema, José Luis Morales and some guy called Iago Aspas (who, incredibly, was also the league's top-assister). A sixth, Antoine Griezmann, was aged 30, and of the four players to score the most goals, the average age was 32.2, with the youngster in the quartet, Villarreal's Gerard Moreno (who would fail to score against the Reds in May 2022), sneaking in at the age of "just" 29. (All ages calculated as of the summer of 2021.) Of those, Aspas could be seen as a shining light, at 33: a late-bloomer, who retained his tenacity and desire. He is nothing short of a phenomenon in Spain – but in a team where he's settled and valued part of the setup. In 2021/22 he scored 18 league goals, four more than in the whole of 2020/21, to mean he's never scored fewer than 14 *La Liga* goals in a season with Celta, dating back to 2015. Only Benzema scored more this past season.

In the Premier League, the average age for the top ten scorers was the more logical 27.9, which is just above the average age for a top team (26-28 is usually the average for title-winning Premier League; never below 25, never above 30). Only Jamie Vardy was older than 30 – he was 34, with two others scraping in at 30.

At the time of revisiting this, towards the end of 2021/22, eight Premier League players had 12 or more league goals. For six of the players the age-range was 28-37, with Harry Kane turning 29 in July. The other two, Diogo Jota, 25, and Ivan Toney, 26, are hardly kids, either. Bukayo Saka, 20, stood a goal behind, on 11. (The joint top-scorers as of the end of the season, Salah and Son, were both aged 29.)

A year ago, Robert Lewandowski led the Bundesliga charts by such a distance that he broke the all-time record, with 41 goals. He was aged 32. By the age of 33, at the time of writing, he'd played the same number of games as in 2020/21 (29 in the league, 40 overall), and whilst down nine league goals (a measly 32), he was only down from 48 to 46 in all competitions. Being in the league's powerhouse team clearly helps, of course. In 2020/21, four of the top-11 scorers (four players were tied in 8th place) were aged 31-33, and seven of the 11 were aged 28 or over; but a few youngsters, like the freakish Erling Haaland, brought the average down to 27.5. Still, old-guns led the way.

Four of the top-ten scorers in *Serie A* in 2020/21 were in their 30s, with Juventus' Ronaldo top-scorer, aged 36 (another good personal season, but the team were starting to suffer). Zlatan Ibrahimović, 39, missed out on the top ten by just one goal, with 15. Seven of the ten were aged 28 or over, and the average age was over 28. One more goal for Zlatan, and the average would have approached 30.

The average age of the 17 players who scored 20 or more goals in those four major leagues was 29, and 46% of the players (six of 13) who scored 21+ were in their 30s.

Of course, some of these older players would also have been penalty takers (and you can probably take a penalty aged 40 as well as aged 20, as it requires no stamina or speed; indeed, conversion success rates for penalties peaks at age 32-33), but Bruno Fernandes and Harry Kane were in the aged-27-and-under club in 2020/21, along with other penalty takers, so the same applies there. It's not like all the younger goalscorers were scoring only open-play goals.

Lewandowski was better than ever, at 32, and Suárez, who looked leggy at Barcelona in an ageing side, won the title for Atlético, aged 34. Karim Benzema, at 33, just had the 2nd-best season of his career. A year later, Benzema bettered it: 27 in the league, and 44 in 46 games overall. He led the scoring charts in Spain, aged 34 (ahead of Aspas, aged 34); Lewandowski in Germany, aged 33; Salah and Son in England, aged 29; Ciro Immobile in Italy, aged 32.

Immobile helps prove a key point about a player's stability at a club and the role that plays in longevity, and getting the best out of him. A success in Italy, he flopped badly in a year under Klopp in Germany. He then flopped on loan to Sevilla, and didn't do much on loan back in Italy, with his old club Torino, in the second half of the same season – where he couldn't quite rediscover his magic touch; a total of ten league goals across three clubs in two seasons. It's hard to then explain why he suddenly scored 23 league goals at Lazio the next season, but he has remained at the Rome club ever since. Despite that good start at Lazio, his three best scoring seasons all eclipsed that first season, with 36 league goals in 2019/20, and 41 in all competitions in his second season. In 2021/22 he bagged 27 league goals in just 31 games, and 32 in 40 in all competitions (his third best in six prolific seasons in Rome).

Therefore, Immobile was not Immobile in Germany, nor in Spain. He even wasn't Immobile back at his old club Torino, perhaps returning with the shame of failure, having left as a man on a mission. Again, we can look at whether or not Lazio (complete with ex-Reds Lucas Leiva and Luis Alberto), as a team, are doing as well as they *should* be, with just one top-four finish in Immobile's time at the club, otherwise bobbing between 5th and 8th (they finished 5th again, ahead of Mourinho's Rome rivals, Roma). Would they suffer if they lost Immobile's goals, or would they do better as a *team* with a different attacking dynamic?

In Germany, Lewandowski is nearing 350 goals in eight seasons with Bayern, albeit he said it will be his last at the club, despite a year left on his deal. Clearly Lewandowski has proved to be a vital player rather than just a goal-machine – but even then, doubts about his attitude started to arise. (After Mané joined Bayern, Raphael Honigstein wrote, "A source close to a veteran player told the *Athletic* the team expect Lewandowski to move on. Quite a few have grown a little tired of his public posturing, to say nothing of the return of his egotistical streak on the pitch.")

In England, Salah, with 23 league goals, was ending his fifth season at Liverpool, and Son Heung-Min, also with 23 goals, had been at Spurs for eight seasons. Running riot in Spain, Benzema had been at Real Madrid for *thirteen* years. Immobile, top-scoring in Italy, had been at Lazio for six seasons.

Prior to that, Ronaldo's best seasons at Juventus were years two and three, after a fairly prolific but not mind-blowing first season. His best seasons at Real Madrid were years 2-6, again after a healthy start. When he left, he'd just scored 44 goals in 44 games – yet Juventus were on the slide, with too much focus on feeding their main-man's ego.

Messi was slightly different in that he began his career with Barcelona at such a young age, and as such, was never going to be posting elite numbers aged 17 or 18, given that almost all goalscorers start to get really prolific only once in their 20s. But then he had a mind-blowing *ten consecutive seasons scoring between 40 and 70 goals*. Even when he left, he'd just bagged 30 league goals in 35 games. In Italy, Romelu Lukaku led Inter Milan to the title with 24 league goals, one better than his first season. The top scorer in France, Kylian Mbappé, may only be 23, but he had been at PSG since 2018.

Still settled at the same clubs, Salah, Son, Lewandowski, Immobile, Benzema and Mbappé led the scoring charts in the main five leagues. Meanwhile, super-scorers Messi, Ronaldo and Lukaku, having moved clubs in the summer of 2021 (with Messi and Lukaku making it clear that they happier where they had been), are well behind their prior peak output. Interestingly, young Dušan Vlahović was flying for Fiorentina in his third and fourth seasons (nearing a goal every game), but started life at Juventus only fairly well after a £70m move, at a goal every other game, even when in a better team.

In May 2022, Ian Hawkey wrote in the *Times*, "It's not quite the outlook Vlahović signed up for in January, having rejected the idea of moving from Fiorentina to the Premier League – Arsenal were keen; Ralf Rangnick says that he pushed for Manchester United to make an offer – to become a generation-defining centre forward with Italy's most decorated club. Juventus told Vlahović what he wanted to hear, when, four days after his 22nd birthday, they handed him a No 7 shirt recently vacated by Cristiano Ronaldo. "He's right up there with the best," [Massimiliano] Allegri said, "alongside Erling Haaland and Kylian Mbappé."

In an interesting addition, Hawkey notes how a certain striker scored a lot of goals but also saw his acquisition as a costly mistake.

"But then last season [Juan] Cuadrado had a different No 7 to aim at: the striker who averaged more than 30 goals per campaign from 2018 to 2021. For all that Juventus's executives look back on the Ronaldo years as an expensive folly, he left big boots for any young tyro to fill."

(Plus, why would you take the shirt that has extra weight, like a ton of lead, sewn into the number? Comparisons are already going to be drawn, with the idea to reduce pressure, not ramp it up.)

To be his best, Vlahović, like almost every other striker, needs to spend time at the same club, to generate understandings and match wavelengths. Antoine Griezmann, despite the £100m move (which, to my mind, was ludicrously over-hyped, and the showbiz nature of it saw him put too much pressure on himself), never scored as many for Barcelona in a campaign as he did in each of his five seasons at Atlético; Eden Hazard disappeared without trace at Real Madrid. The settled stars, as the biggest fish in their particular ponds, wilted with the move to the highest strata of club, with £100m+ price tags adding to the pressure.

Just as I often bang the gong for the value of a settled side and squad (all that shared knowledge, understanding and camaraderie) – at least until it naturally ages out – this shows that you cannot just transport an elite goalscorer into another team and see him repeat his output. Sometimes the goal tallies can immediately go up (see Salah at Liverpool), but the general trend appears to be that even older strikers, who seem to defy the ageing process, benefit from time, and a team set up to suit their needs; and that, once moved to another arena, their age can quickly start to show. Once aged 35 or 36, there isn't the time to spend two or three years settling and adapting; the whole point of United signing Ronaldo was to fire them to the league title immediately.

Many of these elite club goalscorers also have merely 'very good' international records; in part due to playing for less successful nations. Yet even Messi, Mbappé, Agüero and Benzema, for elite nations, are/ were nowhere near as prolific as in club football: dropping to a goal every two-to-three games, when often at almost a goal per game for their clubs; Immobile is closer to one-in-four for Italy. (Of his 15 goals for his country in 55 games, the first was against Holland; the rest against Israel, Macedonia, Liechtenstein, Albania, Finland, Armenia, Northern Ireland, Lithuania, the Czech Republic, Turkey and Switzerland.)

A settled setting, and consistent selection, can make a *huge* difference. Even ageing strikers can thrive if the team is set up to meet their needs, albeit a veteran striker's impressive goal output can sometimes come at the cost of the team scoring even more goals without them. That's always the key factor: is the *team* successful?

The Fast-Improving Luis Díaz
When Liverpool signed Colombian Luis Díaz in January 2022 – bringing forward a deal planned for the summer as Spurs and others sniffed around – the Reds bought another fast-improving attacking player, whose goal return (if not his scintillating displays) fell below the standards he had started to set at Porto. Of course, by the end of the season he'd played more games than anyone else *in the world*, according to official studies; he tired a bit in the run-in, as you might expect.

In 2017, with Atlético Junior, he scored just one goal in 23 appearances, aged 20. A year later, he scored 16. Before long he was signed by Porto, and scored six and then six again in his first two seasons. Then, he had 14 in 16 league games when Liverpool swooped (as well as going from one goal for Colombia in his first 16 caps to seven in his next 19). His four league goals for Liverpool in 13 games was an *exact* mirror of Luis Suárez's return, eleven years earlier, after a similar January move. It's unlikely that Díaz will replicate the 30-goal seasons of Suárez, but it does suggest that his finishing – with a bit more luck (he was denied in all manner of ways in his first half-season) – could see him getting 20 goals a season.

Liverpool fan and TTT subscriber Jorge Echeverri explained to me in vibrant detail how he, a Colombian, became a die-hard Red, well before his now famous compatriot; and how Díaz is sparking greater interest in Liverpool in his homeland.

"The decade my father spent in London in the 1930s, his death when I was six years old, and my status as an only child combined in such a way that it was unavoidable for me to travel to England from Colombia once I finished my degree in architecture. The year was 1978 and, a few months later, I was already enrolled in the LIFS (London International Film School) in Covent Garden.

"My passion for Millonarios, the team that I had followed since childhood weakened due to the distances, and the delays with which I got its news. It is worth mentioning that the team received its name in the years that in Colombia were nicknamed as 'El Dorado', where many star players from Argentina immigrated to Colombia, because of a strike in their local league. Among them was Alfredo Di Stefano, who played for Millonarios, and contributed to defeat Madrid at the Bernabéu 4-2. The artistry exhibited during the match was his ticket to play in Spain. Madrid bought him and, in a way, together with the end of the strike in Argentina, brought about the beginning of the end of those golden years in Colombian football.

"Nevertheless, as the months passed away, my love for the sport was still in good health and I followed with curiosity the steps that Ossie Ardiles and Ricky Villa were taking at Tottenham. Of course, my interest was due to the empathy with which all South Americans learn about the careers of their countrymen in Europe and, more so in those days, when the two Argentines came to be the forerunners of the handful of players who today parade through the English stadiums. In addition, and although the matter could be contradictory, the World Cup in Argentina was fresh in my mind, where a mantle of suspicion covered the victory of the hosts' 6-0 win over Peru. It is significant that while the fans celebrated the goals that sent their team to the final, the sportswashing dictator Jorge Rafael Videla and his military filled planes with political opponents to throw them to their deaths at the mouth of the Río de La Plata.

"('They are disappeared, they are gone, they have no identity, they are not dead or alive, they are disappeared,' said Videla, the President of the Military Junta in 1979.)

"It was against this background that I learned one September afternoon that Bob Paisley's Liverpool had beaten Spurs 7-0. Curiosity piqued, for the next three years I soaked up both the absurd dominance the team exercised over others, and the characteristics of its host city: its affiliation with progressive ideas, its particular accent and, especially, the animosity towards Manchester United, a sentiment that I had shared since the years in which that team had played the intercontinental finals against the Argentinian Estudiantes de La Plata.

"However, my return to Colombia marked the rebirth of my love for my local team and a distancing of what was happening in the English league. Except, of course, for the attention I paid to the 1984 European Cup final where Bruce Grobbelaar's 'spaghetti legs' captured my sympathy. Later, Hillsborough and the treatment given to the tragedy by the police and certain media, as well as the gradual deterioration of Colombian soccer, colluded in such a way that the balance ended up tilting in favour of the Reds. Of course, this was influenced by my need to support the team that my feelings – not my reason – chose with all my soul. The rest is history: while the attention I paid to the tournament in my country was in a tailspin, my passion turned to Liverpool.

"Thus came the years in which Rafa Benítez took charge of the team and their resurgence on the world scene. The attraction was such that I had to make the peregrination to Anfield as a commandment. That afternoon Liverpool won 2-1 against our suffering neighbours even though Milan Baroš saw red. It was not by chance that an ex-girlfriend who in those years lived with a Basque cameraman, and whose parents were friends of Xavi Alonso's parents, sent me the shirt that one of my daughters wears.

"In Colombia as in other countries – I am thinking of Egypt before the arrival of Mo Salah – the fans that Liverpool normally had were low in number. The vast majority of my fellow countrymen, followed, and follow, Barcelona and Real Madrid, and when it came to English football, Chelsea, United, and, to a much lesser degree, City. Not even the resurgence of Liverpool in the hands of Klopp managed to change that state of affairs.

"All this has been altered with the advent of Lucho Díaz to the Reds. Today, the newspapers and the radio give permanent accounts of his deeds, and those of the team, in much greater numbers than that of the ailing internal tournament, even more so as the national team has been eliminated from the Qatar World Cup. Not in vain, a few days ago, a serious magazine in the country – Cambio – published an article by the journalist (anthropologist, professor and researcher) Weildler Guerra. Because he exposes my ideas about Lucho much better than I do, I allow myself to quote him:

"'Díaz's talent has become a source of national pride, since members of a country or a social group also have a collective self-esteem.'

"Lucho's father, Manuel Díaz, had a soccer school, and his son accompanied him to training sessions as a child. This provided him with a community to learn from and a teacher who saw in his son a kind of rough jewel that he had to polish. In 2015, Díaz was part of the Colombian indigenous team that went to Chile, where he showed his exceptional skills and potential as a player. "

"When Luis Díaz was asked where his magic for soccer came from, he responded spontaneously: 'From La Guajira. It comes from my roots. I always played soccer in my town, in my homeland.' This reiteration of his links with La Guajira makes us evoke the sense of aesthetics among the Wayúu (the indigenous group predominant in the arid lands of this region of Colombia). For them it is not enough to possess material wealth. Human performances must be ornate. When a necklace or a mule is delivered in compensation, these constitute the luxury of payment. Consequently, the simplicity and naturalness of Luis Díaz as a human being adorn his talent as a player."

Therefore, if before it was almost impossible to find a person wearing the red jersey, now its presence competes with that of the other teams and I don't think I'm wrong if I say that they already outnumber the others."

And to think, Díaz, while hitting the ground running, surely has other gears to find.

Darwinian

A late addition to the high-profile 'striker moving to a new club' list is Darwin Núñez, about to turn 23 as this book goes to print; bought by Liverpool for a fee rising to £85m.

He started his career with Peñarol in his native Uruguay, scoring one goal in 10 games as a teen, before three in three at the start of the next season, that saw him whisked off to Almería in Spain. He bagged a further 16 goals that season, in the second tier; Luis Suárez told both Barcelona and later Atlético Madrid to sign the young man, whom he saw as 'special'. Núñez moved instead to Benfica, scoring just six goals in his debut campaign of 29 league games (and a decent amount in the Europa League), to do okay. The next season, 2021/22, that all changed: he scored 26 in 28 league matches, as well as six in ten (two against Liverpool) in the Champions League. Again, another striker exploding into goals after a slower first season.

Now, will he need a season to adapt to Liverpool, like so many other strikers who have moved clubs recently? Or will he slip in seamlessly like Mo Salah or Sadio Mané – albeit the latter top-scored with just 13 in his debut campaign. In Mané's case, his third season with the Reds was his most prolific, followed by his sixth and his fourth.

(Again, how will he fare at Bayern Munich? It can't hurt going to a totally dominant side in a weaker league, but replacing a phenomenal goal machine in Lewandowski might take some adjusting to.)

Andrés da Silveira Stein, whom I spoke with just before the end of the season, is surely going to be excited about the Núñez signing. Stein is the aforementioned fan born in Mexico City to a Uruguayan father and Brazilian mother. "So, you can really say I am a Citizen of the World," he told me. "I've traveled a lot across these three countries. I've been living in Montevideo since 2006, but also lived here from 1987 to 2003. Been married for five years and have a child of four (who I hope follows my footsteps into being a Liverpool fan).

"I've been a Liverpool fan for well over 30 years, I started following the club through the few bits of English Football we got here, when we had Ian Rush, Jan Mølby and Kenny Dalglish, I remember that last title before it became the Premier League. It also happened at the same time that I started playing *Championship Manager 2* on the PC and was in love with how good our players were. Then kept playing as Liverpool in every edition of the game, you can say I followed Liverpool through gaming those first 5-7 years, football through the TV was hard to come by."

"I've followed Liverpool as best as possible, not always possible back at that time, I didn't have Cable and the Internet was a dream over here. But I kept up as much as possible. Thankfully it has improved a ton after the 2000s arrived. Klopp's charisma and the team's swagger still keep the following strong, but we simply can't get organised to create a fan club. Uruguay is a tough place for things like that."

"Liverpool started to take off in Uruguay mostly with the arrival of Luis Suárez and later Sebastián Coates. (I will never get over the fact that he failed to get his career going with us, such a talent, I am happy though that he's Captain of Sporting and beloved by the fans and recognised by the press, but I digress...).

"The early Rodgers years were a bliss in terms of being on TV and getting more fans and followers over here. I got plenty of friends to follow and talk about the Reds. Nowadays it retains a strong following here, but it's not the same without a Uruguayan player. Getting Darwin Núñez would certainly rekindle the Uruguayan fans' love for Liverpool."

I'm guessing that Andrés will be rather delighted that his compatriot has signed, and *should* be Liverpool's next big star. Darwin has the pace, height, power and finishing skills to do it all. It may take the new no.27 a while to settle, but Liverpool do have a record of integrating players quickly, as long as they are physically ready, and as long as there are only one or two being added to a settled team at a time, lest the vital cohesion be lost. (Signing him before preseason should also help.)

The Anti-Dickhead

Two key players – both now in their 30s – that Jürgen Klopp was fortunate to inherit were Jordan Henderson, who went from something of a whipping boy to the FWA Footballer of the Year in 2020, and James Milner, a player I thought looked too slow for Liverpool when he pitched up in 2015, aged 29, on a free transfer but big wages. It didn't help that he was in a slow team back then; but as pace was added to the side by Klopp, Milner's nous and leadership became vital. In June 2022, Milner joined Henderson in the MBE club.

After Liverpool beat one of Milner's old clubs – Newcastle – 1-0 in late April 2022, Klopp was overjoyed with the player voted man of the match. "He's a role model. I have told him, I can tell the whole world – nothing we have achieved in the last few years would have happened without James Milner, it's as easy as that. Whether he was on the pitch or not, he's set standards in a way not a lot of people can set standards, and it educated all of us. Milly played a great game today. I loved this game – and he played a massive part in it."

Asked about Milner after the game and whether he has met a fitter, more dedicated professional, Klopp said: "No. But it would be interesting to look at Luka Modrić, is he not 36 as well? It's a good generation! But, it is difficult to be fitter than Milly."

Milner and Henderson continue to set the tone at Liverpool, and the hope has to be that the next generation of leaders take the mantle from a duo who cannot go on forever. While there are only über-professional players at Liverpool, some – often the strikers and flair players – are more mercurial and emotional; or focused on their own game (but still as part of the team) rather than *leading* the team.

Henderson has done some successful off-field campaigning, but it never came at the expense of his football. (Obviously, had his form suffered in the aftermath of such efforts, then he would have drawn extra criticism.)

In the *Times*, in June 2022, Matthew Syed wrote about how James Milner – having just signed a new one-year contract with Liverpool – was on a par with Rafael Nadal as "beacons of sanity in a world obsessed with egos".

"This [Nadal] is a player who cooks for himself and his family at grand-slam events, who goes to the supermarket to buy ingredients, and who remains grounded by surrounding himself with trusted friends.

"He studiously avoids getting sucked into controversies and spats, and rejects the superficial temptations of what has come to be called celebrity culture. And isn't this one reason why, despite a series of physical injuries, he has sustained the mental equilibrium to stay at the top?

"I would place James Milner in this category too, another sportsman in the news this week having signed a contract extension with Liverpool. Milner may not have the stellar talent of Nadal but he has made the most of his potential through hard work, sacrifice and solid dependability. He has the eighth-most assists in Premier League history and in the 2017/18 Champions League made nine in a single campaign, beating the record at the time of eight. Like Nadal, Milner is 36 years of age. And like Nadal, he is the last person to be seen in the roped-off sections of nightclubs or gracing the pages of gossip columns. Indeed he hardly ever gives interviews at all.

"Both men are sometimes described as dull but doesn't this show just how off-kilter our culture has gone? I once heard a PR expert saying that Nadal should do more to elevate his 'brand', but this is the point: neither Nadal nor Milner is remotely interested in becoming a brand, and therefore they are incorruptible."

It could also be a reason why Milner seems so at ease with himself, comfortable in his own skin. The lack of a brand means a player can just be a human being, as crazy as that might seem in 2022.

Perhaps the lack of genuine superstar talent helped keep Milner grounded; he was never so fêted as to invite fawning adulation, albeit he did break through at Leeds United aged 16, and as such, could have been led astray. A solid family background helps, as seen with Harvey Elliott, who first played in the Premier League at a similar age. Despite some expensive moves and playing for big clubs, Milner was never the centre of attention.

Wide-eyed in the red fog the day after defeat in Paris, Milner said to Jordan Henderson, filming on the open-bus parade, "Mate, what am I fucking seeing?! Wow!" The vice-captain later suggested that the response from fans lining the streets influenced his plans.

"I felt that after the parade and that played a part in my decision-making also," he noted on the penning of the new deal. "It's a unique club. Now this is signed, I'm already looking forward to getting back with everyone, refocusing and going again. It's a brilliant dressing room to be part of."

Many of that squad seem more like quiet leaders, albeit a couple have now departed. Players such as Joël Matip, Joe Gomez, Ibrahima Konaté, Roberto Firmino, Alisson and Fabinho, seem obsessively focussed, but fairly introverted. They're not weak guys – quite the contrary – but they're understated and a little quieter. Naby Keïta, Takumi Minamino (who joined Monaco in July 2022 for more than twice what was paid for him) and free agent Divock Origi are very quiet characters, as is the super laid-back Caoimhín Kelleher. Alex Oxlade-Chamberlain proved very likeable and sociable, without being a big talker on the pitch. Meanwhile, Kostas Tsimikas looks absolutely maniac on the sidelines whenever Liverpool score (and even more so when he scored the winning penalty in the FA Cup final shootout), which is great to see, but he's not necessarily as boisterous when playing.

Quiet leadership is important, but Henderson and Milner will bark instructions and gee everyone up. They are not afraid to put a foot in, or to confront opposition players, such as when Henderson took to routinely protecting Liverpool's penalty takers as goalkeepers and opposition players tried to disrupt the focus of Mo Salah or Fabinho when faced with a spot-kick. Trent Alexander-Arnold has a fierce will to win, but can lose his composure at times, and is another who is mostly quiet on the pitch. So many of these players lead by example.

There could be a danger that signing lots of nice guys (even if they are dedicated and determined) makes the team 'soft', so there need to be a few senior pros who will show the team will not be bullied; something Virgil van Dijk does in a very laid-back kind of way. (At times he looks disgusted if he has to chase a forward for more than five yards, as if he should already have won the ball by then, or that the striker was just being plain rude by thinking he could outrun him. But he also stands up for teammates being physically intimidated.) Thiago is very vocal, but often when berating himself for a loose pass (ditto Matip, who often has a running commentary with himself). With van Dijk, it's often just a look that tells teammates to up their game. Diogo Jota is also fairly aggressive in his manner, without being a hardman. Harvey Elliott and Curtis Jones also seem to have big personalities, which helps when so young and trying to break into such a successful side.

Having Jürgen Klopp on the sidelines also makes up for the relative on-pitch 'politeness' of his players, in a way that a quieter manager may not suit this same group of players. The trouble with outspoken individuals is how they may not sublimate their egos for the benefit of the team (and may ignore instructions), even if there will be occasions when you'd want that kind of authority, independent thought and ability to go it alone. The issue is, you often can't choose *when* these players will go rogue or not, and whether it will be helpful or harmful.

Of course, it's fairly similar at Manchester City, where players have to fit into the manager's system, and where, as seen with his run-ins with Ibrahimović at Barcelona, ultra-big personalities are not really helped. Criticism came Guardiola's way after another Champions League exit, but the levels of success and consistency shown over the years (even with the outrageous budget) still made City a team that, just like this current Liverpool side, will be remembered for generations to come; even if, perhaps having a younger Vincent Kompany back at the Etihad would make them even more of a force, with a bit more personality. Plus, of course, Liverpool are widely believed to play with more *emotion*, as purveyors of a slightly less robotic style of football, even if both teams share many of the same qualities. While most neutrals still hate Liverpool as part of a generational loathing, it still seems that most prefer the Reds' style.

Perhaps Andy Robertson is one of the few players aged below 30 who fits the Milner/Henderson profile. He is someone who will literally ruffle the feathers (well, *hair*) of a Lionel Messi. And in terms of setting the standards for training, various players could be quietly assuming that role, if they copy the template set by the captain and vice-captain. The standards can be set without fanfare, after all.

Another interesting addition is Díaz. While yet to show the excessive, line-crossing will-to-win of a fellow South American *Luis*, Díaz has the same street-fighting football style as Suárez, full of aggression, zest and determination, albeit even more pace. Díaz seems a humble guy, having come up the hard way (which tends to toughen players up and make them appreciate what they have), but he shows opposition full-backs zero respect. He seems a perfect fit for Liverpool.

Darwin Núñez has that fire and desire, too; that pace, that determination, that never-say-die spirit. After the African affairs, it now seems that Liverpool are edging a bit more towards Latin America, via Portugal, where new director of football, Julian Ward, spent part of his career.

On a shopping expedition, Núñez opted against a fancy modern phone for one that would just do the basics. According to ex-Red Maxi Rodríguez, who played with a young Núñez at Peñarol, the striker was a 'fighter', who, according to quotes in an *Athletic* article, "always turned up early and seemed to push himself further than any of the club's youngest players".

The anti-dickhead will turn up early, keep working hard. Timekeeping is a vital aspect for respecting the group as a whole; not keeping anyone waiting *for you*. That's why Klopp sees it as a non-negotiable. Núñez turned up exceedingly early for his unveiling at the AXA training ground, as further proof of his attitude.

One bonus of focusing less on African signings is the lack of AFCON impinging on the schedule, which, at best, has proved inconvenient when played during the European winter. That said, one clear anti-dickhead – and reigning AFCON champion – left in June 2022, and Jürgen Klopp bid Sadio Mané a very fond farewell.

"He leaves with our gratitude and our love," Klopp said. "He leaves with his status among the greats guaranteed. And, yes, he leaves in a moment where he is one of the best players in world football.

"But we must not dwell on what we now lose, instead celebrate what we were privileged to have. The goals he scored, the trophies he won; a legend, for sure, but also a modern-day Liverpool icon.

"Since he first stepped through the door, he made us better. If someone had told us in that moment what he would go on to contribute and achieve for this club, I'm not sure it would have been possible to comprehend in that moment. Not the scale of it at least. Sadio made it all possible."

Núñez, 22, and Díaz, 25, freshen up a fast front-line, to make it *even quicker*. (Plus, the tricky Fábio Carvalho is a speedster, too.) If the pair click, interchanging on the left with one cutting inside and one going outside, then we can hopefully expect a lot of flame-red fireworks.

Goals Galore – A New Club Record

A record-breaking season of goals – 147, to mirror the maximum break in snooker (which also involves a lot of reds) – started at Norwich, first game, after just 25 minutes: a back-to-front move that saw Virgil van Dijk, after winning possession, lay the ball to James Milner, who pinged the ball out to the far side, and Trent Alexander-Arnold. His low pass-cum-cross into the box was miscontrolled by Mo Salah, but, in the first of his many assists (this one inadvertent), it fell straight to an alert Diogo Jota, who swept the ball under the keeper. Salah then assisted Roberto Firmino for the second, and the game was won when, lurking on the edge of a packed box at a corner – at which Liverpool's giants were being blocked and man-handled – the Egyptian opened his own account as the ball fell to him, and he curled it towards the top corner.

It was fitting that Jota scored the opening goal. Although his season petered out, Jota was by far the top scorer of the Reds' vital opening goals in games: ten, to six from Sadio Mané and five from Mo Salah. Next came Ibrahima Konaté of all people, with three; tied with Taki Minamino, albeit the Japanese's goals were in lesser competitions, bar the vital strike in league game 37 which took the title race to the final day. In terms of scoring the 'winner' (the last goal in a one-goal victory), Mané did so four times, with Salah and Divock Origi on two apiece. (Origi got a two-for at Wolves, when his injury time opener was also the winner.)

In a fast start to the season, Jota and Mané added two more in the next game, at home to Burnley, whilst a Salah penalty rescued a point at home to Chelsea in the third match, as the Reds sat third on goal difference, with Manchester United top, also with seven points.

In all competitions, the first sixteen games saw 12 wins, four draws and, perhaps not required for the mathematically minded amongst you, no defeats. By the time the Reds travelled to West Ham in early November, they had scored 42 goals. They added two more that day, but the team balance in that initial third of the season was not quite right, with opponents allowed numerous good chances; conceding three goals to David Moyes' team, to suffer a defeat, and shipping two or more goals against AC Milan (eventual Italian champions), Brentford, Manchester City (understandable), Atlético Madrid (also understandable), and Brighton – a draw from a 2-0 advantage, where, back for a game in my old season ticket seat, I saw Mané make it 3-0 and the huge sigh of 'this is done' to fill the stadium, only for VAR to chalk it off (rightly so, on replays), and for the whole stadium to deflate. West Ham, Brighton and Brentford scored a total of eight against the Reds in those three games.

To me, the midfield balance seemed a bit wonky, with what looked like one holding midfielder (Fabinho) and two more advanced midfielders, one in a kind of inside-left position and the other (Harvey Elliott or Jordan Henderson) the inside-right. In the absence of Gini Wijnaldum, there was no one in the midfield to keep possession in a simple but reliable manner, and the new formation allowed for attacking overloads on both flanks, where Andy Robertson and Mané on the left, and Trent Alexander-Arnold and Salah on the right, would be joined by a wide central midfielder, to make various passing triangles possible. As an attacking strategy, it worked wonderfully, but obviously it left the defence – itself a bit rusty – a bit more exposed.

Right from the start of preseason, Liverpool were pressing hard and attacking with pace and fury, but it left the team a bit more vulnerable to counterattacks; especially with all of the Reds' centre-backs either coming back from serious injury (Virgil van Dijk, Joël Matip and Joe Gomez), or in the case of Ibrahima Konaté, new to the league. Matip had a full preseason, but van Dijk did not. Yet the Dutchman started the season in the team, alongside Matip, and had to find his match-legs game by game. It often takes months of playing after almost a year out before fitness and sharpness return to elite levels, and in van Dijk's case, he was now 30, which meant some natural slowing down could be masked (or made worse) by the ACL damage. It looked like he might never be the player he was before the injury.

Fears of permanent decline, however, were arrested by the time 2022 was well underway, as his individual statistics improved massively (as did the team's overall defensive metrics), to reflect his return to peak condition, with the pace of old still there when called for. Alongside him, Matip was consistently good, and Konaté impressed on virtually every outing; yet the defence only really solidified after a 2-2 draw at Chelsea in the opening game of 2022, with a succession of clean sheets and a maximum of one goal conceded in games right up until April. (When Man City twice scored two goals against the Reds, in a league draw at the Etihad, and a Liverpool win in the FA Cup semi-final; and in between those two matches, Benfica scored three at Anfield, albeit against a heavily-rotated Liverpool side 3-1 up from the first leg and coasting into the semi-finals.)

The Reds then kept clean sheets against Manchester United, Everton, Villarreal and Newcastle United, before the Spanish team, in the semi-final second-leg, grabbed two before half-time to set up a thrilling final quarter of the tie.

Between Chelsea in August and Wolves in December, Liverpool scored a minimum of two goals per game. Fourteen wins, three draws and the defeat at West Ham were part of a sequence where, after having lost in London, the Reds won four on the bounce. This run included some astonishing results, and some of the best goals you will ever see; guaranteed Goal of the Season contenders, whatever the year; and the best deservedly *did* win the award. In total, 57 goals were scored in those 18 games, at a rate of 3.2 per match. Incredibly, four or five goals were scored in each of the games against Porto, Watford, Manchester United, Arsenal, Southampton and Everton in this sequence. At this stage the defending, as a team, was still mixed, but the club's all-time goalscoring record was already a possibility.

Over the festive period, Jürgen Klopp's men, after a run of eight wins on the bounce, hit a sticky patch, due to Covid and injuries, with just one win in six, albeit two of the 'draws' were League Cup ties – one a draw with Arsenal that set up a second-leg win at The Emirates, and another the late 3-3 comeback against Leicester in the quarter-finals, that the Reds won on penalties (in a game in which a particularly obnoxious James Maddison knee-slid in celebration to the Kop, which is about as acceptable as Michael Fagan breaking into Buckingham Palace to sit with the Queen on her bed). Yet just a few days later, the Reds put in perhaps their limpest display of the season at Leicester in the league, to lose 1-0, as part of a three-game 'slump' that included draws at Spurs (with some *atrocious* officiating decisions going against an under-strength Liverpool) and Chelsea. With Salah, Mané and Naby Keïta heading off to AFCON, and Liverpool soon falling 14 points behind Man City in the table (albeit with two games in hand), it felt – to me, at least – that the title race was over.

But if you include the penalty shootout victory over Chelsea as a win rather than a 0-0 draw, then the Reds won their next 12 games in all competitions, usually by one- or- two-goal margins, except when putting six past Leeds at Anfield. A month after departing, Mané returned victorious, Salah crestfallen, after the two met in the final of Africa's major tournament, which spurred the former to a prolific run of goals – often when playing centre-forward – and sent Salah, miles ahead of everyone in the Premier League scoring charts prior to the tournament, on a bit of a drought. Still, before they went away the team was scoring a lot of goals, which it continued to do whilst they were absent, and continued to do when they returned.

The only change was the arrival of Luis Díaz, who didn't start with many goals, but did see shots denied by blocks on the line, the woodwork and great goalkeeping. It felt like he would create and score even more, once settled into the team patterns. Signed at the end of January, he didn't exactly provide cover for the absent African duo (Keïta, as an attacking midfielder, had returned early after Guinea were eliminated), who were back a week-or-so later.

It perhaps helped that Liverpool's games during AFCON were Shrewsbury Town (cup), Arsenal (cup), Brentford, Arsenal (cup), Crystal Palace and Cardiff City (cup), meaning only two league games. The Reds scored 16 times, *sans* Salah and Mané, with eight different scorers. These included teenagers Harvey Elliott, upon his return after serious injury, and Kaide Gordon; both getting their first goals for the club at the Kop end. Alex Oxlade-Chamberlain bagged two, both assisted by Andy Robertson, and Jota scored three, all assisted by Trent Alexander-Arnold. Cup specialist Takumi Minamino grabbed two, while Virgil van Dijk and Roberto Firmino notched one each. The remaining four goals were scored by Fabinho, who scored more that month than he had since arriving in the summer of 2018 – although two of the four were penalties.

Fabinho later popped up with a vital goal in Villarreal, to turn around the Reds' rapidly souring Champions League semi-final situation in May, which was his 8th of the season.

I'd written back in August (and also in the previous season) how I'd found it strange that the Brazilian regularly stayed back at corners, as the covering 'defender' – albeit that job has to go to someone quick enough, and able to thwart attacks, with the centre-backs naturally pushed up into the opposition box. Two more candidates for the role in most teams would usually be the full-backs, but they either took the corners or, if on the other side of the pitch, were positioned to re-deliver anything cleared in that direction, almost like a second corner. While height is vital for defending in general, height isn't usually necessary when facing a counterattack from your own corner – it's almost always just about sprinting. As such, others were finally found to fill the role, and Fabinho – while not an aggressive header of the ball or an outstanding leaper – had joy when finally allowed to stay forward at corners, causing danger, and notching a few goals as one more 6'2" (at least) player to deal with.

TTT writer Mizgan Masani noted the lateness of Liverpool's goals: "One of Klopp's main strengths is to instil a never-say-die attitude in the team. Irrespective of the situation, this team goes till the final whistle to try and change the result in their favour or further secure it. The timing of goals is a good measure of that.

"The 2016/17 season saw only six goals scored in this period, which kind of made them predictable. Teams were able to know that Liverpool got tired after the 70-minute mark and did not create or score much. However, things changed from 2017/18 season onwards, they are now averaging 16 goals per season in the period between 76 and 90 minutes. They have won and drawn a lot of games by scoring in this block of time. Goals in this period also help in closing the opposition down and not allowing them to have much time to strike back. It also shows the growing mental strength of this side to keep going until the final whistle is blown."

By early May, the average distance of a Liverpool goal – from scorer to crossing the goal-line – was just 10.5 yards, or closer than a penalty. (Albeit this average discounts penalties, all 12 yards, as well as own goals.) This was from the 114 scored in the two main competitions: Premier League and Champions League. Fewer than 10% were scored from further out than 18 yards: a sure sign that expected goals and shot locations had meant working better chances closer to goal than taking potshots from outside the area, albeit players still succumbed to the temptation, and occasionally it paid off. (It's worth it at times, just to vary things.)

The goals from more than 18 yards out were: Porto away, Roberto Firmino, 36 yards; Porto at home, Thiago Alcântara, 31 yards; Newcastle at home, Trent Alexander-Arnold, 29 yards; Brentford away, Curtis Jones, 26 yards; West Ham away, Alexander-Arnold, 22 yards; AC Milan at home, Jordan Henderson, 20 yards; Atlético Madrid away, Salah, 20 yards; Atlético Madrid away, Keïta, 20 yards; Crystal Palace at home, Keïta, 19 yards; and Watford away, Mané, 19 yards.

The distances may suggest spectacular strikes, and some were beauties (both of Alexander-Arnold's, Keïta's volley against Palace, Jones' thunderbolt at Brentford) – but there were all types of goal. Even then, the pick of the bunch, in terms of technique, was Thiago's, where, from 31 yards, he cut across the ball from a cleared set-piece and sent a shot zipping, about 12 inches off the grass, across some invisible surface, into the far corner. (After this sequence of games, Luis Díaz scored from distance against Spurs, via a big deflection.)

The furthest, Firmino's, was perhaps the most enjoyable in certain ways, needing only the old Benny Hill theme tune to highlight its comedic value. The entire move was a delight, in different ways. Curtis Jones picked the ball up deep in his own half and, closed down by players including ex-Red Marko Grujić, managed to dribble brilliantly, albeit *in the wrong direction* – jinking back towards his own goal, and seemingly into trouble. Somehow he turned, turned again and turned once more, and out of nowhere hit a long pass that bounced 20 yards over the halfway line. The Porto defender seemed set to clear it, but Firmino anticipated it better, and leapt to take the ball on his thigh, wrong-footing the defender, who swiped at thin air. At this stage, the Brazilian was about 45 yards from goal, which would normally mean a lot of work to do; but inexplicably, the Porto keeper was himself now almost 40 yards from goal, and stranded. By the time Firmino got to the loose ball he'd sent himself a bit wide – but also wide of the keeper – and swivelled to hit a shot that was more like a golf putt from some distance beyond the green.

It's been noted that a powerful shot can travel at well over 100mph, albeit the speeds are a bit debatable. In terms of how fast someone can run, Usain Bolt was once recorded at 27.8mph. The Porto keeper, Diogo Costa, could perhaps run at 15mph, at full-pelt. Roberto Firmino's shot, from 36 yards at an angle, was therefore possibly hit at 15.01mph. Cue the comedy chase by a man trying to catch a football that was *fractionally* faster, over 36 frantic yards. He eventually scooped the ball away as he slid onto the goal-line, but it just had crossed by the time he got a hand to it. At this stage, Luis Díaz's Porto had got the score back to 3-1, but this killed the game; albeit there was time for Firmino to have another goal initially chalked off for offside, then allowed via a VAR check (something we'd later see happen against the Reds via Darwin Núñez). Diogo Costa was perhaps the most calamitous keeper the Reds faced in Europe, until the semi-final, and the uniquely strange Geronimo Rulli of Villarreal, who punched every easily catchable ball and dived out the way of most shots.

Rulli even allowed Liverpool to seal a 3-2 win in the second leg when, channeling his inner crazy Costa, he too charged out of his goal, almost to the centre-circle. Sadio Mané, just inside his own half and therefore onside, ran through, chasing a Keïta pass, and beat the stranded keeper to the ball. Mané skipped past the covering defender and ran down the inside-left flank, towards the goal, as the keeper and defender raced back towards the line; again, the Benny Hill theme music would only have improved it. Casually, Mané, upon entering the box, rolled it in, with a bit more pace than Firmino's effort, to rack up another win. The two opposition players could never quite get there.

Fifteen of the 114 goals involved ten or more passes; four of them with 20-25, and a further one – Díaz's first Liverpool goal, against Norwich – after an incredible 34 passes. Interestingly, these 15 goals included one away at Arsenal, another away at Everton, and two away at Manchester United. (Also, at home against Arsenal, AC Milan and Porto.) As such, almost half came in big games, against quality opposition (and, er, Everton). Just over half (eight) were in away games.

If the most startling two results were the 5-0 and 4-0 wins against Manchester United, the two best individual goals came against Manchester City and Watford. Indeed, while individual goals can sometimes be fetishised ahead of more complex team moves, these were so outstanding as to warrant special admiration. A fantastic volley can often just be one single moment of contact with a ball, perhaps after one good pass (albeit it could be meeting a clearing header, for example). The more complex moments, the greater the skill and difficulty.

After a below-par first half, Liverpool began testing Man City at Anfield, and Salah already had an assist in the game – setting up Mané – before his majestic solo triumph. By then City had equalised, and Curtis Jones got himself the simplest of assists by giving Salah the ball and watching him go. João Cancelo jumped in front of Salah, trying to nick the ball, but Salah, with his back to goal, a few yards infield on the right side and about 25 yards from the byline, turned him expertly. Phil Foden then appeared to push Salah in the back as Bernardo Silva slid in. Beautifully, Salah used the sole of his boot to just inch it away from the permanently scowling Portuguese, and accelerated past the prone player. Faced now with Aymeric Laporte, Salah predictably – too predictably at times – tried to cut inside, as he does 99 times out of 100. But then, when he bluffed and checked onto his right foot, Laporte was helpless. With both Laporte and Rúben Dias desperately sliding in, the Egyptian hammered the ball home from the tightest of angles, with the right foot he should trust more often. The jink from left foot to right foot essentially fooled elite defenders and created space in a packed box against a team that rarely conceded chances, let alone goals. At this stage, Salah had taken himself onto a whole new level, to be regularly heralded as the best player in the world at the time. While the AFCON would effectively curtail his individual form (perhaps allied to the tiresome media-hashing of contract talks), his brilliance in racking up 23 goals (in addition to multiple assists) by the time he departed for that competition on 3rd January put Liverpool in a strong position in the league and the Champions League.

In this imperious form, he managed to score a similarly jaw-dropping goal against Watford, in a 5-0 win that preceded a 5-0 win at Old Trafford, as part of a sequence of ecstatic, orgiastic football. Indeed, just before the Watford win came a 5-1 win at Porto, too. Given that it was Watford and not Man City, the goal has to be downgraded a little, but Salah picked up the ball in a similar area – from a successful Reds press by Firmino and Keïta – and three Hornets converged on the Liverpool no.11. Again he did the soft shoe shuffle, to roll the ball forward and then backwards, before going to shoot with his right foot from an almost identical angle to the goal against Pep Guardiola's man. But this time was a double-bluff, cutting back onto his favoured left foot to curl the ball into the far corner (as such, that part of the finish – the position within the goal frame where the ball entered the net – was identical).

Later in the season, a goal by Rafa Silva of Benfica (from just before his team was due to meet Liverpool) went viral, when he collected the ball on the edge of his own box and ran the length of the pitch to score. But aside from the admirable pace and determination, he mostly ran in a straight line, straight past players who were never close enough to put in a challenge, until one *finally* made one in the box. It felt more like a player in rugby or the NFL sprinting clear. Salah's two goals, by contrast, were in packed boxes, and involved deft skills in tight spaces and incredible changes of direction. (This is always why I rate John Barnes' 1987 goal against QPR as one of the best I've ever seen: the way he gets the ball on the halfway line, sprints forward, but then, when confronted by the opposition block on the edge of the box, shifts his balance and body-weight – with a physics-defying grace – one way and then another to go past two England centre-backs and slot past the England keeper.)

A beautifully hit shot – even one like Thiago's against Porto – can be a thing of wonder, but it's just one moment of contact with the football. Against Watford, Salah manipulated the ball eight times; against City, *ten* times. Had any of these touches been fractionally less perfect, the ball would have been lost. There was not a lot of pitch to play in, and almost no space. At that point in time he was operating in a sphere of his own.

And then, after scoring two in the cauldron of Atlético's Metropolitano (the venue of the Reds 2019 Champions League glory), he went to Old Trafford and bagged a hat-trick.

'Deserved Goals'
In 2010, Finnish subscriber Aki Pekuri wrote an article for *The Tomkins Times* about his model called 'deserved goals' – a kind of precursor to expected goals. Two years later he wrote another article, this time about the role of luck.

"I realised it is the tenth anniversary of my TTT article about getting luck on our side," he told me in March 2022, "and oh boy have we got it!"

"I don't even remember how and where I originally started reading your articles, but at least the reason is still crystal clear – literally in-depth analysis based on research and data. You definitely were a trailblazer in the field of football analytics, or should I say football transfer and manager performance analytics. You used to write for the official Liverpool FC website, right?"

As Aki notes, indeed I did, from 2005 to 2010. I also co-wrote a purely statistical Liverpool FC book with Oliver Anderson in 2006,

The Red Review, which included a lot of things that became mainstream a few years later (hockey assists, adjusting everything to per-90, distance of shots that led to goals, with/without comparisons, and so on). Of course, since the big data revolution, much of it (and anything I could do now) is miles behind expected goals and, further ahead, the AI algorithms analysing football. It all became very professional and *gigantic data* in the interim.

"Your texts provided clarity to what was happening and I was hooked. At the time I was also finishing my Masters thesis in 2009 after spending six months in University of Sheffield year earlier. And oh, the first child was born. Career-wise I somehow ended up becoming a researcher and stayed at University of Oulu further six years until 2015 when I completed my dissertation.

"A sort of book also, that. But honestly, I have presented my chapter in *These Turbulent Times* more proudly and way more broadly than my academic output."

[*These Turbulent Times* is a 2013 anthology of some of TTT's articles since the site's inception in 2009, by, other than myself: Lee Mooney, Andrew Beasley, Dan Kennett, Daniel Rhodes, Graeme Riley, Bob Peace, Krishen Bhautoo, Daniel Geey, Mihail Vladimirov, Paul Grech, Neil Jones, Ted Knutson, Simon Steers and others, many of whom now work within the game, if no longer writing for TTT.]

"By the way, it was a Commodore 64 game called *FA Cup* that made me a Red. The idea of the game was to choose a club and a tactic for each match to simulate through the match. Options were A, B or C meaning attacking, balanced, defensive and once I figured out that A works for Liverpool FC I won the cup nine out 10 and was so happy about it. It was 1990 or 1991 so I was eight or nine years old. I still own the cassette.

"Nowadays I still watch every LFC match but reading and analysis are almost limited to browsing through Twitter before going into bed. Yet I still dream of finding enough energy and courage to make a career shift towards data and analytics. It is also nice to think ifs and buts regarding my early work and to notice how relatively advanced the models and thinking were back then.

"I see my 'deserved goals' in 2010 as the same concept as xG nowadays but of course with less advanced model and assumptions. If I recall it correctly, in that luck article I only separated normal shots from clear-cut chances and valued them with a single number. For betting I based my model to shot maps which was enough to beat bookies in most leagues bar the Premier League.

"Without coding skills it was just too time consuming to maintain as I manually entered each shot from each match over multiple leagues to 8x5 matrix table. That was the accuracy, the field was divided to 40 parts that each had a unique value i.e. probability of scoring, aka deserved goals aka xGs. These days as daughters are grown up I have more time that I am allocating to local football.

"After Covid restrictions in early 2020 we registered our team to northern group of the Finnish 5th division. Everyone was just eager to get out and do sport again, and I ended up making a comeback after a 20-year break. Not that I ever played in the senior team or any division even when younger. I just quit when I was 18.

"Last year we were promoted from the 4th to the 3rd division and I have given up a playing role as training has intensified. My role in the first team is now to look after money that we don't have, and as team leader handling all the general or administrative stuff. No one is paid a penny and my deal is that I am allowed to participate training anytime!

"To secure playing minutes at more appropriate level I gathered another group of players and registered the reserve team to the 5th division again. There I am also a treasurer and team leader but it seems also a manager. I am still undecided whether I should play as a 10, 9, 8 or 6. Maybe I will choose that Juan Riquelme role as we are both slow.

"Anyway, I live in a city of Kemi, just at the southern border of Lapland region, with 20,000 habitants. The club Kemin Palloseura has quite a nice history and in the summer we celebrated our 90 year anniversary. In 1985 the club won bronze in the 'Finnish Premier League' and 1986 was runner-up in the cup. I guess the glory part ends here, but I am fine with that and learned to be patient with LFC. The most successful player from KePS as the club name is abbreviated, is Hannu Tihinen who played eight games for West Ham in 2001. I watch basically all games comfortably from my own sofa. Locally there is just one bar that shows football, but there is no real following behind any club so one must bring his own friends to raise atmosphere.

"In bigger cities and especially in Helsinki there is a good following and multiple sport pubs to watch matches with other Reds. I used to go to those when my work required weekly travelling couple of years ago. The official LFC supporter club Finland is also more active in south where cities are bigger."

Steven Wilson, 54, is a Pacific Islander who has lived in Texas for the past 25 years. For him, football is becoming more fun.

"I enjoy football more now than in my early life. I used to play all sports and watched all sports and knew baseball, American football, basketball far more than football. But now my life (outside of family) is centred around football. Not only am I the President of the OLSC, I am President of a local youth club. I am on the board of the Austin Soccer Foundation (promoting grassroots football). I referee, all the way to the collegiate level."

[At this point I felt tempted to ask if he wanted a job at the PGMOL.]

"I am a licensed coach and have coached for 10 years. I have played semi-pro and traveled around Europe playing and I still play twice a week. I really can't explain the reasoning for losing interest in the other sports, but it probably coincided when my love for the Reds started."

Norwegian Jan Ove Knudseth reminded me of the reason so many Scandinavians love Liverpool.

"English football actually means a lot to Norwegians. It started back in 1969 when the national broadcasting company started broadcasting English football matches every Saturday. There are many Norwegians, myself included, who are more passionate about English football than Norwegian football. More than 50,000 Norwegians (or 1% of the population!) are members of the Norwegian Liverpool fan club."

Just as this book was about to go to print, Joel Rabinowitz ran an article on his Substack (*The LFC Journal*) about 'the Liverbirds Svalbard' that caught my eye, and seemed worth quoting.

"In one sense, it's not all that surprising – there are Liverpool supporters clubs in pretty much every major town and city in mainland Norway, and indeed dotted throughout the other Nordic nations. During the 1970s and 1980s, following a decade in which The Beatles had catapulted Liverpool into the international spotlight, Scandinavian state broadcasters first began showing English football. Naturally, Liverpool made the cut for TV slots more often than not, given their status as the dominant force on the domestic and European stage under Bill Shankly and Bob Paisley at the time.

"As such, millions of Norwegians, Swedes, Danes and Finns developed a strong affinity towards Liverpool, and that has been passed on over multiple generations since.

"... What sets the Liverbirds Svalbard apart, though, is their unique geography; they are the northernmost supporters club on the planet, a hotspot of Liverpool passion on a frozen island in the High Arctic, where you're more likely to come across a reindeer or a polar bear than a Man City or Chelsea fan.

"...Ronny Brunvoll, who moved to Svalbard in 2012 and began supporting Liverpool in the 1976-77 season, details the typical match day routine: 'Depending on the day and kick-off time of the match, we meet for a pint or two at Karlsberger Pub [which does a special cut-price beer deal specifically for Liverpool fans on match days]. Then, we'll move on to Barentz Pub to watch the match itself. For cup finals, we usually arrange some kind of parade with lots of flags, banners and music, which involves either climbing up a mountain together or heading out on snowmobiles. It's a community with a lot of pulse – it was the first thing I checked out when I moved here, and it has become like my second family.'"

The cup finals of 2022 famously saw Liverpool draw blanks, but the football in recent years will have kept even the Svalbard crew warm.

Then there's British-born Nabs Al Busaidi from Oman, Supporters Representative for Africa and the Middle East, as part of the Official Liverpool Supporters Club (OLSC) system; who, despite that, knows a thing or two about the bitter cold. Nabs is considered to be the first Arab to walk to the magnetic North Pole, to climb Mount Vinson in Antarctica, and to row the Atlantic Ocean. On a trip back to the UK to see a couple of Liverpool games (amongst other things) towards the end of 2021/22 he met the Prime Minister at 10 Downing Street (poor Nabs), and on another day, met James Milner (lucky Nabs), before seeing the Reds play Spurs. (I know which *leader* I'd rather meet.)

"There were pockets of international OLSC fans all around the stadium, but Oman were right at the bottom of the Kop near the corner flag, with Idaho, Glasgow, Ireland, Norway, Wisconsin and a few others."

The following day he was also a guest at the Manchester City game at home to Newcastle, whose fans sang "We're richer than you / We're richer than you / We've got Saudi money / We're richer than you".

Headers and Volleys

The Reds' first header of the season came via Diogo Jota, able to flick on, at the near post, a Kostas Tsimikas cross to open the scoring against bulky, bruising Burnley. The cross was inch-perfect, for Jota to dart in front of Ben Mee, and for the ball to dip just at the point where James Tarkowski, nearer to the Greek, could not backpedal fast enough. For Liverpool's 5'9 (Mo Salah, Sadio Mané) and 5'10 strikers (Jota and Luis Díaz), and even Firmino at 5'11", there are several key aspects to the crosses, that helped the Reds, aside from when sending bigger players up for set-pieces, to lead the league in headed goals.

Now, this is such a difficult art. There has to be pace on the cross, but a slower cross enables defenders more time to jump, and a keeper more time to gather. It cannot be too looping, as taller defenders, and the keeper, will be able to take it at its highest point. And like a free-kick over a wall, it has to go over the defenders and dip down in time.

If it's going over the head of a 6'4" defender, and there's another 6'4" two yards behind (in a line, as the ball travels from flank to centre), it has to drop rapidly.

When Spurs came to Anfield to snatch a draw in May, they defended with three tall centre-backs, albeit none was an out-and-out giant. Also dropping into the space were Pierre-Emile Højbjerg, 6'1", and Rodrigo Bentancur, 6'2". The wing-back, Emerson Royal (6'0"), cramped the box too. All three of Spurs' strikers were 6'0-6'2", and so made all the corners Liverpool won harder to deliver; Virgil van Dijk getting up well just twice, to head wide, then head against the bar. Otherwise, the 11 corners and 50 crosses were mostly suited to the way Spurs were playing. They had no one over 6'2" in their lineup, but they had almost no one under 6'0". Spurs were defending so deep at times that the Reds' backline was 20 yards inside *their* half.

(Incidentally, this summer, at the time of going to press, Spurs have signed a 6'1" winger, a 6'1" forward, a 6'0" midfielder and a 6'7" goalkeeper. Antonio Conte's winter signings were a 6'1" winger and a 6'2" midfielder.)

There were no headers from any of the Liverpool strikers to trouble Hugo Lloris (a certain Darwin Núñez would have been ideal for Liverpool), and despite 22 shots, a staggering *twelve* were blocked. While Spurs may still have opted to defend deep, that Liverpool *now* have a 6'2" striker will mean that teams who do so are going to face a striker who can get above their tallest defenders in a crowded area.

In the *Sunday Times*, Jonathan Northcroft talked about Liverpool and headers, albeit it's worth starting with a general point about Núñez's underlying numbers:

"Back in 2020, the leading scouting consultancy Driblab congratulated Benfica for spotting the potential that lay in Núñez's seemingly innate knack of selecting shots with a high xG (expected goals) and finding a high volume of touches in the box. In other words, the data showed that here was a young forward with the priceless old ability to be in the right place at the time, and know when to try and score."

Next, the issue of headers, and how Núñez had doubled his tally of three the previous season: "... It suggests he is really beginning to learn how to use his height and gift for arriving on to balls played into the box. And which team scored the most headers in the Premier League in each of the past four seasons? Yep, Liverpool. Mané was responsible for several of those and heading prowess has been an overlooked element in his game. He is 22nd on the all-time Premier League list for headed goals, level with Kevin Davies and Marouane Fellaini.

"With Mané set to quit Anfield … there will be a need to replace not only the considerable off-ball and on-ball skills Mané offers, but also his effectiveness in the air. Only six of Salah's 156 Liverpool goals have been headers, after all – though Luis Díaz has a surprisingly good aerial-goals record, and Diogo Jota was level with Danny Welbeck and Harry Kane as the top scorer of headers in last season's Premier League."

Núñez has a clever way of pulling away from defenders to the far post, which would suit the way Liverpool already score from headers. If playing against two centre-backs, he can lose both and go up against a smaller full-back.

While Núñez is not yet an aerial *dominator* (that can come with time), he did score several headers for Benfica that were not like any Liverpool tended to score, where he got up high against a tall defender close to goal and headed home via what was essentially an aerial duel. That's the bonus of being 6'2", and being in the Premier League will teach Núñez, just as it taught a young Kevin Davies and Peter Crouch, to become so much more dangerous with added age, power and experience. Height is just the starting point: a great leap, anticipation, strength and heading technique all matter – and as with anything else, more experience helps with aerial duels – but they will always be best on someone 6'2" rather than 5'9". What more can Liverpool get from a springy 6'2" striker with heading power than they got from the clever Sadio Mané? As well as open play, Núñez has to add a threat at set-piece situations.

As TTT alum and *Anfield Index* podcaster Dan Kennett noted, Liverpool "finished the season with 206 shots from set pieces. The data goes back to 2011, and the previous highest in the Premier League was 180!" The Reds "ended with 19 goals, which is one every other match. It's a crazy volume." Liverpool now have an extra 6'2" player to help convert that volume into a goals tally that matches the more prolific (but according to xG, *fortunate*) Man City from their set-pieces.

As Liverpool's title hopes faltered, Spurs were packing the box, and there was no space to shoot, and with three narrow centre-backs and two narrow full-backs, no space to drop an ideal cross. The Reds' final passes were hurried, and many of the shots were taken too slowly, as if trying to be too sure. It perhaps made sense that the equaliser came from a deflected Díaz shot, as deflections are one of the bonuses of keepers wrong-footed when they can't see past their own defence. Liverpool don't often shoot from well outside the box (and it's dumb when defenders do it from 40 yards), but this was a game where it had to be an option, providing – as was the case here – that there was enough space to get a meaningful shot away. The scooped passes, dinked crosses and other ways the team had been using to break past a resolute back-line just weren't working (although again, Núñez will help in the future), as Spurs were extremely well organised, tall and committed, after a week to prepare, while the Reds had a midweek Champions League semi-final in Spain (and almost no club ever wins all its league games after its Champions League knockout ties. It's where points are most likely to be dropped).

Against two centre-backs, the crossing will find more gaps, unless the full-backs are very narrow and, as some teams do, a back six is formed by the wide midfielders. It helps that in Trent Alexander-Arnold and Andy Robertson, Liverpool have two of the best crossing full-backs in world football. But with three smaller strikers, there have to be a high number of crosses played in, for just a few to land perfectly. With Origi 6'1" but not especially aggressive in the air (most of the time), Liverpool haven't had a target-man under Klopp since the sale of Christian Benteke. Yet the target would not be from deep balls (albeit it's an option from goalkicks and hurried clearances), but from crosses. Benteke, rightly sold, didn't have Alexander-Arnold and Robertson feeding him. Núñez's aerial figures *could* go through the roof with that kind of delivery; as well as freeing up Jota, Díaz, Firmino and others if Núñez is marked in open play by the taller defender. Aim a cross for Núñez, and even if just over his head, Jota or Díaz could be making the run in behind, to head home.

Liverpool's first 39 goals of the 2021/22 season – Premier League and Champions League only – contained just two headers. The second came at Brentford, in the 3-3 draw (another Jota bullet-header), albeit headers had *created* goals, such as a repeat against Crystal Palace from the previous season, when Mané mopped up the loose ball after a header from a corner. Indeed, Liverpool scored three from corners against Patrick Vieira's team at Anfield, each with a shot from a second ball. After Mané's goal, van Dijk headed it on and Mo Salah volleyed home from close range. Then Naby Keïta, after the keeper punched Salah's corner to send it outside the area, hit a sublime first-time volley that absolutely flew into the far corner. Indeed, this was a tactic Liverpool were making good use of: the long-range shooters placed just outside the area, to smash home the loose ball; Jordan Henderson had just done the same to seal a 3-2 win over AC Milan in the Champions League group stages (catching his shot just after it bounced, so arguably on the half-volley).

Goals 40-45 contained three headers, after just two in 39, then came another 15 goals from non-headed sources. Mané and Jota shared these three headers: the Senegalese at home to Brighton and Arsenal, and the Portuguese at home to Atlético Madrid. As such, there were just five headers in the first 60 main-competition goals. Then followed 15 of the next 55, to more than treble the rate scored aerially.

By goal 59 (excluding the domestic cups), only Jota and Mané had scored with headers. Goal 60 saw Divock Origi head home away at AC Milan, to become the third. Then the variety really began to show: in order, the scorers were Jota, Robertson, Fabinho, Alex Oxlade-Chamberlain, van Dijk, Firmino, van Dijk, Díaz, Jota, Konaté, Konaté, Robertson, Origi, Díaz; and to show the variety of how they came about, they were, in order, scored from: open play, open play, open play, corner, open play, corner, corner, corner, open play, open play, corner, corner, open play, corner and open play. Nine different scorers, and none of them Mané.

Some of the headers were admittedly almost on the ground: Oxlade-Chamberlain's at home to Brentford, and Robertson's stooping far-post steal against Everton, to send the ball past a despairing Pickford. Then there was the rising, majestic, powerful leap by Origi in the same game, to generate power on Díaz's brilliant but wayward overhead kick, in putting the ball just out of reach of a similarly despairing Pickford (late-on, at the Kop end, not for the first time).

By early May, some 20 of the 115 goals scored by Klopp's men in the Premier League and Champions League were headers. Several more were volleys. It was a team that scored all types of goals. None would be better than Mo Salah's two solo goals in the autumn of 2021, but plenty would be more important. The future will mean new ways to attack, different ways to score goals. Losing Mané, Origi and Minamino will mean some lost shared understandings, but if anything, the Reds' front line will be even quicker.

A different type of attacker has been added in Fábio Carvalho, an elusive, skilful attacking midfielder who physically resembles Philippe Coutinho, but also in the way he moves and finishes; yet has more pace, and presses harder (and who seems a better finisher than Coutinho was aged 19). Teenage right-back Calvin Ramsay delivers a ball almost as well as Trent Alexander-Arnold, but while not the same kind of expansive playmaker, can go past opponents with a variety of twists, turns and tricks. And while it's surely too soon to expect first-team minutes, 16-year-old Ben Doak, who played for Celtic against Rangers in 2021/22, is an express train of a winger with a great first touch, who finishes with aplomb. The more graceful Kaide Gordon should be back and stronger after injuries following his winter breakthrough, and the same applies to Harvey Elliott, who, aged 18, began 2021/22 in the team on merit.

Losing Mané will be a blow of sorts, but Darwin Núñez, in particular, offers a different kind of striker, with the physical attributes of Divock Origi, but as a key distinction, the aggression of Luis Suárez.

You can never predict the future, but at the very least, with Salah choosing to sign a new deal, it should prove interesting.

At the Other End

At times, Alisson Becker proved a one-man goal-prevention machine; albeit in 2021/22 his goals *scored* fell (from one to zero), and as such, maybe it's time Jürgen Klopp sent him up for set-pieces again.

While he has so many strengths as a goalkeeper, including his passing (even if he occasionally takes a fraction too long to release the ball), the Brazil international made a massive difference to the Reds' shot-stopping. His quickness and alertness when sweeping also allowed the team to play higher up the pitch, which has myriad benefits.

Having hovered around the 65% mark across various keepers between 2016 and 2018, the save-percentage for Liverpool keepers did not drop below 70% once Alisson donned the gloves. In fact, it was above 75% in 2018/19 and the same was true in 2021/22.

Of course, save *difficulty* is not taken into account here. For that, there is the 'post-shot expected goal' metric; i.e. also taking into account where the ball is heading within the goal frame (i.e. top corner, low centre, and so on).

Unfortunately, the figures for this metric are not available prior to 2017/18, but that first season of data saw underperformance in shot-saving (-1.4) by the Reds' keepers: Simon Mignolet and Loris Karius sharing glove-duty in the league that year. Since then though, there has been massive over-performance: an average of +4.25 in that time, which is without doubt one of the best returns in Europe. The title was won in 2019/20 when Alisson missed 12 games earlier in the campaign: his figures were just about the right side of neutral (+0.6), whereas Adrián, who did make some important saves, had a minor negative score (-1.0). When Adrián deputised, the defence was not as solid – there were hardly any clean sheets – but the results were mostly wins due to impressive attacking play, and digging out late wins when the games were tight. (And a bit of luck, too.)

Another factor behind Alisson's greatness is his sweeping abilities. He is assured of coming out of his area to make interceptions and snuffing the danger out, enabling the defensive line to play as high as possible in order to squeeze the life out of the opposition, as pointed out to me by Mizgan Masani via some research on the Brazilian. Prior to his arrival, Liverpool's keepers were making an 'action' outside their area at a rate of about 0.5 per game. That rose to 1.0 per game once Alisson arrived and stayed steady for the first three seasons, and then jumped to 1.5 per game in 2021/22.

The other factor about Liverpool's high line and sweeper-keeper is that Alisson is by far and away the best one-on-one specialist in the Premier League. Statistically, it's not even close. In data shared by analyst John Harrison after the 34th league game, Alisson had faced 47 one-on-ones, at a rate of one-and-a-half per game; and he had denied eight goals (7.79) more than 'expected'. Two keepers (Robert Sánchez of Brighton, who almost put Luis Díaz in hospital, and Wolves' José Sá) stopped close to five goals, and then the other 17 regular goalkeepers listed weren't even denying three (albeit that's still better than zero, obviously, with nine keepers, in total, denying more than one goal better than expected).

Manchester City's Ederson, by contrast, was virtually neutral: as many saves as expected. That said, despite his team actually playing with a higher line than Liverpool (based on data over the course of the season), he had only faced 27, or less than one per 90 minutes. (Interestingly, when City could only draw at West Ham a few games after this data was published, he was twice beaten by Jarrod Bowen in one-on-one situations.) It just needed teams to try and get in behind City more often, but the way they kept the ball meant it was easier said than done. Of course, Ederson is a thoroughly modern keeper, whose incredible passing suits City – but if teams can get through to face him, he's not *that* special. At the other end of the scale, Everton's Jordan Pickford ranked worst out of the 20 keepers to play the most minutes for their club, at 2.42 more goals conceded than expected on one-on-ones.

Now, one-on-ones are just part of the keeper's repertoire – but clearly, given most clubs face between one and two per game, an important part. These are, by definition, *big* chances.

If you average all the post-shot data over the seasons since Alisson arrived – so, for all situations – and reduce the pool to a minimum of two seasons (to remove outlier José Sá), then the Reds' custodian leads the way, at an average of +4.3 – or in other words, based on shot *difficulty*, he saves more than four goals per season above the average expectations. Hugo Lloris, Alphonse Areola, Łukasz Fabiański, Bernd Leno, David de Gea, Nick Pope and Martin Dúbravka follow, all between +3.0 and +4.1.

For years regarded as the best overall keeper, it's interesting that de Gea in 2021/22 was merely average at stopping one-on-ones, while in five seasons he dealt with the ball outside his area 51 times, compared to Alisson's 178 in just four seasons. (Ederson had 172 in five seasons.) And despite his height, de Gea, when faced with 250 crosses across the latest season, made just eight claims, at 3.2%; compared to Alisson's 17, at 9% (from 188 crosses). As with Cristiano Ronaldo, it seems that Manchester United could have an elite specialist at both ends of the pitch, but where their styles do not mesh with modern football: Ronaldo does not press and obviously cannot make as many runs off the ball aged 37, while de Gea is a reactive goal-line keeper, who does not cut off things like through-balls and crosses at the source, which are vital to playing a higher modern line. (And spending almost £100m on a slow centre-back not suited to a high line was another weird move, but that's United's problem.)

One other observation about Alisson that I want to highlight is his *stillness*. This may seem like an odd quality for a footballer, but he produces the finest saves with the least flamboyance, and is calm and focused until forced into action. I spent the season amazed at the praise heaped on Pickford and Arsenal's Aaron Ramsdale, both at least two inches shorter than Alisson, who I labelled 'chaos keepers'. Both have their qualities, and make some stunning reaction saves – but neither is tall enough to get to shots into the corners (and as such, they make 'spectacular' tip-over saves from efforts taller keepers would just catch), and both run around their area, shouting, high-fiving, or chasing the referee halfway up the pitch. They look particularly good at double-saves, given that they are agile and quick to their feet, but they charge about, commit themselves early, and seem to rely on adrenaline and all-action – when the best keepers like a quiet game. To me, it's no coincidence that both came to prominence in relegated sides, with lots to do.

With one game to go, Ramsdale ranked 38th out of the 41 keepers to play in the Premier League in 2021/22, having conceded 4.6 goals more than expected. Yet people thought he was the best in the league. Every time I saw him I noted how erratic he was. (He's still fairly young, mind.)

With my suspicions that you ideally want a keeper over 6'3" (just as you want centre-backs who are over 6'2" – I'd always go at least 6'4" if you can find the talent to match), it's interesting that all of the keepers who saved more goals than expected in 2021/22 averaged out at 192.4cm in height, or over 6'3", while those who performed worse than expected averaged at 190.1, or 6'2" – even if there were outliers in each category, and things like age and just *general ability* are also going to matter, too. The peak ages for all goalkeeping save percentages are between 28-30, so right where Alisson sits in 2022, in the sweet spot between experience and agility, before reactions start to dim. Once in the mid-30s it will also be more difficult to race to the ball as a sweeper-keeper.

In basketball, the chances of making it in the NBA famously double with each extra inch of height. So someone who is 6'3" has twice the chance of someone who is 6'2", but half the chance of someone who is 6'4". This rule of thumb stretches up to around 7'5", after which any additional height is often down to diseases including Marfan syndrome (with issues falling within chromosome disorders, genetic disorders and endocrine disorders). Football is not basketball, of course, with the goal being on the ground and not in the air; but height can be vital – a lot of the game takes place in the air, and a goalkeeper or defender has to try and leap as high as possible to deal with certain situations, with a keeper's height also helping increase his reach. (Also, the goal itself *begins* on the ground, but rises to 8ft.)

Several years ago I looked at the aerial win percentages of players in the Premier League, and those who won the most were the group that averaged a height of 6'5" or more. Then, with each inch of height taken away, the success rate dropped, down to about 5'9", where the results became noisy.

Again, there were outliers within each height band, but as I noted in 2015, tall centre-backs and tall keepers (as well as a tall defensive midfielder) can really help protect the area, especially against crosses and the long-ball styles still favoured by some English teams. Where Liverpool were clever was in finding tall players for these positions who were also elite *talents* – not just giants, but technically excellent, and crucially, also quick. That said, it's where they paid a premium: Virgil van Dijk and Alisson, the club's two most expensive purchases of the Jürgen Klopp era even when adjusted for inflation, and with Fabinho not exactly cheap.

That said, Joël Matip was a bargain on a free transfer, and so far, Ibrahima Konaté looks like a steal at around £36m.

Plus, in Darwin Núñez, whose fee with add-ons could top those paid for van Dijk and Alisson, Liverpool have paid a premium for another tall player, who should not only help to score goals, but at 6'2", do some solid defensive duties at those all-important set-pieces.

Déjà Vu: Chelsea In the Cup Final

The action-packed but goalless 90 minutes at Wembley; the extra-time, with tired bodies and minds wary of making an error; and the penalty shootout, going beyond the five initial takers into sudden death. Though later unused, Takumi Minamino as the top scorer for the Reds in the run to the final; Luis Díaz a contender for man of the match; Ibrahima Konaté with Romelu Lukaku in his pocket; James Milner on as a sub to rack up another big occasion on one of the longest CVs in football.

We'd been here before, three months earlier, and the result was the same: Liverpool players in red running like lunatics to celebrate, only with the victors' keepers in green and not yellow this time. The shootout differed too – both teams had their first-choices in goal, whereas the previous final involved their backups, albeit the Chelsea one cost a world-record fee and supposedly specialised in penalty saves. In May, Liverpool were without most of the takers of those best penalties: Fabinho, Mo Salah, Virgil van Dijk, Harvey Elliott. Instead, Sadio Mané took one, with his success in Senegal shootouts not replicated domestically, given his poor spot-kick record with the Reds.

Weirdly however, fully in yellow for the entire game (bar the keeper in grey) were Chelsea, choosing their away kit, apparently due to Thomas Tuchel's superstitions (or was it a conscious effort to downplay their owner's Russian guilt by looking a bit more *Ukrainian*, especially with the blue tracksuit tops?). It made no difference: Chelsea were beaten in full yellow, just as they had been in full blue.

Yet it was another reminder that, in the season of tons of big wins, at the pinch points, it ultimately came down – good and bad – to very fine margins. Liverpool had hit the woodwork in normal time. César Azpilicueta – an especially narky player for someone who looks so angelic – hit the post with his penalty. To win the two domestic cups, Liverpool and Chelsea each took 18 penalties; Liverpool won 11-10 in February and 6-5 in May, with Chelsea missing three (Kepa Arrizabalaga, Azpilicueta and Mason Mount) and Liverpool missing just one (Mané).

It also called to mind Manchester City's recent Champions League semi-final defeat to Real Madrid, where Jack Grealish, on as a sub and with City leading the tie by two goals in the last minute of the second leg, went at speed into the box, dummied ex-Chelsea keeper Thibaut Courtois and naturally assumed that when he struck the ball past him – from a wide angle but into the gaping net – it would be a goal;

instead, it was cleared off the line by a rapidly-appearing defender, and even then, almost hit Phil Foden to bounce in. Grealish then hit another shot that Courtois saved with a leg so outstretched that it was the studs on his boot that deflected the shot narrowly wide. You can pick apart what happened *next*, but City were a millimetre or two from killing off the tie, before Madrid's incredible two injury-time goals took it to extra-time. Pep Guardiola was once again a 'fraud', overthinking things, when in fairness, the sub he sent on (albeit one that cost £100m) did almost everything to take them into the final. It's part of the reason football is such an amazing sport, as a dominant rugby, basketball or NFL side could clock up 50 or more 'points' when on top and thus clearly see their reflection as the better side in a landslide score. In football, the low-scoring nature makes most games more likely to be on a knife-edge, even if no one ever sees certain comebacks heaving into view. (As luck would have it, Courtois would soon do the same to Liverpool in Paris. Still, it felt less galling and painful to lose to the Spaniards than it would have to be beaten by City, for various reasons, although it helped that Sergio 'Pig's Heart' Ramos was long gone.)

The mood after missing just a couple of penalties, *had it happened*, would have totally changed the view of Liverpool's domestic cup finals, and indeed, the season up to that point. Even a moment of clarity from Alisson could have been overlooked: remembering to clutch the ball as it bounced back towards the goal after his fantastic strong-wristed save from Mount. (In one famous shootout a keeper ran off to celebrate after the ball hit the bar, but the ball then bounced down in the six-yard box and span into the empty net.)

"We played 240 minutes in two finals against maybe the most dangerous attacking team in the world and it's 0-0", Tuchel said afterwards, in his assessment of a team who had by this stage scored 140 goals in the season.

A beaming Klopp said: "We are mentality monsters, but there were mentality monsters in Chelsea colours as well – it was one penalty. Chelsea played outstanding but in the end there must be one winner and that was us today.

"… I couldn't be more proud of my boys, the shift they put in, how hard they fought. It was an incredible game, a nerve-wracking shootout, my nails are gone."

Klopp became only the second manager to win all three domestic trophies as well as the European Cup/Champions League with the same club, following on from Alex Ferguson. Klopp did so in six-and-a-half years, whereas it took Ferguson 13. (Obviously Bob Paisley's six league titles and three European Cups – and three League Cups – in just nine years remains the best pound-for-pound achievement in English football, especially as he inherited a good Liverpool team, but not one that was dominating Europe.)

Spotting It

All 18 of the Reds' spot-kicks in the cup finals had been on target, with one saved. In a previous shootout (the League Cup quarter-final against Leicester), Taki Minamino was the only player to miss, blazing over. In that game, five of the six were scored, including one by Alex Oxlade-Chamberlain, who didn't even make the bench for the FA Cup final. In total, 24 shootout kicks were taken in the domestic cup run, with 22 successes. The scorers were: James Milner (3), Fabinho, Virgil van Dijk, Trent Alexander-Arnold (2), Mo Salah, Diogo Jota (3), Divock Origi, Andy Robertson, Harvey Elliott, Ibrahima Konaté, Caoimhín Kelleher, Naby Keïta, Alex Oxlade-Chamberlain, Roberto Firmino (2), Thiago Alcântara and Kostas Tsimikas. It meant a 92% success rate, with just two misses, with sixteen different players scoring; and 100% of the efforts were on target.

Penalties will always remain *something* of a lottery, as just like paper/scissors/stone you can be thwarted by the perfect guess of your opponent; keepers have to dive before the ball is kicked to reach the corners, and as such, they *may* simply dive out of the way. Whatever direction they dive, they can make a deliberate save, or the ball can just hit them. But it's also something that can be worked on, even if the pressure cannot be replicated. As with any skill, the more practiced, and the more composed in the heat of battle, the greater the chance of success.

"We work together with a company, four guys, their name is *neuro 11*," Klopp said after the final. "They got in contact with us two years ago … One of them is a neuroscientist and he said 'we can train penalty shooting' Really. And I said: 'sounds interesting, come over.'

"German guy, we met. We worked together and this trophy is for them like the Carabao Cup was."

Klopp also took personal responsibility for Sadio Mané's miss after he asked the forward to change his mind, based on how the Reds' striker knew Chelsea goalkeeper Edouard Mendy from their time at Senegal. (And indeed, two successful penalty shootouts against Egypt in 2022.)

"Sadio's penalty was maybe more, for sure at least 50 per cent, my responsibility," he said. "We have to let the boys do what they think they do but with him I said 'he knows exactly the goalie so do it the other way around.' Like very often in my life I realise it was better to shut up. But we still made it."

A day after the final, Daniel Harris of the *Guardian* wrote, "In August 1974, Liverpool beat Leeds United 6-5 on penalties to win the Charity Shield – the first of 26 shootouts in which they've competed. Of those, a quite ridiculous 19 have been won, including two European Cup finals, two FA Cup finals and three League Cup finals. Two of them have come this season, at the end of goalless draws against Chelsea. On the face of things, what happened in, say, Rome in 1984 has nothing whatsoever to do with what happened at Wembley on Saturday. But an overall success rate of 73.08% cannot possibly be a coincidence, and instead speaks volumes about Liverpool's mythology and self-mythologising – veins into which Jürgen Klopp has tapped so astutely. Of course, all professional footballers are capable of beating a goalkeeper with a free shot from 12 yards, but Klopp has given those who play for him confidence, entitlement and aggression, their sense of history and destiny bordering on the messianic – and they are not finished yet."

On Twitter, Geir Jordet (whose bio says 'Football psychology researcher, consultant, speaker. Professor Norwegian School of Sport Sciences') made some widely-shared observations regarding the two managers' approach to the penalty shootout.

His tweets, starting from the second, read: "At around 60 seconds after the final whistle, Klopp already has made his selection and approaches each penalty taker to tell/ask him what shot to take. He does this one-on-one and often cements his ask with his trademark HUG. The asking process is intimate, safe, and loving.

"At 1.30 min, Klopp is done with his rounds, the team is gathered in a huddle, and he gives a short but passionate speech. At 1.45, he finishes and the team breaks up the huddle. At 1.50 min, Tuchel is still revising his notes, and eventually making his way into the huddle.

"Tuchel spent the first 1-2 minutes seemingly revising his selection, and (probably) from the corner of his eye sees that Liverpool has already finished their huddle before Chelsea has even started it. He then moves to the middle of the circle BEFORE he is done with the plan.

"Entering the circle of players before you've completed the selection is what happened to Gareth Southgate in the 2021 Euros final – you're late, not ready, become reactive, and what could have been a smooth final reminder to the team becomes erratic, rushed & stressed.

"In the huddle, Tuchel then asks players about the shots, publicly in front of the whole team. There's plenty of group pressure when done in this way, the chance of honest responses from the players drops, and it creates further stress that carries on to the shootout itself."

This is interesting, as Mason Mount clearly looks uneasy; agreeing to take a penalty, but under duress. You don't need to be a body-language expert to see his lack of conviction when *put on the spot*, as it were.

Indeed, Mount had already drawn attention to himself before the game. "It's definitely time for us to win a final at Wembley," he had said after the semi-final against Crystal Palace. "For me, it is five finals, so we have to put the pressure on us to step up. We remember those defeats, and now it is time to get payback."

It felt like Mount had all that in his head as he took the fateful penalty, which would have been fine had Alisson dived the other way – but was at a good height for a keeper who guessed correctly, and in no way unstoppable. Players are under enough pressure *already*, and the key has to be to do everything to minimise it. The more you say that can come back to haunt you, the more it inevitably *will* come back to haunt you, especially in key moments. (As such, I'd have preferred that Mo Salah had not tweeted and spoken of wanting revenge over Madrid for 2018 – it just handed Carlo Ancelotti's side the power that silently *seeking* retribution would otherwise have offered. It's a bit like AC Milan in 2005, touching the trophy – it's beyond superstitious, and can be seen as a signal by the opposition, about getting ahead of yourselves. Indeed, ex-Red and Madridista Fernando Morientes told Liverpool players in Istanbul before the game: "Please don't touch the cup, because it is not our cup yet.")

Geir Jordet's tweet thread continued: "While Tuchel is still in the process of selecting and asking his players, Klopp has finished all his administrative duties and spends his time spreading warmth, love and good energy; even taking a moment to have a laugh with van Dijk.

"Because Liverpool finished their huddle early, they step into the mid circle first, and get to pick position. They pick the side closest to their bench, which enables staff to give further instructions during the shootout & maintains closeness to the warmth of the manager.

"Jürgen Klopp's Monsters of mentality are not born, they're made. Proactive preparation, composed execution, and warm/loving communication tend to give the best possible foundation for performance under extreme pressure. Liverpool was up 1-0 before the shootout had even begun. 9/9"

Of course, all these details would be irrelevant if Mason Mount guessed correctly about Alisson's dive, and Liverpool's next taker failed. Even so, it feels like the attention to detail helped, even with some natural outcome bias.

My long-time friend Adrian Mervyn was at the final, and messaged me from Wembley. "It was interesting to see Alisson grab the ball after each pen and hand it to our next taker with a word of encouragement. Knowing the attention to detail of our analysts, I'm certain that they had come up with that solution after Kepa's shenanigans in the League Cup."

Whether or not it was the analysts who decided it, it was another human, *psychological* component. Jordan Henderson had begun to do the same when goalkeepers tried to psyche out Mo Salah for spot-kicks during games, by blocking their path to the Egyptian. Indeed, rather than it be mind games, it's almost anti-mind games – a chance to cut out opponents' shithousery.

I'd been offered a chance to join Adie, but was not well enough to take up the offer of a ticket from Matt. I first met Adie – son of two Liverpudlians who moved south many years earlier – in 1994, when I joined a friend's Sunday League side (before I moved to another side in 1996, which led to me playing semi-professionally with the better half of that team also playing together for the same non-league side). I'd spotted Adie wearing a Liverpool shirt, on a training ground in Hayes, west London, that is now opposite a film studios in which *The Imitation Game, Stan & Ollie, Ted Lasso, Peep Show, Black Mirror* and various other films and TV shows have been shot.

I've written before that I grew up in an area near Heathrow Airport that had about a dozen clubs within a 10-15 mile radius, but none closer; and how none ever quite lured me in. Even at school, no two people seemed to support the same team. I was taken to Fulham by friends for my first game while still in primary school, had a father who was a lapsed Brentford fan and an aunt who bought me a Queens Park Rangers kit (while Spurs' Glenn Hoddle had been born in my home-town, which meant I liked them, too), I still gravitated most significantly towards Liverpool at that young age, as a glory-hunting kid – for whom the glory swiftly disappeared when, aged 19, I attended my first game at Anfield in October 1990, a 2-0 victory against Derby (at whose art college I was then studying, and so I managed to get a ticket in the away end by visiting the Baseball Ground).

At the time of my first game, Liverpool were reigning league champions and producing the best-ever start any club had enjoyed in the English top-flight: eight wins on the bounce. Little did I know that, league-wise, that was the best it was going to get for another 30 years. (Still, that made the wait all the sweeter.) The 100% winning start to the season ended the very next game, in a 1-1 draw at

Norwich. The Reds remained top until January 1991, but soon Kenny Dalglish resigned. Liverpool regained top spot on a couple of occasions, but the final time was immediately after my very first away game: a record-breaking 7-1 win away at Derby County, on March 23rd – still in with the Derby fans, albeit they began applauding at 5-1, making it a little easier for me to blend in. A week later, Queens Park Rangers won 3-1 at Anfield, and it was 2nd place all the way, with Graeme Souness returning to the Reds as manager four games later.

Ray Wilkins was in that QPR side, and he was another from my hometown, although his move to Manchester United in 1979, when I was eight, thankfully never tempted me to follow them, nor Chelsea, whom he had been captaining until then. Perhaps, as a kid, with a good touch and a penchant for a pass, I modelled myself on those local lads Hoddle and Wilkins, albeit looking back, I gained only the singing voice of the former and the hairline of the latter.

Finding Liverpool
Chris *Tango* Tang, 47, is a Liverpool fan originally from England (Luton), but now living in Hong Kong, "where my parents are from originally, before emigrating to England in the 1960s".

He is "… married, with two young boys, aged four and two respectively. I've been a Liverpool fan since the age of four (1978), simply because my two older sisters supported them. I remember we had this Division One ladder where we would change the positions of teams after the week's results, that got me into the habit of looking at the weekly results."

Tango's tale is amusing to me, as one of my earliest memories is having a similar (maybe the same?) ladder, pinned on the hallway at the top of the stairs outside my sister's bedroom.

Malaysian Mark Tan Hong Kheng has been supporting LFC since 1978, "when I was a nine-year-old," he tells me. "Those were the days when we used to get *Shoot!* magazine at the local newspaper store in Kuala Lumpur. I was starting to be interested in football then, more playing than watching, and saved up pocket money for some issues of *Shoot!* In the magazine then, they had the folded cardboards which had the league positions and each club had a cardboard tab that could be inserted and placed in a holder for the league position that club was at for that week."

Okay, I'm starting to see a pattern here! It turns out that *Shoot!* may have been handing out the equivalent of cocaine to children to get us hooked on the addictive wall-chart in the late 1970s. Weirdly, when this book led me to recall the wall chart, the thing that stuck in my mind was Clive Walker scoring two against Liverpool for Chelsea, as it meant my older sister temporarily became a Chelsea fan; my total confusion at her abandoning Liverpool seared into my memory. It seems – unbeknownst to me until a quick google – that these League Ladders date much further back, and were prevalent. I had always put the start of my own Liverpool fandom at the sight of Kenny Dalglish leaping the hoardings at Wembley in 1978, when the Reds won their second European Cup. But the Clive Walker game was 7th January 1978, and I recall already being tied to the Reds. The tactile nature of those league ladders, and the physically interactive way that you had to change the league table, felt so much stronger than just glancing (or staring) at a league table. Also a hook to me was my first Panini sticker album in 1979, and loving the Liverpool page. By that stage I was *hardcore*, to my little mind, at least.

Research shows that the team that is successful when we are eight or nine years old is likely to be the one we stick with. I too felt hooked by then.

Mark spoke for me when he said, "I enjoyed putting that wall chart together and it amazed me that each week, Liverpool were constantly on top. That got me keen on the club and their relentless dominance of the league back then captivated me. I guess I was a young glory hunter supporter then. Mind you, Man United was still the bigger and more popular club in Malaysia at that time and I actually knew more Man United players' names than Liverpool players' names. Nevertheless, that was the time I got hooked on LFC and being young and impressionable during those years, the interest did rise and wane with the seasons but my heart always came back to LFC. It was a solitary decision made by a young boy and I didn't know anyone else then of my age group that supported LFC. I can't say I had any family or friends influence me at all in that decision.

"I mostly watch the games physically alone at home as the games are broadcast at a late night hour in Malaysia (eight hours ahead of the UK). But I'm never 'alone' as there are three mainstay chat groups that keep me company before, during and after the game:

"My friend in Kuala Lumpur and three others in Singapore are the first chat group – this is the group of us who went to the 2005 final in Istanbul and will forever have that experience bind us together as the highlight of our time in supporting Liverpool. It was the best night of our lives!

"The 2nd chat group is a group of LFC supporters all over the world, most of whom I have not met. Other than our support for LFC, the other commonality we have is that we all graduated from the

University of Chicago Booth School of Business. Even though I've not met them I'm quite certain some of them are also TTT subscribers. I can tell from their intelligent comments.

"The 3rd group chat is made up of the core four founders of our social league team, Desa Hartamas FC ('DHFC'). The four of us started our social league team back in 2000 and now carry on playing in social leagues well into our 50s and are united by our ardent support for the Reds.

Meanwhile, Andrew Chow, in Singapore, fell in love with the Reds after the FA Cup final from the year of my birth. "Supported Liverpool since 1971. Loved the way 'we' played despite Arsenal winning the double. Also Shanks' ethos really appealed to me."

Some were born into it, quite literally. For those of us who grew up outside Liverpool, it was never preordained; albeit plenty of Merseyside kids ended up supporting Everton instead of Liverpool, or vice versa, to go against their parents or siblings.

Jill Adamiecki, one of the long-standing subscribers to TTT, moved *into* being a Liverpool fan. "I went to Liverpool University in 1972 nominally a Man Utd fan, principally because I fancied the football shorts off Georgie Best! Within weeks I had fallen in love with the city and the Football Club – the Red version obviously and I have followed them to a greater or lesser extent, through thick and thin, of which there has been plenty of both, ever since. So this is the 50th Anniversary both of my fandom and of making excellent friends I hope to meet up with later this year."

A great memory for Jill was an FA Cup final almost 50 years earlier. "Watching the 1974 FA Cup Final on a black-and-white TV in my student flat with two neutrals, a Liverpool-hating Forest fan and a Newcastle supporter. The reception was so dodgy one person had to keep their foot on a certain floorboard and another had to hold the aerial up in the air and the change of personnel was carefully timed for when the ball was out of play. On the final whistle we ran into the street and all the trestle tables came out with food and drink, and 'Liverpool for the cup' cakes, and the party went on until the next morning. The next day – I presume – we followed the bus along the Boulevards to the reception in St George's Square and *honestly* Kevin Keegan leaned from the bus and blew me a kiss. Yeah right said my daughter, until 32 years later I got a text 'Stevie waved to me from the bus!'"

Still a couple of years shy of 70, Jill is not in the oldest cohort on the site. In a comment on *The Tomkins Times* in late 2021, on a trip down memory lane about football and music, Jack Kirwan noted, "I'm 78, so much further down the line by far than even you. I grew up with Buddy Holly, Jerry Lee Lewis, Eddie Cochran, Chuck Berry and the like. My memories of great Liverpool FC teams go back to Bill Shankly's early/mid-1960s wonderful lads, who won the Second Division, First Division twice, and FA Cup for the first time ever, all in five years. And they were treacherously robbed of a European Cup Final as well as reaching the final of the Cup-Winners' Cup.

"I was late in developing an interest in football, as my father and uncles had no time for it. From the age of 13 I was obsessed with aircraft. (I still am, in case you wondered.) Then I saw Everton vs. Liverpool in the semi-final of the Liverpool Senior Cup at Goodison Park, and was instantly smitten.

"I first went to Anfield to see them play Manchester City – who still had the legendary Bert Trautmann in goal – a bit later, and still remember the sense of awe as I reached the top of the outside concrete steps to be confronted with a swaying, seething mass of extremely vocal supporters on the Kop for the first time.

"After that, I never missed a match.

"On Good Friday 1964 I watched at Anfield with my brother as Liverpool opened their Easter programme by beating a very good Spurs team (basically still the one that had won the double in 1961) 3-1. Then that evening we went to the Orrell Park Ballroom to see the amazing pumping, pointillist piano-playing of Jerry Lee Lewis.

"Next day a group of us motored in a hire car to Filbert Street to see Roger Hunt and Alf Arrowsmith finally break our Leicester City hoodoo in a 2-0 win. Arrowsmith was unbelievable that season, scoring 15 goals in 20 games and showing striking power that defied explanation. Whereas Roger Hunt used a scattergun shooting-on-sight technique that often resulted in goals, but also sometimes in facial injuries to spectators behind the goal when he got it wrong, Arrowsmith's shooting was hard-struck, but deadly accurate. He was to shooting what Xabi Alonso was to passing.

"Then, in the first few minutes of a Charity Shield 'friendly' vs. West Ham, he was crocked. He had bad cartilage damage, which never properly healed (he had water on the knee, for instance) and his career was over at just 21. It still pains me to think about that loss of such a fine player, so young. (Like Sir Roger and several others of that side, he's no longer with us.)

"He was actually replaced by a substitute (Phil Chisnall, newly arrived from Manchester United in the last ever such transfer), the first time this had ever happened. Subs didn't get introduced into competitive fixtures for another two years, which is why Gerry Byrne had to play for almost two hours with a broken collarbone in the FA Cup Final the next year."

On May 3rd 2021, Allen Baynes had started some of the older subscribers thinking. "I have just realised that today marks the 60th anniversary of my first Liverpool FC game. It was a warm May evening as I walked from home less than a quarter of a mile from Goodison. Yes, it was a derby game, the final of the Liverpool Senior Cup. We were in Division 2 and this was the only way to play the Division 1 Blues. Ian St John made his debut and scored a hat-trick, sadly the other lot got four.

"It started a great football journey which has been the backdrop to my life. I couldn't have realised then that it would lead to League titles, League Cups, FA Cups, European trophies galore and a World Club Cup. I have been there to se them all raised aloft by captains from Big Rowdy Yeats to Hendo. Fantastic memories, and massive elation."

JDay's first game was, "21st November 1959, the month before Bill Shankly arrived, my dad and his mate, who was a Red, took me to Anfield to watch us beat Leyton Orient 4-3. We were at the front of the paddock and remember distinctly the absolute wonderment at seeing those red shirts so close. It was love at first sight.

"Funny thing is, my dad was an Evertonian and took me to Goodison the week before. I have absolutely no recollection of that game."

The earliest attendance on the site belonged to *Snatch*, in a short comment referenced earlier in this book, but worth repeating: "My older brother took me to Anfield in April 1950 as a birthday present. I hated the experience, it was frightening. My mother was not impressed when she found out. Fortunately I was not permanently damaged, although it was not until I was at secondary school that I went as a regular. I was seven years old."

Then there's American and site legend Jeff – a font of American and European sporting knowledge – who wasn't born *into* Liverpool FC, but found it via his advanced studies in England.

"The first game I went to in England in the fall of 1965 was to Anfield. If you want to talk about a shock, I got one that day. The place was full and people were cheering and applauding and trying to support Liverpool from the time the lads came on the pitch until the final whistle. In addition, when Liverpool did something of note they ground erupted and I want to note when Aston Villa did something of note the crowd also applauded. I had never seen anything like this in my life, and I had been to World Series games in New York City. I also want to note it made more sense to go from Cambridge to London to watch a match than it did to try to get to Liverpool regularly, and I went to matches, I am certain, at West Ham and Tottenham and Arsenal, and in the '70s to QPR, and the experience was nothing like Anfield. My experiences at Anfield from 1965 until the last match I attended over the Christmas period in 1994 was nothing like I experienced anywhere in England and for that matter on the continent as I lived in Turin and Barcelona."

Prior to launching TTT, Jeff had been emailing me for a couple of years to point out how awful the Reds' then-owners were. But he also constantly spoke highly of what John W Henry and co. had done with Boston. From the start, he made it clear that to compare the two ownerships via nationality was crazy. (Which reminds me of the Liverpool fan who, in 2007, emailed me in a state of anger that Liverpool were going to sign *another* Fernando. Torres, he said, would surely follow his namesake, Morientes, as someone who would never shine in red.)

Another American, Erin McCloskey, was on TTT from the start, and someone I met in person, along with her Liverpudlian husband, at a London-based website get-together to watch Liverpool play Newcastle circa 2011. (I have to 'circa' a lot of things these days, including my age, the current year, and what day of the week I think it is.)

Her first sight of Liverpool playing was against Roman Abramovich's Blues, relatively early in his ownership. (Again, Chelsea keep popping up, beyond the references to the cup final.)

Born in Corvallis, Oregon, Erin has lived in NYC for the past 20 years. She "grew up playing soccer as a kid and always loved the game, but we didn't have a lot of exposure to professional/foreign leagues in small town America in the '70s/'80s/'90s, so I didn't have a team I followed. In 2004 I met a Scouser at a party in NYC and we started dating. From the very beginning we were spending all of our weekend mornings at the pub watching Liverpool (and every other match that was on TV). I fell in love instantly with LFC, the city of Liverpool, and that Scouser who is now my husband."

In 2022 she told me that, "My first ever live LFC match was actually away at Stamford Bridge in 2006. We lost and were repeatedly threatened with bodily harm as we left the ground, but it was still absolutely magical. A few days later we hopped the train up to Liverpool to see my husband's parents and I went to Anfield for the first time, playing Newcastle. I was in awe. I got so choked up during *You'll Never Walk Alone* that I could barely sing along for fear of bursting into tears. It wasn't just a song. It meant something. It was important. And I was so fortunate to be a part of it.

"When I first became a supporter, the matches weren't readily available on television or online, so going to the pub was the best way to see everything. We developed a little community of other supporters who went to the same pub, one of whom became one of our closest friends (Hi, Dave!) We went to the NYC LFC supporters' pubs a few times and that was a lot of fun, but we decided we kind of preferred our smaller pub with our smaller group that wasn't quite as manic. Once we started having babies, heading to the pub at 7am on Saturday was no longer possible (or desirable!) and fortunately by that point all of the matches were easily watchable on television in the US, so it has become more of a family thing (along with way too much Twitter!) That said, the husband and I made a point of watching the 2018 and 2019 Champions League finals at the terrific Carragher's pub in NYC. At those times you just really want to be in the midst of the crowd!

"I have also been part of several online LFC communities, starting with RAWK in the '00s. Once one Mr. Paul Tomkins set up his own community, I moved over there. I also joined Twitter in 2009 specifically for LFC content and engagement. I can be a lot more obnoxious and brainless on Twitter.

"While the vast majority of matches are on TV in NYC, I'm fortunate as a supporter in the US to have been able to attend quite a few matches in person over the years. Because I married into a Liverpudlian family, we visit fairly regularly. It does involve a lot of travel, but it is always combined with family. The biggest challenge is getting my hands on tickets when we're there!"

How have her feelings towards football changed? "I don't think it's more or less, but I definitely enjoy football differently as I've gotten older and had a family. Now that I've had two kids along with a hectic career, I don't have the time or ability to focus so much on football on a daily basis. I used to be on RAWK or TTT every single day (sometimes while at work – shock/horror!), having lengthy discussions and debates about the club, the players, the league, etc. I still watch every match, I still read all the news, but I'm less drawn into all the controversies and arguments. I think that allows me to just enjoy it a bit more. Of course that also coincides somewhat with a more stable and successful period for the club (kids born late 2011 and 2014), so who's to say if it's the chicken or the egg."

I wondered, as I had with the other Liverpool fans I interviewed, how Covid affected their celebrations in 2020?

"I still feel sad for the players and the locals that their celebration of that monumental achievement was so dampened by Covid. They all deserved so much more. The entire city deserved *so much more*. For me, Liverpool FC was the one real bright spot in that misty haze of 2020. Experiencing [albeit not herself catching] Covid in the US epicentre was frankly terrifying. A couple of blocks from my house there was a Covid tent hospital in Central Park. The place where I played football with my kids a month prior was now a fenced-off death farm. Parked next to it on Fifth Avenue was a refrigerator truck for the dead bodies. It was absolutely surreal. Football was something 'normal' to think about it. Even though the season was so hugely affected, we had that massive points gap to gloat over during the shutdown, and once the season restarted it was like a little bit of joy coming back. I worried about the players and their health, but I was also ecstatic to have a return of that huge source of happiness each week while still being mostly shut in our home. Like a little glimmer of light in that dark tunnel."

Erin and her husband also played a small role in helping to oust Liverpool's previous owners, the 'cowboys' Hicks and Gillett, who had acquired the club via a leveraged buyout in 2007, which placed the debt of the purchase back onto Liverpool FC (which the Glazers did with Manchester United – to ongoing *huge* debts – and Burnley's new owners recently did, and it still makes no sense how such a financial manoeuvre is allowed). Before long, Liverpool were in serious financial trouble. "In 2010, when we were in the throes of the Hicks and Gillett nightmare, we all knew that they were going to every bank looking for money because they had leveraged the club beyond its capacity. My husband and I both work in banking in midtown Manhattan and one Tuesday afternoon while sitting in my office I got a call from my husband. He said, 'I'm getting coffee right now and I'm looking at Tom Hicks and his son sitting on a bench outside.' He quickly snapped a grainy Blackberry photo of them and texted it to me. They were right off Park Avenue, next to Deutsche Bank and JP Morgan's main offices. I immediately tweeted the photo, giving the context, and boy did people do their thing. JPM and Deutsche leadership was flooded with emails and messages from around the world, telling them not to give money to the charlatans who owned LFC. I like to hope it actually had some effect. It was literally on the front page of the *Wall Street Journal* the next day! It felt like we were actually helping the club from afar, in some small way."

Before long, Hicks and Gillett were gone, and whether or not people still like or trust FSG, the club is a paragon of self-sustainability, and on-pitch success.

Mike Hajialexandrou, 57, lives in London, the son of two Greek Cypriots. "I was in Istanbul, at Barcelona 4-0, both incredible. I was also at Hillsborough. There was nothing great about that day, but the work we put in to save lives made me proud to be a Red.

"In the 1980s, we might get a lot of abuse from Scousers in the crowd. For not being Scousers, taking their tickets (you could rock up at the turnstile easily then!) and being fair-weather. No one makes those comments anymore. 57-year-old guys turning up with their kids in the last 20 years have not been fair-weather. If you want to be a global club, and Liverpool are one of only two in the UK, then you have a global fanbase. We belong to the Liverpool family. It can mean more in desolate parts of the world because it's not so accessible. *You'll Never Walk Alone* is about everyone, not a select worthier few."

He obviously also feels some kinship for the ultimate hero of the Reds' 2022 FA Cup final.

"Tsimikas is Greek, as is Sotirios Kyrgiakos. We are proud of them because they are both warriors and play for the team. Tsimikas has stimulated Liverpool interest in Greece, just as Klopp has in Germany."

Back to Wembley
I first met Matt Clare, from Cheshire and who did his degree in Liverpool, but now living in London, at what was then my new Sunday League team, in 1997. I'd just given up playing semi-pro after just a year due to then-undiagnosed health problems (I was finally diagnosed with Myalgic Encephalomyelitis in 1999), and so, with Adie, the three of us went to virtually all home games together from London, getting our season tickets grouped in the Lower Centenary Stand, as it then was.

We also attended quite a few of the London and Midlands away games, as well as the occasional one further afield, such as to the brand-new, space-age Reebok (but it's a lot to ask when it's already a 400-mile round trip for home games at least 19 times a season, and you're also going to Anfield for cup games and European fixtures.) We also did Roma away in 2001 – a quite wondrous couple of days in very sunny February (as well as being constantly pelted by Roma fans during the game) – and Barcelona in 2007 (the 2-1 win, Messi, Ronaldinho, Xavi and co. defeated by John Arne Riise and Craig Bellamy's golfing skills); with Istanbul and Athens too, although the other two guys managed various other trips as well, including to Kiev, Madrid and Paris, and many beforehand.

Matt was the friend who paid for the ticket and flight for Istanbul at a time when I was too ill to work a proper job, and yet to make a penny as a football writer (indeed, I was travelling in the hope of a great final chapter to my first Liverpool book, and that duly arrived). His son Henry, now 17 and for a decade or so until recently, alternately on the books of two different clubs (one Premier League), now joins his dad at the game whenever possible – including a fairly horrific time in Paris.

For the 2022 FA Cup final, however, Adie – with Matt also unable to attend – was on his own. At least, in terms of people he knew.

"When Kostas scored the winning penalty I ended up in a huddle of four complete strangers jumping up and down and shouting," he told me, afterwards, when sending me a review of his experience. This, alone, is par for the course – a goal celebration is a chance to grab anyone in the vicinity. However, "on reflection, this probably wasn't a good idea as a few days after the semi-final [following similar scenes] I contracted Covid for the first time! Then, when the huddle disbanded one of the guys grabbed my head and planted a kiss on it! The things we do in the heat of winning the FA Cup.

Though going to league games and even European finals since the 1970s, "I worked out that this was the fifth FA Cup final I've been to. The first was in 1986 when Merseyside came together. It truly was the friendly final and I remember seeing loads of Reds and Blues heading to Wembley together. Unusually for me I had a seat for that match from my Dad's season ticket. He was unable to go as he was out of the country. It was quite close to the Royal Box and I had a brilliant view of all the goals."

(Of course, no view could have been better that day than the camera in the net, just behind the line, hit by Ian Rush's game-killing goal. "Is this three? It is!")

Decades later, in the stands of a rebuilt Wembley, plumes of red pyro drifted over 30,000 Liverpool fans. "ABSOLUTE SCENES!!!!!" tweeted Dua Lipa, Arsenal fan but adoptive Kopite, as her song *One Kiss* once again reverberated around a celebrating travelling Kop.

Later, in the changing room, third-choice goalkeeper Adrián wheeled around a joyous but stricken Egyptian Moamen Zakaria, who sat with the FA Cup in his lap. Zakaria, as an ex international colleague, was there as Mo Salah's guest; diagnosed in 2020 with with ALS (amyotrophic lateral sclerosis), he beamed with joy as the entire Liverpool squad danced around him.

Football has its problems, but sometimes it's a great way to bring people together.

A Decade Ago

With the previous day's successful final in mind, TTT subscriber *Egremontcosmo* shared on the site some memories of an earlier FA Cup final, which showcased the journey the club had been on since 2010. (I was not at the 2012 FA Cup final, but did attend the successful League Cup final earlier that year.)

"With regard to some of the comments about the blue plastic flag wavers. I was at Wembley for the 2012 final. The only tickets I could get for me and my mate (an old-school '70s/'80s Villa fanatic but with distinct Liverpool sympathies whenever we weren't playing each other) were in the Chelsea 'end'.

"We got to Wembley just before midday and strolled around what passes for a selection of pubs in that locality. Already rammed, wall to wall, with happy, singing Scousers. I remember a bloke selling dodgy badges, etc. running the gauntlet, foolishly thinking he was going to take the Mick out of the biggest Mickey-takers on earth. Everywhere was joy and hilarity and my mate's face was a picture – he kept saying how it took him back, and how this was a proper football club (and despite all the games he'd been to in his life, he'd never been to an FA Cup final).

"When the time came, we went into the stadium and took our seats. The contrast, even as the ground filled up, was barely believable. It was like being in fucking *IKEA*. Both of us kept gazing longingly across at that old familiar sea of red, wishing we could be there. All the noise and energy was from that side. The Chelsea end? I've sat in doctors' waiting rooms with more atmosphere – and they were winning!

"My old mate is no longer with us – he passed away just before Christmas last year – and it's at times like this I think of him the most. He'd have absolutely loved what happened yesterday. Like he said: a proper football club!"

Had Liverpool won that final then Kenny Dalglish's sole full season during his second tenure would have looked very different, even if it might not have saved his job. It was also a season of narrow misses, with record-breaking hits of the woodwork, but league decline in amongst all the tiring cup games. Those two cup runs included games against Chelsea, Manchester City (two legs), gritty Stoke City, Manchester United, Everton and Chelsea again. Andy Carroll came close to taking the 2012 FA Cup final to extra-time.

I felt Dalglish unlucky to lose his job, albeit John Henry had phoned me out of the blue in March to discuss Damien Comolli's role, and ask my view on the various names FSG had been recommended as a potential replacement. (I later got blamed on Twitter by some morons

186

for Dalglish losing his job, but as one of those who pushed to get him the job in the first place – or rather, to at least be spoken to – his position was obviously not raised to me, and I wouldn't have felt comfortable passing comment; which is one reason why I never wanted to be officially connected to the club, beyond remotely writing a weekly column for its website from 2005 to 2010.)

All I remember from the call was that Johan Cruyff and Louis van Gaal were seen by the Americans as likely to be too difficult to work with, and I had nothing to add on the pair, beyond it sounding like what you'd generally hear in the media about the Dutchmen. (That said, I do remember 'advising' Henry to stick with Jordan Henderson, whom I felt could not be judged when playing right-midfield to balance the team, as a young newly-arrived player, who I felt had a lot more to offer than was obvious to the naked eye. Comolli always said he was sacked because of signing Henderson, but the impression I got was more the overall failure to communicate. Of course, what Henderson *did* wasn't always clear even to long-term watchers of the game, and still wasn't to some outsiders, years later.)

My sporadic advice was always offered just as a fan of the club. I made it clear from the moment John Henry approached me (initially via Facebook, which I ignored thinking it was a hoaxer) that I had no interest in club politics (especially after inadvertently getting caught between the 'warring' Rafa Benítez and Jamie Carragher in early 2010), nor any kind of paid role. Henry's original idea was that I could sit next to him to help explain the game to a neophyte, but I wouldn't have wanted that attention. The only 'rewards' were a ticket in the director's box – against Chelsea (who pop up yet again), when Fernando Torres scored two in late 2010 (which I was too unwell to attend and gave to Adie) – and something sent to my dying father from Aston Villa owner Randy Lerner in 2011, organised by Henry (my grandfather briefly played for Villa after WWI, albeit it's another team I could have supported but never felt drawn to). Plus there was the lunch Henry paid for in Liverpool soon after buying the club; given that his research about a club he'd never heard of led him to my books on Amazon, and duly wanted to meet, I did take the steak meal.

In 2012, I offered no real opinion on Comolli, as I wasn't the one working with him, but it was clear from what I was told that the Frenchman wasn't doing his job in keeping the owners in the loop as to general football thinking. (I don't think Comolli did a bad job overall, and the later development of Henderson turned a 'flop' into another success.) While not discussing Dalglish, Henry admitted that he'd recently been over in Liverpool for a week and seen the Reds prepare brilliantly to play Brendan Rodgers' Swansea, only for Swansea to control and win the game. He found it baffling. Maybe that's when Rodgers first entered his thinking, prior to meeting him that summer.

It does make me wonder if, in this day and age, the ability for a manager or director of football to make a flashy presentation or to gift-of-the-gab it to an owner is as important as actual job skills. Of course, these managers do constantly have to sell themselves and their ideas to the media (as well as fans), to buy themselves the time to build success. Increasingly, management is about adjusting perceptions and controlling the mood; managing expectations, without killing them.

Writing about cricket, Michael Atherton has noted how those who do the best Powerpoint presentations often get the top jobs, and it's a sense I get with football too. For all my years writing about the game (over two decades and more than a dozen books), and having been a county-level player in my youth, a semi-pro for a season, and all the time as a season ticket holder at Anfield, I'm not sure – despite the ability to *pontificate* – that I could tell anyone which manager or director of football to choose (as I made clear in 2010 and 2012 to Henry). I'm just not tapped in to that entire well of information.

I could tell with increasing certainty that Hodgson was a terrible fit, and that Dalglish would surely lift the unbearable negativity around the club as a caretaker, if offered the role (which his family had told me he was open to; or, to at least be spoken to whilst ostracised at the Academy). But beyond that, I don't have access to the working methods of the professionals all across Europe, and have no idea of the minutia involved at the elite level of coaching and management. (Sometimes I worry that I know just enough to be dangerous, as the saying goes. Thankfully no one acted on my hard-hitting suggestions that Liverpool immediately replace Virgil van Dijk with Phil Jones, and retrain Alberto Moreno as a goalkeeper instead of buying Alisson, using the £66m saved to invest in Salomon Rondon, Paul Dummett and Ali Dia.)

Ultimately, it's often the way individuals sell themselves to clubs and owners that gets them the job; especially if the owners and directors are new to football.

With that in mind, it's interesting to ponder if Jürgen Klopp had to make a Powerpoint presentation to get the Liverpool job. Somehow I doubt it.

Indeed, at that point, Liverpool needed to sell the 'project' to *him*; which they did by analysing how unlucky his Dortmund side were in his final season, courtesy of Ian Graham's computer modelling, and facilitated by Michael Edwards (both of whom joined via Spurs, and

Comolli). They proved Liverpool to be a serious club, unlike the 'Disneyland' Ed Woodward had promised Klopp in 2014 when trying to lure him to Manchester United.

In the summer of 2015, I wrote that the top two names in the frame, Klopp and Ancelotti, were suited in different ways, albeit despite what happened in 2022, it's clear that the Italian would never have matched the German at Liverpool. Indeed, I wrote that summer that Rodgers should be retained *unless* he could be replaced by Klopp, if such a coup were possible – but it just felt unattainable to me.

Unexpectedly, I was invited to meet some other members of FSG in Liverpool in October 2015 (Henry was there and said a brief hello, for the first time since 2012), to discuss their excitement about having just procured Klopp. I'm still not entirely sure what the purpose of the meeting at the Titanic hotel was, as I opened with my usual gambit of noting that I don't want to get involved in club politics; and I'm not really a journalist, who looks to make contacts. (Contacts are a double-edged sword, as you can find yourself being more generous to them, as you'd expect, whilst at the same time you can gain more information to be better informed about them. I can't say that I got to 'know' John Henry, for example, but unlike some of the FSG Out brigade on social media, I certainly had spent time in his company and taken his calls and emails and odd times. I got the sense of someone who really wanted to learn how to 'win' at football, but I can't talk of the purity of his motives, as I cannot read minds nor see into people's souls. To me, wanting to make Liverpool's *winners* is what mattered most.)

What was clear from that meeting, however, was that, in those initial weeks, they all felt Klopp was even better than they'd expected, and were bubbling over with excitement. (It was also put to me that they were serious about winning the biggest trophies, and it not being about making a profit; the former subsequently delivered, in spades, and the latter an ongoing issue that will linger until if/when they sell.)

Also around that time, Michael Edwards, as an apparent regular reader of my work, emailed me, unsolicited, and at that moment, and again in brief discussions over the following years, he too would sing Klopp's praises to the hilt – albeit everyone seemed frazzled and burnt-out post-Covid.

(While it had been *mooted* for a while, I was, however, still shocked when Edwards emailed me well in advance of his stepping down to explain what was happening, and to express, with sincerity, how perfect he felt his replacement, Julian Ward, would be for the role. In early 2020 I'd also been offered a very brief glimpse at Liverpool's scouting software, which threw up the name Diogo Jota; but I didn't think any more of it at the time, as it seemed a bit left-field – until he signed several months later.)

Again, I can't say that I 'know' Edwards, but he seems like a genuinely likeable guy to me, as did everyone else I've met or spoken to connected to Liverpool. Maybe that's part of some grand hoodwinking process, but Benítez, Henry, Edwards and others all made swift private gestures in times of difficulty for me that suggested real decency.

One of my proudest moments was receiving a photo of *Mentality Monsters* from Edwards, the book sitting on his desk at Melwood. I don't think it sycophantic to point out that he eventually led the world in his job. The same can be said of Klopp (whom I've never met, despite my attempts – or perhaps *because* of them – to hang around the L4 area in lederhosen). I only met Rafa Benítez after *he* suggested it, five years after he joined the club, so I didn't need any extra reasons to believe in his qualities as a manager in 2009. In 2010 I'd already heard about the great things FSG (or NESV as was) did at Boston via Jeff and others to take them seriously as potentially successful owners – and while all of these people made mistakes, they all proved world-leaders at Liverpool.

By contrast, all I got from Christian Purslow and co., however, was to be put on a blacklist of 'enemies of the club' in 2010, for opposing the hapless George Gillett and Tom Hicks when it became clear to me (somewhat belatedly) that they were a pair of utter buffoons.

(When it came to that regime, I'll paraphrase Billy Bragg: "if you've got a blacklist, I want to be on it", from 1988's *Waiting for the Great Leap Forwards*. We duly got our great leap forwards.)

I'd also been approached by Brendan Rodgers' assistant to meet with them at Melwood late in the 2014/15, but I gave that one a miss, as I wanted to try and remain objective, especially after the swiftly ensuing 3-1 home defeat to Crystal Palace and the 6-1 pasting away at Stoke, which came before any plans could be made; before the early 3-0 home defeat to West Ham in the following season, which, along with the confused transfer situation, tipped me from 'let's see' into the 'we need a new manager' camp. He remains the most difficult Liverpool manger to assess, I've found, given the chaotic highs and lows of a shortish tenure, and the sense – at that time – of a polished performer rather than someone genuine and relaxed in his own skin; with the addition of the backroom wars over transfers.

I do have to add that I think Rodgers, now aged 49, is a far better manager now than he was then, with the Liverpool job perhaps coming too soon for him (and it seems the intention was to pair him with an experienced director of football). It's both a testament to his improvement and a fairly damning indictment of his *overall* record at Liverpool that, having managed lower-budget Leicester for 168 games, his win percentage there (48%) is close to the 50% he achieved in 166 games at Liverpool, with the 2021 FA Cup thrown in with the Foxes – compared with no trophies (or finals) with the Reds; while his 70% win-rate at Celtic in 169 games shows a consistency, at this point, of games managed, if not win rates, as he won *everything* north of the border – but mostly only as expected (albeit achieved with greater domestic domination, mixed with a continued underperformance in Europe, which is a bit like Pep Guardiola at Man City).

Rodgers' Anfield tenure remains a baffling mix of highs and lows, but I'd also like to state, once again, that the run-in failure in 2013/14 – another Chelsea connection to this chapter (as well as the fact that he coached there) – was just one of those things. I don't believe you can ask a team that has essentially only got one way of playing – gung-ho, to great success – to suddenly change the way they play in the final games. Maybe it would have worked, but it seems fanciful to think it could operate at that level.

The team had not yet evolved to be able to switch like that, and in the end, never would (losing the attacking verve when trying to be more defensively resolute in 2014/15). Although it resulted in no trophy, the 2014 run-in was one of the most exciting periods in the club's history, with almost every league game from the start of January to the end of April won. It also presented me with my first chance to sit inside Anfield back in my old season ticket seat *for a game with the title on the line that day*, as the Reds beat Newcastle, but Man City won their game. (An experience I'd repeat in 2019, but miss in 2022. Obviously no one was in that seat when the title was won in 2020.)

Yet even Klopp's predecessor was part of the process, with the near title success in 2013/14, and 2014/15 implosion, all adding to where the club would end up; including the improvement and massive profit delivered by Luis Suárez, which, as I've noted many times, led to the purchase of players who would later help lift the Reds back into the Champions League, albeit under new management (and players like Emre Can, Adam Lallana and Divock Origi, bought with the Suárez money, were appealing to Klopp, as players previously on his radar at Dortmund. None of those may have excelled beyond moments or cult heroism, but their procurement contributed to Klopp thinking he could work with the players at Liverpool.) Even the wrong paths taken led, circuitously, to Klopp. If Comolli was the wrong man in some ways, he was the right man in others, courtesy of those assistants and players he brought to the club.

And so, with Rodgers appointed in 2012 and unwilling to work with a director of football – torpedoing the idea in his first press conference – Liverpool lurched from the transfer committee successes without Rodgers' input (Philippe Coutinho, Daniel Sturridge) to the muddled thinking and transfer chaos of the next few years; but at the same time, avoided a potentially calamitous appointment of an unsuitable director of football in 2012 (such as van Gaal, *had* FSG been keen), who might have taken the club in entirely the wrong direction, as opposed to leaving the role open, which allowed for an internal promotion.

Yet, in the summer of 2015, Klopp aside, *it was all there.*

By 2015, Edwards, backed by people like Graham, was ready to transition into the director of football role, and Klopp had been successfully seduced.

If the warm months of the spring of 2014 felt like a brief summer fling – flirting with exciting football and title races – this has proved *the real thing.*

Quadruple Possibility Rumbled On

It was 14th May, and after winning the FA Cup, the quadruple was still on. The Reds were three points behind City, who were due to play at West Ham the next day, with the Reds' 37th league game (and 61st of the season overall) pushed back to Tuesday, away at Southampton. "The quadruple thing is absolutely outstanding that we can talk about it. It's crazy," Klopp said after the FA Cup final success. "It's out of this world – this was game number 60 in an intense season."

The earliest it could be *mathematically* out of reach was May 17th. Manchester City went to West Ham on the 15th and, despite coming back from 2-0 down at half-time (with great pressure but lucky goals: one deflected, one an OG), missed a late penalty at 2-2; while West Ham fluffed three huge chances on the break, two at 2-1 up and one at 2-2. Had their penalty gone in, City would have been six points ahead, with Liverpool having just two games to play (and City themselves still with one, at home to Aston Villa). The goal difference had swung in recent weeks, to +7 in the Citizens' favour, which would be hard to pull back in the time left. Still, the game at Southampton – ludicrously arranged on a Tuesday when Wednesday would have been fairer – at least gave the Reds the chance to narrow the gap, even if the injuries to key players were mounting and about half the team had to be in the 'red zone' for muscle issues after 120 minutes at Wembley.

According to a BBC article by Chris Bevan at the start of May, the Reds had already taken the *possibility* further than any club in English football history. (It was an excellent article, but with the weird opening gambit of "Whether you love Liverpool or loathe them…", as if that should matter).

Having already won the league title quicker than any team in English football history (it would have been in March 2020 but for Covid delaying the season, and still took fewer games), and racked up the two top points tallies for a European team reaching a Champions League/European Cup final, Klopp now took an all-fronts charge later into the season than any team in English football history. These are stunning achievements.

Chelsea in 2006/07 had previously lasted the longest, until Rafa Buddha Benítez sat Zen-like at Anfield during the penalty shootout in which Bolo Zenden helped despatch his old club – Chelsea, yet again – from the Champions League semi-final. The Blues finished 2nd in the league, and won both domestic cups; their quadruple hopes ending on May 1st 2007. Prior to that, Manchester United on 19th April was the furthest it had been taken, while Man City's 2019 and 2021 vintages saw their quests end on April 17th. In 6th place were Burnley's 1961 side, whose hopes ended on 15th March. Incredibly, Liverpool's previous best efforts lasted only until February, albeit they did otherwise rack up a lot of trophies; an early FA Cup exit often the main problem – never getting past round five in the seasons when there was league, European and League Cup success.

"This is the Reds' 24th attempt at a quadruple in the 47 seasons it has been possible since the League Cup was established in 1960/61 – the joint-most with United, who were denied an attempt in 1999/00 when they did not take part in the FA Cup," the BBC article read.

"While Liverpool won one of the required trophies in seven of those seasons, did a double of some kind in four more and managed one treble of the league title, European Cup and League Cup in 1984, until this campaign they had never even reached March still in with a chance of all four."

Winning the FA Cup meant that, with the minimum of finishing a narrow second in the Premier League and runners-up in the Champions League, the season could not be seen as a failure.

In the *Guardian*, Jonathan Wilson noted: "Just a League Cup? After playing every possible game this season, after keeping the possibility of a quadruple alive longer than any side has before? However great the achievement to have come so close, that would have been an extreme disappointment."

That was the key: not the FA Cup *per se*, but the possibility, however remote (due to Manchester City's points advantage and Real Madrid's European know-how), that the Reds could still land an unprecedented *four* major trophies in the same season.

Days later, a Liverpool team depleted by injuries to the key men in the spine (van Dijk, Fabinho, Salah and others), and with nine changes essential after 120 minutes in searing Wembley heat, went behind at Southampton to another goal that involved Martin Atkinson ignoring a clear foul on a Liverpool player (a trend), and yet a team containing so many 'reserves' without much recent football overturned it, slamming in 25 shots to turn the game around to a 2-1 win. Harvey Elliott, Ibrahima Konaté and a surprisingly sharp Roberto Firmino on his first start in many weeks all shone, while Taki Minamino smashed home the equaliser – his final goal for the club.

Of course, Liverpool didn't necessarily help their league campaign by needing the game to be put back from the weekend to Tuesday *due to* the FA Cup final, but while momentum is wildly misunderstood, you also can't untangle the intangible benefits of a great cup run if, at the same time, you're motoring in the league. (You'd probably expect Minamino to be less likely to have scored in this vital league game if he hadn't bagged so many in the cups.)

It can all feed into each other, allowing the manager to keep players in the zone (but also rotate judiciously), yet also provide extra obstacles. This one was, yet again, hurdled.

It meant that the quadruple challenge would now be taken to the final domestic day, against Wolves at Anfield on the 22nd May, six days before the Champions League final in Paris. With a point advantage and a +6 goal difference, and with City's opponents, Aston Villa, playing Burnley just three days before the final Sunday of the season, it was in the hands of Pep Guardiola and his team, but Liverpool would not go away.

This Liverpool Side Is Among the Best the Game Has Ever Seen

It's not just a red-eyed fan like me who thinks this Liverpool side is one of the best the game has ever seen.

Writing on the *Athletic* in April 2022, Michael Cox noted: "Before this weekend's title showdown between the clubs, Manchester City manager Pep Guardiola named Jürgen Klopp's Liverpool as the toughest side he's faced – which is quite a big statement when you consider that Guardiola has previously been up against the likes of Jose Mourinho's Real Madrid, Klopp's Borussia Dortmund, and Luis Enrique's Barcelona.

"But the more you think about it, the more it makes sense.

"OK, Mourinho's Real were lethal on the counter-attack and boasted peak Cristiano Ronaldo. Klopp's Dortmund played at a famously ferocious tempo that made it difficult for opponents to settle. And Luis Enrique's Barcelona featured a front three of Lionel Messi, Neymar and Luis Suárez – surely the greatest attacking trio we've witnessed in recent years, and among the best of all time.

"In comparison, Liverpool aren't quite so intimidating in one particular area. They're outstanding on the counter-attack through Sadio Mané and Mohamed Salah, but not quite as ruthless as a Ronaldo-inspired Real. Liverpool play with intensity, but not as much as Klopp's former side Dortmund – a deliberate decision from Klopp to create a more sustainable style of play. And although Liverpool's front three is exceptional in terms of individuals, whether it's Diogo Jota, Roberto Firmino or Luis Díaz completing the front three, it's not quite Barcelona's 'MSN'.

"The difference with Liverpool, though, is that they're nearly as good as those three sides in all three respects. They're true all-rounders – and the problem with facing Liverpool is that it's difficult to identify any major problems.

"The aforementioned sides had greater strengths but more obvious weaknesses.

"Mourinho's Real Madrid were overly aggressive in terms of breaking up the passing of Guardiola's Barcelona, getting themselves in trouble with referees, depriving themselves of midfield guile, and tiring because they spent such lengthy periods chasing the ball.

"Klopp's Dortmund were also prone to fatigue late in games because their approach depended so much on energy. They, again, lacked the technical quality in build-up play relative to other great sides of that period.

"Luis Enrique's Barcelona sometimes lacked defensive commitment from the three attackers – compared to Liverpool's attackers, at least – and therefore weren't always particularly compact. Guardiola gambled against that iteration of Barça – unsuccessfully, as it turned out – going three-on-three at the back because he believed his side would be able to overwhelm Barça elsewhere.

"But with Klopp's Liverpool, where's the weakness?"

Later in the piece Cox concludes, "Guardiola and Klopp have again great teams to rival their efforts in other countries. Their only drawback in terms of greatness is that they haven't won even more honours than they have – which is, of course, primarily because they've been great in the same era."

A month or so earlier, Ryan O'Hanlon on *ESPN.com* noted several reasons why he felt Liverpool in the past few seasons under Klopp had been historically elite.

"In terms of points, it's not close: You play to win the games, and sure, fine – whatever. Through 26 games, the 2019-20 iteration of Liverpool had won 25 matches and drawn one for a total of 76 points. That's the most at that stage of a season, by seven points. For context, Manchester City won the league last year with 86 points, and Manchester United finished second with 74. This year's version of Liverpool 'only' have 60 points through 26 matches, the 19th-best total in league history and less than they had in 2018-19 (65), too."

"…When it comes to assessing team quality, you know what's even better than real goals? Expected goals, baby! *Stats Perform* has advanced data for the Premier League going back to the 2009-10 season, and here are the 10 best expected-goal differentials through 26 games, in ascending order:

10	Liverpool	2019/20	+31.25
9	Man City	2020/21	+31.33
8	Chelsea	2009/10	+33.47
7	Man City	2012/13	+33.76
6	Man City	2011/12	+33.88
5	Man City	2018/19	+42.16
4	Man City	2021/22	+43.35
3	Man City	2019/20	+44.02
2	Man City	2017/18	+44.82
1	**Liverpool**	**2021/22**	**+46.60**

"Two things: Manchester City's run is incredibly impressive, and through 26 games, by this very powerful metric, Liverpool appear to be maybe the best Premier League team of all time. At least, they're controlling the creation and suppression of chances better than any side ever has."

"… In addition to one of the best coaches of the 21st century, a world-class one-on-one shot-stopper, an impeccably composed behemoth of a centre-back, an undefeated midfield pairing, and the best full-back duo in the world, Liverpool finally have the one thing they've lacked over the past five years. Not having it prevented them from keeping pace with Man City while competing on multiple fronts in previous seasons, and without it, they weren't immune to a devastating injury crisis that tanked their performance last season. Now, they have the thing that allows you to still be in the mix for four trophies come the beginning of March.

"Perhaps more than any other reason, Liverpool are as good as they are right now because they finally have *depth*."

In mid-October 2021, James Gheerbrant wrote of Liverpool in the *Times*: "Something is happening with this team. And it's not a fluke, a quirk of the finishing gods. Liverpool's 22 Premier League goals this season have come from chances worth a cumulative 20.4 expected goals (xG, a measure of the quality of a chance). So far, they are averaging 2.55 expected goals per game. In their past four seasons – in two of which, let's not forget, they amassed 97 and 99 points – that figure fluctuated between 1.8 and 1.95. This attack has been one of the world's best for the past few years. Right now, it's pouring on chances like it never has before.

"It's true that eight games is a small sample. But we can trace Liverpool's improvement back a little further than that. If we include the last nine games of last season, beginning with the 3-0 win over Arsenal at the start of April, Liverpool have been creating, on average, 2.21 expected goals per game, across a span of 17 matches – almost half a season. (And that's without even including the two Champions League matches that Liverpool have played this season: eight goals against Milan and Porto, from 2.7 and 3.4 xG respectively.)

"To put it in context, that is in the same ballpark as what Manchester City were creating at their absolute peak under Pep Guardiola: they averaged 2.11 xG per game in 2017-18, 2.24 xG the following season."

In late June 2022, the *Times* ran a piece analysing league performance against spending. "Manchester United were the worst-performing club in the Premier League last season based on their return from spending on transfers and wages, according to an analysis by football finance experts.

"Liverpool, who finished second in the Premier League table, came out best…"

Man City ranked 6th.

"The analysis, carried out for the *Times*, is based on figures reported in clubs' most recent annual accounts to measure spending on wages and amortisation, which breaks down transfer fees over several years (for example, a £20 million signing over four years would be recorded as £5 million per year). The sports intelligence agency, Twenty First Group, then used the figures to calculate "expected points" — how many points a club would be expected to secure over a season given their spending.

"Omar Chaudhuri, the chief intelligence officer at Twenty First Group, said: 'As in all football around the world, in the Premier League last season there was a clear positive correlation between investment in wages and transfer fees, and performance on the pitch. Better players cost more money, and so clubs who can and do invest tend to finish higher in the league'."

"United's wages and amortisation costs were £24 million more than Liverpool's, so they should have been expected to win three more points than the Merseyside club.

"'That they won 34 points fewer is both a reflection of Liverpool efficiency and Manchester United's inefficiency,' Chaudhuri added. 'Liverpool won 18 points more than expected given their spending, and Manchester United 19 points fewer.

"'These were the best and worst performances in the league in terms of points won compared to expected, and illustrates the degree of over and underachievement beyond a difference of only four league positions between the clubs.'"

Luke Edwards, the *Telegraph*'s Northern Football Correspondent, wrote at the end of April 2022 that neutrals should have been cheering Liverpool towards the quadruple.

"You can continue to try to hate them if you must. If your tribal loyalties will not allow it, or your view is so soured by past grievances that you cannot look beyond your prejudice, you can dismiss this idea as preposterous, but it is impossible not to like this Liverpool side.

"It is a team you cannot fail to enjoy, such is the brilliance with which they take the game to their opponent, with no fear or mercy offered.

"They are wonderful to watch – a whirlwind in red, combining elite skill and technical magnificence with diligence and hard work; a collective work ethic that embodies everything important to and desired in team sport.

"...They face a formidable foe in Manchester City, but even in that ferociously intense competition between two tremendous sides, the neutral will probably choose red for the simple reason they are not owned by a nation state looking to sportswash its global reputation.

"As for Jürgen Klopp, he is a manager, even if you twist your face at some of his antics, particularly his rudeness and lack of grace in defeat [harsh!], you also know you would simply love him if he was the manager of your team. There is no greater show of respect you can give an opposition's manager.

"His charisma, his passion, his ability to unite a team with its fans and, of course, his coaching ability and man management, no club in the world would pass up the chance to employ him if they could."

"Some will still bristle at that, but like so many others I have tried to dislike this Liverpool team because old habits die hard. It is not possible, not if you are fair and honest about it. If you like sport and appreciate and celebrate greatness, you simply have to admire what Klopp and his players have done. What they continue to do.

"If I can admit that, anyone can. I grew up in an era when it was anyone but Liverpool. A primary school in east London dominated by Liverpool shirts. I supported Everton to be contrary, a brief flirtation it must be said, but battle lines were drawn."

Amen to that.

Football, and the Value of Community, Family and Friendships

What follows in this, the penultimate chapter, are a series of short sections written by subscribers, in response to questions I posed regarding the importance of football (and Liverpool FC) in their lives; and its connection to friends, family and community.

Rather than simply quote passages, I thought it made sense to run them as supplied.

Alex Tate

In May 2011 I felt I was simply tired; full-time job, part time study, married with a young daughter around two-and-a-half years old. After many tests I was diagnosed with cardiomyopathy. My heart was simply not pumping effectively, it was twice the size it should have been and my lungs half full of fluid.

"It's as bad as it gets," said Dr Taylor. "But with medication and even a pacemaker we can get you right."

"Good," I replied, "I've some studies to finish and a little girl I want to see grow up."

Dr Taylor very stoically nodded and winked at me.

Within five weeks, one operation and one session of chemo later, I was back at work. But the treatment had affected my ejection fraction, the percentage of how well the heart pumps. From high risk category of 38% I was soon down to 30%.

Over time this gradually got lower. My pacemaker would wi-fi information daily to my cardiologist who knew what was happening before I did. In August 2017, after various life changes, a transplant was raised and paperwork started.

By October the effects were noticeable, by January I'd reduced my work from four full days to three half days. My daughters went to stay with their mum full time as I couldn't look after them. Even caring for myself was a struggle. Early April 2018 I made the call to the hospital and within hours I was in emergency. Had I left it any later I may not have made it through.

There was six months of multiple operations and more trauma than is expected before I returned home in September 2018. While I had a new heart, I was up for new kidneys too; mine had failed during the transplant and therefore dialysis three times a week was part of my life.

Recovery was slow but then halted when in January 2019 I went into a more local hospital with an infection, and around five other serious ailments. This four-month stay culminated in a diagnosis of lymphoma of the liver. I had three months of chemo, the latter two took me so close to death it was a familiar feeling for me.

A few months later I was in hospital, no surprise, and the nurse wanted to wake me at 4am. I asked, "Sophie, can you come in at 5am instead?" Having explained to her why she smiled and said I should ring the buzzer and she'll come along.

Sophie saw me watching my phone – Barcelona vs. Liverpool – and asked if it was on the internet. Upon replying *Yes,* she set up the computer in my room with her ID and I watched the game on a bigger screen. Such was my involvement in the game she asked what was going on. It transpired she was off to Porto next week and on to Barcelona to see her bother. I urged her to go to the Nou Camp. She didn't make it, but was back in time for the second leg, put the game on the computer again for me where I got to see *corner taken quickly.*

By July 2019 I was given remission and started work on returning to study. A different qualification to the one when my heart went. Is there some correlation?

Thankfully now, with great support from my medical team, yogis, fellow students and the very best friends and family, plus *The Tomkins Times*, I am approaching four years since transplant and am fitter than

I have been in years. Healthier? Well, this is a completely different issue.

I hope to graduate this June, coinciding with heart and cancer anniversaries, and continue the rebuilding of my life. For what is now the third time!

* * *

March 2011. Andy Carroll finally wore a Liverpool jersey in a competitive match, a 3-1 win over Man Utd, which only slowed their title bid rather than derailing it. Any win over Man Utd is welcome, a Kuyt hat-trick and a little rejuvenation under new owners bade well.

The semester break brought an opportunity to study intensively in an aid to complete my MA, and I chose Sports Journalism. While the study took a week on campus the actual writing lasted much longer.

With online news becoming much more prevalent beyond the main media channels, and I was already a member of *The Tomkins Times*, my cohort was tasked with keeping a blog updated several times a week for a couple more months. So I took the issue of Carroll costing £35 million and searched for a club whose whole match day squad was of similar value. This was only an exercise in interest and not to prove anything. Some of the Leicester fans on the forum I joined questioned their squad equating to Carroll's fee, disagreeing vehemently amongst themselves over the *Transfermarkt* assessment of costs.

TTT was about two years old and various members had already provided great articles for the site; *Beez*, or if reporting in *The Liverpool Echo* known as Andrew Beasley, had written one on Andy Carroll and I wished to cite this in my work, as well as one on TTT.

Beez and I had music in common as well as Liverpool FC and I feel this moment drew us closer, both fledgling writers giving each other support. Despite a couple of trips from Australia back to the UK to see my family we've not met.

I have met *Gary the Spud* and his family, though. Just before the end of the 2010/11 season I was diagnosed with cardiomyopathy and spent a large amount of time off work and in hospital, even finishing the semester from my hospital bed. To aid this concerning time Gary sent a dozen DVDs full of music which he felt I'd like. Music here had drawn Gary and I together and this arriving in the post was a real boost.

The music theme continued as our first meeting led to trawling a number of record shops in London, a pastime I had greatly missed since leaving the UK in 2002. Our families went on the London Eye and our eldest daughters, both around three years old, gibbered on as if old mates.

Our friendship extends beyond TTT and over the years we've both dealt with highs and lows, and sometimes communication in a long distance friendship can give you a great uplift regardless of how you feel.

Donny G wrote a piece for my parenting blog and we've exchanged emails since, most recently there's been more due to the hardships Donny has faced.

A mind-bending early morning telephone call with *Leeberolf* span me out for the rest of the day.

My brother put up Andrew Chow and his friends at his hotel, enjoying themselves by raucously taking over the pool in celebration of a cup win for Liverpool, a highlight on his trip over from Singapore. My brother works elsewhere now.

Closer to home, and again through music, *Fady* and I used to get together to watch games at each others houses, and show off our record collections! He and his wife relocated overseas and then once back in Australia settled in Sydney to be closer to Alison's family. But we've caught up when he's in Brisbane.

We did go to the pub once to watch the Merseyside derby. Our venture out was to meet Krish who was over for a holiday. Unfortunately it was a drab 0-0 but through TTT it was another display of the reach our community has.

I'm not the only recipient of support through these world wide friendships. My health conditions have been documented and many people ask how I am, offer support or have given advice. So while the above are friends with stories, there's many others from simple interaction on TTT who I enjoy reading their posts whilst knowing a little bit more about them than a common red allegiance.

Tash and Dowdy

Tash (Taskin) and I grew up literally as next door neighbours. He's about three years younger so, although he was was born after his family moved in next door, I was so young that I can't recall a time when he wasn't there. We lived in a quiet area of Swindon where the neighbours were all pretty close and, despite the age difference, we spent the vast majority of our younger years hanging around together; building dams at the brook that ran alongside our street, going to the park and, of course, playing football.

My brother is five years older than me and had spells 'supporting' Spurs and Leeds – but eventually came to the right decision about the Reds! I guess his early allegiances were fleeting and reflect either their relative success or popularity as clubs or, in Spurs' case, the fact our uncle was offered (but declined) trials with them. But I've supported Liverpool as long as I can remember and my earliest, albeit rather vague, memories are of the '74 cup final. Not sure when Tash got into football first although I do recall him being fascinated by the '78 World Cup and having a t-shirt of the mascot (Gauchito?) which he absolutely loved.

In many ways, Tash was like the younger brother I never had.

Then, Notts Forest had their spell of success and another neighbour became a fan of theirs. Tash won't thank me for saying this but he 'wavered' for a while so it was Liverpool 1 Forest 2 for a relatively short period of time in the local fan stakes but I didn't give up. I mean, he could only have been six or seven after all and eventually common sense prevailed and he became a firm Red.

After that, I reckon 80-90% of our conversations, and there were a lot of those conversations, were about Liverpool FC. We'd dream of going to games when we were older, talked about what posters etc. we wanted to adorn our bedroom walls and any news or trivia we could get hold of. Given we lived miles from Liverpool and had no internet, mobile phones and the like back then, I'm still amazed how much information we managed to glean, most of which came from newspapers, *Shoot*, *Match* or *Football Handbook* magazines and probably various other sources that I've simply forgotten.

Our local youth club organised a trip each season to a First Division match and my 1st LFC trips were away games at Chelsea and Villa in the late '70s but Tash was too young so didn't go to these. I think his first was at Coventry in '85? I've still got the ticket stubs from all of them and I reckon he has too although I've not asked him. It was a great day and there must have been four or five other neighbours, probably all younger than Tash, who'd followed our lead into supporting the Reds, that also went. I still have a photo taken in my back garden, hours before the coach was due to leave, where we are all wearing kits, numerous scarves each (even though it was a warm spring day!), badges and carrying all manner of flags.

I was given a book about the history of the club and read it in a day. I lent it to Tash and he did the same although it was only a paperback, albeit with 'shiny' paper, and the glued spine wasn't the best so when it came back the next day, half of the pages were loose – presumably where he'd opened it out flat to read. Normally that would have driven me up the wall – especially if a sibling had done it – but, as it was Tash, and it was about LFC there was never a problem. Of course, I still have the book on my shelf at home and never look at it without automatically thinking back to those days. It's one of those "if I close my eyes I'm right back there" moments, so vivid are the memories and, more to the point, emotions of that time!

Once I could drive, we ventured to Southampton and The Dell. Our first away game 'on our own' and I have great memories of parking up and walking to the ground. I think that was the day Kevin McDonald broke his ankle attacking the far post – about six yards from us and I can still hear the crack of his bone shattering.

We also went, with the youth club, to Wembley for the '87 League Cup Final when, disappointingly, Liverpool – for the first time – lost a game in which Ian Rush had scored. It was a strange day as it turned out our tickets were in the Arsenal end, which didn't bode well given we were decked in our Liverpool colours. By then, I was 18 and 'deemed' an adult for the trip so had four or five juniors with me that I was effectively responsible for – Tash being one of them.

We weren't the only ones in the wrong end and after several stewards and policemen had simply suggested we go elsewhere, without any practical suggestions of where we might actually go, we walked back onto the concourse, got pelted with beer by some 'cockney yobs', found a steward who advised us to go half way around the ground and wait by a door. After half an hour or so, which felt more like hours, and with kick-off getting close, there must have been 30-or-so of us congregated there. The door opened and we were led down myriad tunnels to god-knows-where. Eventually we saw, literally, a glint of light at the end of a tunnel and we walked out onto the sandy track around the edge of the pitch. It was essentially a maintenance tunnel that led out opposite the famous tunnel end and gave us what was the closest thing we'd ever experience to the buzz the players must feel when they walk out to the noise of the waiting crowd. This was only 15 minutes or so before kickoff so most fans were in place for the game. We were led around the perimeter and let into the LFC end. Sadly we didn't get the result we wanted but I'm sure we'll both always remember walking out of that tunnel into the bright sunshine and cacophony of noise!

Our first game at Anfield was Rush's last game (first time around) against Watford. I think one of Tash's school mates' mum won the tickets in a prize draw or something similar and, thankfully, they asked me to be the 4th for the trip – with the aforementioned mum borrowing a colleague's car for the drive to Liverpool. We left home stupidly early, as you had to in those days, and when we got to the first major junction – the M5 at Gloucester – she got on the wrong carriageway and we headed south towards Bristol, having to turnaround at the next junction and head north instead! We did make it to the ground in time and were there to see Rushie score, what we thought, was his last ever goal for the Reds, racing clear late on to slot home at the Kop end. All very poetic and a fantastic memory for us all – not a bad way to start the list of visits to L4!

My family had moved house in '86 but we kept in touch and, after Tash left school, we played in the same Sunday league side that I'd introduced him to. But, we lost touch in the early '90s after I married and had started a family – life just getting in the way as it does from time to time. Unbeknown to me, Tash moved to Barcelona and it was by pure chance that we got back in touch in mid 2006.

I'd been on a work event in London, involving several beers, and got the train back. I hailed a taxi for the trip home and got talking to the driver who seemed a good bloke. From the name shown on his ID card, I guessed he was of Turkish descent and sure enough he was. When I mentioned I'd grown up next to a lovely family of Turkish Cypriots, and mentioned the three children's names, he replied "I know Şeniz [the middle of the three], she works for a charity I use". The conversation went on and I asked him to pass my business card (it's all I had on me) to her as I'd love to catch up with Tash again. A few weeks later, I was sat in our Bristol office when an overseas call came in, from Tash.

Why am I telling you this? Well, because it's probably the best way I have to explain what sort of friendship we have. Whilst so much time had passed and lots had happened to us both in the intervening years, it was like we'd never lost touch. We simply picked up again where we'd inadvertently left off years beforehand. Obviously he was living overseas so we couldn't meet up easily – that started again in earnest when he'd come over for games and we'd travel up together. At that stage, I had access to two Kop tickets and was on the waiting list for two of my own, which eventually came when the Main Stand was expanded – 18 years after joining the list! Of course, we often talk about other matters including friends, family, childhood memories and current world events but LFC is the glue that binds us together!

When we made the Champions League final in Kiev, we were successful in the ballot for all four tickets. My sons and I were definitely going but my usual travelling companion couldn't make it so I offered the fourth ticket to Tash. The dilemma must've been terrible for him. Apart from the issue of getting flights to Ukraine – we only secured ours a week before the game when we'd all but given up hope of getting there – he had another dilemma. He'd already promised his nephew, who has travelled to games several times now, and a cousin, who was due to be over from the US for the game, that he'd watch with them. It would've been a huge issue for him because family and loyalty to friends is a huge part of what makes Tash who he is.

It's why, when my eldest son and his partner visited Barcelona a few years back, Tash was only too pleased to be on hand to collect and return them to the airport and to help them find their way around the city. I'm sure lots of people might offer to do so but he actually did it.

One thing that perfectly sums Tash up, and in particular his good and caring nature, is that after Hillsborough, he organised a charity football match. Full 11-a-side with a load of his college mates, myself and one or two of my mates. It was intended to be a more significant event than the eight-hour five-a-side game we'd held a few years earlier, for Sport Aid/Relief I think. After all, Hillsborough was just more personal to us and so we decided to play for 12 hours with only short 10-minute comfort breaks every 2 hours on a rolling basis so the game continued throughout.

I was working for Allied Dunbar at the time, and they had a great social club with excellent sports facilities and happily agreed to let us use one of the pitches for the day and the local paper agreed to send someone to cover the story – although for the life of me I can't recall if they ever did!

Not surprisingly, with 22 lads, aged 16-20 years, running around there were some funny moments, such as when someone got caught in the 'swedes', but generally we all kept it relatively serious as it was such a traumatic event. We managed to raise £795. Although it's not a massive sum of money now, it certainly felt significant in those days. All down to Tash and his desire to do something to help people in real need.

Alan in Australia

About 18 months ago my marriage ended suddenly and, thus far at least, acrimoniously. One thing has kept me sane during the past 18 months: my subscription to TTT. Not only does it provide easy access to intelligent, cogent and respectful discussion of all things LFC, but it has also provided a bridge back to human engagement, from which I temporarily withdrew. It's only about three months since I recovered the ability to eat and crap regularly. The previous 15 months I found myself so miserable I couldn't consume much food at all, and when I did I'd usually vomit. (All of this aged 55, eek!)

Happily my resumption of eating, currently two healthy meals per day plus regular bowel movements, has led to a subsequent recovery of my sanity, by and large. I've managed to engage with Family Court processes, and hopefully will soon regain access to my two children, now 11 and nine. (I've even managed to type this with a wry smile rather than sobbing! A major achievement.)

Sadly I suspect my 18-year marriage is over, much to my regret, but hopefully we will recover the ability to co-parent sooner rather than later, notwithstanding the intrinsic adversarial nature of Western Australian family law processes.

These past year or two, I've taken an enormous amount of strength and solace from TTT. Primarily it's your writing which appeals to me, whether it be football analysis, discussion of the insidious impacts of confirmation bias (my own as well as others'), the wonderful Jeff's posts on all and sundry (particularly anything about Dallas, who has become my substitute pet), the sweet reason of Nari Singh, the self-deprecating humour of *Krishaldo* – I could go on for ever. [Alas, Jeff's dog Dallas died aged 13 in June 2022.]

It really is a marvellous culture that you have developed on this site. This is not just the best football blog ever, it's inspiring in so many ways, and has helped me to put my personal woes into perspective.

The site you have created – community is a better description – has been an oasis for me during my own battles with mental health issues.

Alan (born in Wallasey, before emigrating to Australia in 1972).

Beezdog and *AriseSirRafa*
Andrew Beasley

We are often told that people are becoming increasingly isolated thanks to the internet. That we live our lives online rather than in reality, more concerned with likes and retweets and thumbs-up rather than human interaction.

The lockdowns brought about by the pandemic only accentuated that feeling further, yet seven days after the UK first ground to a halt in March 2020 something truly remarkable happened.

But our story begins a little over 11 years earlier. As a fan of Paul Tomkins' writing on the official Liverpool site, I joined his subscription website *The Tomkins Times* in November 2009. It's fair to say it changed my life in more ways than one.

While there had long been online forums in which you could discuss the ups and downs of the mighty Reds, I had never partaken. To put things into context, I hadn't long had an internet connection at home at this point. It was a very different world (for me, if not everyone).

Having spent a few days getting to grips with *TTT*, I was intrigued to see a new thread pop up at the end of my first week as a subscriber. It was regarding stats and the first two posts were from someone going by the handle 'Arisesirrafa'. I approved of the username and the info he provided. Somehow the vital connection was made.

A few months later, *TTT* subscribers in London began meeting up to watch Liverpool matches together. Plucking up the courage to go along — meeting and talking to people I don't know is a personal nightmare — I met *Arisesirrafa*, or Andrew Fanko in the real world, as well as loads of other great people. We started going to matches together, whenever he had a spare ticket, and continued to catch the Reds on TV too. It reached the point where members of the London chapter of *TTT* were going to each other's stag dos and weddings. Genuine friendships borne out of a niche football website.

More was to come though. In 2018, Andrew and his wife Frankie decided to apply to go on one of the hardest quiz shows around, the BBC's *Only Connect*. But they needed a third wheel for their team and knowing I loved the programme they asked me.

If you're a football fan, you often measure your life by matches. The day after I got married, Liverpool won 3-2 at Loftus Road, for instance. And on the day of the Reds' crazy 4-3 victory over Crystal Palace in January 2019, we took part in an audition to appear on *Only Connect*.

I enjoy a good pub quiz. I often guided teams to victory in work quiz nights back in the days when I had a proper job and wasn't a freelance football writer (something else for which I have *TTT* to thank).

But Andrew and Frankie are incredible quizzers — way, way above my level. When we were conducting our audition, with mock questions for the show, they were answering them before I'd barely read them.

Fortunately, I was able to contribute more on the actual programme. Our aim was to win an episode. Do that and we could hold our heads high, and we'd always have the memory of a victory.

Except that we won and won and won again. On the night between our successful quarter-final and semi-final, the Reds brushed aside Porto 2-0 at Anfield in a quarter-final match of their own. I'll leave it to you to decide if the Champions League outweighs *Only Connect*.

Whatever your choice – as if I need ask – it was another major life event marked out by a Liverpool match.

We then won our semi-final the following day, and the final the day after that (with it being broadcast on the eighth day of lockdown). Five wins out of five. Oh *campeoni!*

We later returned to win a 'Champion of Champions' special episode too (which was filmed on the day Alisson Becker scored a remarkable winner at The Hawthorns; I listened to it on the train home and burst out laughing). Using the info from the back of the second *Only Connect* book, only two teams prior to the 007s (for that is our name) had won at least six episodes without losing any. Well, we have now done that too.

I'm a realist. Had I never met Andrew and Frankie they would have gone on the show with somebody else and still stood a very good chance of winning.

But thanks to *TTT* I was part of that journey too, and I now have my name on the *Only Connect* Wikipedia page.

That's not bad going for a fiver a month to join *The Tomkins Times*, is it?

Owen Ravenscroft

I had two tickets to a match I never expected to go to. But who to take? My dad was the first person I thought of. After all, it was he who shaped my entire outlook on the game. However, I settled on my 11-year-old daughter, Alice.

… I suggested we walk around the back of the Main Stand as we have to get to the other end of the ground to take our seats. In doing so, we took in the Hillsborough Memorial. A place where I've been several times, but it never fails to affect me. It was her first time. She didn't really understand, so I explained that when I was roughly her age 97 Liverpool fans went to a football match and never made it home. She asked why, and I said they were tragically crushed to death, but it wasn't their fault. She said 'Oh', and we continued on to entrance S.

We climbed the stairs. She was excited and almost racing up them, and when we reached the concourse I asked whether she wanted a drink and food, or to go and find our seats. She chose the seats, and so we climbed up the U2 entrance and into the cauldron of Anfield. She stood stock still and took it in, then she started the long walk up to the top of the stand. We sat for a while, taking it all in. The pitch looked fantastic. I could tell she was in awe. She grabbed my hand. I said something like "Isn't this magnificent?" and she replied "can we get that food now?"

We headed back down the steep stairs, stopping for a quick picture of Alice with the Kop as her backdrop, back into the bowels of the stadium. What would you like? A sausage roll and a Coke. Lovely. I'll have a Carlsberg and a cheese slice. Possibly the best pre-match warm-up in the world?

We stood and looked over Stanley Park towards Goodison while we ate and Daddy drained his pint. We discussed the rivalry, and the friendship. And then they came. About 200 Everton fans, average age about 20 I'd guess. They looked like they were shouting and were clearly trying to 'give it large'. The police (on horseback) were marshalling them superbly.

... Before we knew it the players were back on their way out. The noise level rose, and Alice was clearly unhappy, complaining about how loud it was. I ignored it, thinking that once the match kicked off she'd be alright. She wasn't, she was clearly agitated, and wanted to escape the furore but she also wanted me to be happy so she persevered. She started clock-watching (ironic, given Everton's tactics).

We got through to half-time and she was mostly fine, although I did allow her to play on her phone for a bit to try to keep her distracted form the noise. We went back down during added time. We hit the stairs just as Jordan Pickford hit the deck with the ball in his hands. I bet he regrets that decision more than we do ours, given Alisson's parody at the end of the match.

Half-time came and went so quickly. We queued for another drink, another Carlsberg for me, a hot chocolate for the little 'un. Probably the best half-time in the world?

And so with a few minutes gone in the second half we went back to our seats. I told Alice that the noise won't stop, so the only way to not be scared is to join in. She starts enjoying the game. Watching. Clapping. Chanting (although when I was singing either "Liverpool, Liverpool, Liverpool" or "Going down, going down going down" it transpires that she was singing "Dorito, Dorito, Dorito").

As the saying goes, all's well that ends well.

Remembered for their Brilliance

"Of course, congratulations should be made to Real Madrid and Ancelotti, because then the trophies speak for themselves and they brought home the Champions League. In 10 years this will count, the showcase and the cup victory. But then I go into detail to analyse: Liverpool had 26 shots, Real Madrid only two. And Vinicius's goal came from a error of Valverde. I repeat, I congratulate Real and Ancelotti, because that's right, but from my point of view, it seems clear to me how lucky they were in the previous matches. I don't know Courtois, who was crazy, how he managed to make certain saves. The thing I really don't understand is why no one pointed out to Ancelotti that they had a bit of luck."

Former Italy striker Antonio Cassano

I'll repeat it yet again:

Teams are not always duly rewarded for their brilliance, but they are *remembered* for their brilliance

Some days you do everything right, and someone or something gets in your way. Luck always plays a part in sport; up to 50%, it is believed, on average. Liverpool did everything to make their own luck, but the other half deserted them.

Jürgen Klopp did not have the ideal preparation for Paris in terms of injuries and the ultra-demanding end to a tough league campaign, with a 120-minute FA Cup final thrown in for good measure, in a season that seemed to go on forever. Then the Champions League final itself was delayed by 36 minutes by the shocking treatment of the club's fans by French police hiding behind black masks and riot gear, teargassing with impunity as if they themselves were a bunch of unruly extremist protestors; only for UEFA (and French officials and police chiefs) to yet again blame the innocent.

What an astoundingly unacceptable pre- and- post-match experience for fans. Thankfully we're not talking about another Hillsborough, but there were *near-Hillsboroughs* in the years before 1989, when fans of other clubs were caught up in crushing bottlenecks that didn't lead to deaths.

It can't have helped Liverpool win the game, either. There was no time for the usual pre-match singing, *as no one was there to sing.* Many who did get in had throats full of pepper-spray, eyes glassed by teargas, and hearts full of fear. The atmosphere was understandably muted. Liverpool's famous travelling Kop was silenced by French bully-boy brutality.

With the post-mortem (not a literal one, thankfully) still taking place, I won't delve into that near-disaster, other than to say much of France was rightfully shamed by the actions of their police force and politicians. It must never happen again, but UEFA – dear old caretakers of the game – only seemed to get agitated and apologetic once it was clear than many sponsors were caught up in the treating of honest fans like rabid cattle.

Undermined

The game, as it belatedly unfolded, could be described as Liverpool attacking versus Real Madrid defending, with one meaningful breakaway deciding the game, as one keeper produced the performance of his life, and the other spent the evening trying to keep himself warm. Once an attacking coach – his Chelsea team were a joy to watch 12 years ago – Carlo Ancelotti's team looked slow, dull and predictable, but managed to defend with skill (and luck), keep possession fairly well in deep areas, and score completely against the run of play.

Post-shot xG is discussed elsewhere in the book, but the difference to standard xG is as follows: xG bases the likelihood of a goal from where the shot is taken (maybe 0.99 if tapping in on an empty goalline; 0.01 from 40 yards). But post-shot xG ranks the difficulty of where the ball goes within the frame: central would be low value, top-corner ('postage stamp') would be incredibly high (closer to 1.0 expected post-shot goals).

According to TTT analyst Andrew Beasley, the giant Thibaut Courtois has, in his career since 2017 (when the metric was first introduced), just three times faced post-shot xG of 3.5 or more in a game: one for Chelsea against Watford (3.5), once against Barcelona, in 2022 (3.8), with the third being his first Champions League final, against Liverpool (3.5). Both other times he conceded *four* goals, right in keeping with the difficulty of the shot placement.

In Paris he conceded zero.

It makes no sense, but an agile 6'7" keeper can obviously reach the places most other keepers can't; certainly if he's having one of those days, which he didn't on the previous two occasions he faced such difficult shots. Courtois likes to stay on his line, sweeping outside his area about 25% as often as Alisson Becker, so he wouldn't suit

Liverpool's high defensive line. Alisson is far superior at one-on-ones, and the best all-round keeper in the world. But Courtois is 6'7" and played a blinder. Like David de Gea, he suits a low-block team, which the best teams no longer use.

A (rare) criticism I have of Mo Salah when the striker is either off form or blindly intent on scoring is that he doesn't go outside his man on his right side enough. He did so when scoring a brilliant goal against Manchester City, which rightly won the Premier League goal of the season for 2021/22. But that day at Anfield he was on top form, and even then it's rare for him to take the outside route. There are times when he's low on confidence or high on desire, and you know he'll try and cut inside, relying on jinks and close control to work a space on his left foot. It can work, but too often it's predictable. But when he goes *right*, it really opens up. The shooting situation is tougher, because he has to use his weaker foot; but it usually buys him the time and space he needs, as defenders don't expect it. A shot with the 'swinger' from a great position is often better than a shot with the stronger foot into a crowd of players.

My maxim has always been that even if you lose the ball, try to go on your unfavoured side at least once each match, to then buy more time by putting doubt in the defender's mind. In some games Salah will cut inside six times in a row and be blocked six times in a row. Only when he's truly on-song will he go outside. In Paris, he did just about everything right, and could have ended the night with four goals.

In the second half, as he turned into the space on his right and hit a shot that was about the same height and power as the one against City, it looked a *certain* goal. It had that unstoppable appearance, fizzing from his foot. When Courtois blocked it, it flew away – and agonisingly wide – at a weird angle; it had hit the keeper's upper forearm, which still made it a great save (as even if it hit his enormous nose – speaking as someone who knows a thing about those – it would have been a great save), but an uncontrolled one: the ball could have gone *anywhere*, off the part of his body he wasn't intending to use (the aim is still always to try and get hands to it, but to take whatever part of the body it strikes if it stays out). Courtois had skill to stop the ball – just to get close to it – but it didn't necessarily merit the luck of *still* sending the ball wide. If it had instead hit him a fraction to the right, it could have gone in off the hard point of his elbow. You can't say that he got lucky, as his job was to make himself big (and he's 6'7" to start with) but you can say that Salah was mightily *unlucky*.

Increasingly in the run-in it seemed like Luis Díaz – perhaps told to up his goals tally – also started to cut inside too predictably, doing the same from the other flank. More so than Salah, he can go outside his man with comfort and perhaps greater speed. That said, cutting inside will see Díaz get plenty of goals.

When he cuts inside, Díaz has a better shooting technique than the Egyptian, in terms of whip and power, so the goals *should* follow.

Above all else, Díaz provided dynamism, assists and created havoc, even if, as the player to play the most games in world football in 2021/22 (close to 70), he ran out of steam in the final. Cutting inside remains vital to the way Liverpool play with inverted wingers, but going outside some of the time has to be considered.

Though he scores a lot, Salah can end up tamely side-footing a high percentage of his chances into the middle of the goal where the keeper is, but the sheer volume of chances he creates by cutting inside means that, if he isn't blocked off, he can get those shots away – but when on form, he sets them wider, and with sufficient power. After AFCON, up until Paris, he either tried too hard or looked mentally frazzled.

Yet by the time of the final, after a much needed break (due to a minor injury) he was raring to go, and Madrid's *outfield* players could not handle him. His first-half near-post flick was denied low down by the big Belgian; his race to the near post in the second half was also blocked on the line by Courtois. A second rasping drive in the second half was also tipped wide, even before the one saved by the forearm. There was one tame first-half header straight at the ex-Chelsea keeper, but it was a snap-chance, made with no time to add any deft direction. In total Salah had six shots on target in the game, the most for any player not to score in the competition's final, and the most he had ever had in a match for Liverpool.

While generally an excellent team player, who always tracks back and makes countless runs off the ball (and sets up chances for others), Salah can have selfish, blinkered periods in games, where he takes too many shots instead of passing; there's a level of 'greed' (or single-mindedness) that's required to be a top striker, but also, times when it can be taken too far. Yet in Paris, every effort was clearly the right decision when it came to going for goal. This was the Egyptian at his absolute best.

Then, to add to the opposition goalkeeper's showreel, there was Sadio Mané's fierce low drive early on, that Courtois tipped onto the post and which, again on another day, may have bounced in off his backside.

That day was not *this* day, as this day was Courtois' day.

Ancelotti said after the game that "…it helped that Liverpool were easier to decipher than the others because they have a very clear identity and we could prepare the way that we did. We knew what strategy to take – don't give them space behind the defence to run into. Perhaps our football wasn't extraordinarily beautiful on an aesthetic level, but playing out from the back to incentivise their pressing wasn't a great idea."

While true, to a degree, it was still a game where his keeper made huge saves, including from runs/dribbles in behind.

Ian Ladyman wrote in the *Daily Mail*: "… there have been some strange observations since Real somehow found a way to beat Liverpool in the Stade de France. Some have said Klopp was 'out-coached' by Ancelotti. Others have made much of Liverpool's failure to score in each of the three finals they have played in this season. They beat Chelsea on penalties in the Carabao Cup and FA Cup finals, of course.

"But here is the truth of what happened in Paris: Real found a way to blunt one of Europe's most ferocious attacking teams but only to a degree. The best player on the field was Real goalkeeper Thibaut Courtois and that – as Klopp pointed out himself – says much about the game."

Klopp knew this only too well. "They scored a goal, we didn't. That's the easiest explanation in the world of football. Harsh, but we respect it of course. When the goalkeeper is man of the match something is wrong. Something is going wrong for the other team.

"I think Madrid had one shot on target and it was a goal. But I understand 100% and respect it 100% that the reason for playing football and having competitions is to win the game."

Sometimes, however, you cannot *force* the win.

With pure irony, John Muller of the *Athletic* wrote that, "On another day, in some other timeline, maybe Real Madrid could have won the 2021/22 Champions League final.

"It would have been improbable in any universe, with the way Carlo Ancelotti's team played, but you can imagine some alternate reality where the movements of bodies and balls are just a little less orderly, where football is a little less fair – who knows, maybe stranger things have happened in a world like that than a smash-and-grab 1-0 win."

The article was entitled: *Only in an alternate reality should Real Madrid be Champions League winners – that's the beauty of football.*

It ends with Muller stating a 5-1 win for Liverpool played out in the *real* universe: "No one could argue the result was unfair. Liverpool had the better of possession, field tilt, shots, and expected goals. They'd played the game in an organised 4-3-3 and pushed into Madrid's half, while Ancelotti's lopsided shape, meant to test the space behind Alexander-Arnold with the Vinicius-Benzema pairing, never really created much threat."

As such, it's slightly worrying to discover that, according to official reports of the game, we live in an alternate universe, but clearly it had been a *weird* season.

In his post-match analysis for TTT, Andrew noted: "A brilliant article by [analyst] Mark Taylor which I often refer to came to mind. He showed if one team has lots of low-grade chances but the other team has a couple of good ones, the latter is more likely to win. So I put the shot values from last night in to the simulator."

What he found was:

A) it was incredibly likely that Madrid would score once from their chances; and

B) it was also more likely Jürgen Klopp's team would score four times rather than none.

"And", he continued, "they had so many shots on target too. Mohamed Salah alone had six. It's the most he's had in a game for Liverpool and from the available data (which isn't great for his early career), the most he's ever had for anyone. The preceding two Champions League finals saw eight on target efforts in total [so, four teams' totals combined], yet the Reds had nine in Paris. To put it into context, there were 29 instances of a team having nine shots on target in a Premier League game this season. Those sides averaged 2.9 goals and 2.45 points per game. Not one of them failed to score and only twice were they beaten. Stellar Courtois, eh?"

Regarding the points made in A and B, it's hard to create lots of 'open space' big chances (like Madrid's goal) when you're playing against a packed defence. Those 'big space' goals often come on the break. Real defended deep to prevent one-on-ones (although Salah still got in), which made sense; they also defended set-pieces deep, which seemed to confuse Liverpool – for all the success of *neuro 11* in terms of penalties, the set-piece deliveries under pressure were very poor in Paris. Liverpool had a massive height advantage at set-pieces, yet did not make use of it.

If a team doesn't give you the time and space for big chances, you have to work a lot of 'pretty good' chances, which Liverpool did, and hit them well, which Liverpool (mostly) did; but if the keeper gets a hand, arm, knee or nose to everything, it can be hard to pick fault. Salah, Mané and Díaz jinked past defenders, and got shots away, and on another day they'd have resulted in goals. After all, Liverpool had scored 147 up to that point, so it's not like there was suddenly a need to have a 50-goal-a-season traditional no.9. (That said, Liverpool did soon go out and buy Darwin Núñez, but had not been expecting Sadio Mané to leave until learning of his plans on the eve of the final.)

Even in the first cup final of the season, Edouard Mendy made a frankly incredible double-save against his Senegalese compatriot, with the second effort as he scrambled to his defeat defying belief; Mané's effort deflecting over, in much the same manner that Salah's best shot was somehow kept out by Courtois.

Dr Phil Barter, a senior lecturer at Middlesex University, worked with *Anfield Index* to run a Monte Carlo simulation to calculate the likelihood of the Reds scoring zero goals in the three finals from the quantity and quality of shots. It found that from the 10,000 'runs' the algorithm sped through, only three times did the Reds draw a total blank. In other words, 9,997 times out of 10,000, Liverpool would have bagged at least one goal. Indeed, the most likely total was seven, which came up 17% of the time; and 15 goals, as a possible outcome, came up three times as often as zero goals.

Because football results can be incredibly random.

In fairness, Alisson had made some incredible saves all season long (some of which helped the Reds reach the finals, including one from Darwin Núñez), but Liverpool found opposition keepers playing out of their skin in these cup finals. In Paris, Madrid had one shot on target, one shot off target and one blocked shot. To make it all the more bizarre, Alisson had just one goalkick to take. Obviously he didn't save the shot from Vinícius Júnior as the striker was turning in a cross-shot that took him and the defence out of the game. But if we measure the game in saves made and goalkicks taken (with goalkicks often following off-target shots or attacking pressure), Courtois was *literally* ten times as busy.

Old, Outdated and Lucky
Madrid's football felt dated, as does football in Spain in general in recent times. It is the only one of the major five European leagues that doesn't do as much pressing or favour as much physical power. Even *Serie A* has moved to fast, fun, frantic football.

Carlo Ancelotti's Real Madrid were like a José Mourinho side from 2005: talented players behind the ball, playing on the break. With elite but ageing passers in midfield, they did break through Liverpool's repeated presses, but often got no further than Fabinho, Virgil van Dijk or the utterly imperious Ibrahima Konaté, who put in one of the all-time great defensive displays in a major final, particular for someone who only turned 23 on the eve of the match. It was harsh on Joël Matip – man of the match in Madrid in 2019, and having his best season in terms of performances and appearances – to miss this final, but Konaté's pace was there to help Trent Alexander-Arnold deal with Vinícius' vicious speed. The winger barely had a touch, but obviously managed the one that decided the game, with the Liverpool right-back caught a little on his heels.

It didn't help that Thiago Alcântara, despite passing a fitness test on his achilles, was not 100% fit (as seen by the fact that he had said in the warmup that he didn't feel right), and Fabinho, alongside him, had just missed three weeks' training, and trained only for three days. Neither played badly, but neither were at their best. And yet to leave them out would have also invited criticism. To play them meant you lost something compared to when at their best; to leave them out would be to lose something, too.

It was harsh on Naby Keïta, told by Klopp during the warmup that he'd be playing, only for Thiago to then assert that he felt capable of playing. Keïta came on, tried hard, but hit an atrocious shot which he got all wrong when trying to use the outside of his boot; but his head could not have been clear. He'd missed the 2019 final with injury; this time he was in the side and then out of it again before a ball was even kicked. It's easy to overlook the emotions of players, but Thiago was in tears before the far less important League Cup final when he pulled up injured; if Keïta felt dejected after being in and then out of the starting XI, he deserves some sympathy.

On the eve of the game, Sadio Mané – usually so smart and sensitive, and a wonderful ambassador – spoke of the "great news" about his future that would please fans, which turned out, bizarrely, that he wanted to join Bayern Munich. The German champions had done the same to Klopp in 2013 when agreeing to sign his star man Mario Götze just before Dortmund met Bayern in the Champions League final. Klopp was clearly unhappy when asked about Mané in his pre-match press conference, but it still wasn't clear to everyone outside the club what Mané had told them.

It seems that Mané was acting as a product of the modern game: *his* fans would be happy, all across Senegal. Liverpool were just the club he played for, for a while. He gave six superb years' service, but went out on the bummest of notes. (Although a goal in the final would have softened the blow; he faded badly after a strong start.)

Given that Real Madrid had much longer to prepare, and fewer injuries, it made life more difficult for the Reds; but even then, they did more than enough to win.

Lions and Lambs

Given the crazy schedule since the start of December, Liverpool perhaps once again highlighted the old Michel Platini saying from his playing days: "The English are like lions in the autumn, but like lambs in the spring" – so much football, played at such pace, that so much is lost by the time the end of the season approaches. In this case, Liverpool had played 63 games, and literally none of those games since AC Milan on December 7th had *nothing* resting on them.

The rest – five months and more – were must-win, to stay in cup competitions and to keep pace in the league. The Reds played 42 games from the start of December – the 4-1 win at Everton – to the defeat in Paris. They played 35 games from the start of January to the end of May, losing only to Inter Milan in the second leg of a tie won in the first leg, and to one-shot Madrid. Two games (Arsenal in the League Cup, Benfica in the Champions League) were drawn at Anfield when the Reds won the away leg. Of the 35, 28 games were won, when shootouts were included (and shootouts meant the game was indeed won).

As of early May, these were the most games played by footballers on the planet, with Liverpool's playing several more since then, and Díaz featuring heavily:

5. *Michael Ngadeu (Gent & Cameroon) – 60 matches*
4. *Sadio Mané (Liverpool & Senegal) – 60 matches*
3. *Mohamed Salah (Liverpool & Egypt) – 60 matches*
2. *Joe Aribo (Rangers & Nigeria) – 63 matches*
1. *Luis Díaz (Liverpool, FC Porto & Colombia) – 64 matches*

(And, of course, Salah's games included half a dozen periods of extra-time, while Mané and Díaz also played multiple games that went to penalties.)

Liverpool won 80% of their games in 2022, and lost just 6%, with only 3% actually proving a *meaningful* defeat; i.e. the one in Paris, as opposed to the one against Inter. They won 16 and drew two of their final 18 league games, with the draws away at Man City (a very good result) and at home to Spurs (not normally a disaster). The notion that they 'threw away' the title was as ludicrous as Ancelotti 'schooling' Klopp.

While Madrid had plenty of time to prepare, with *La Liga* giving them an extra two days by playing their final game on the Friday, Liverpool had to play virtually every three days for months, and then had just six days to get ready for Paris. And that week did not go as well as hoped, with injuries and Mané's bombshell.

Although they beat the combined might of PSG, Chelsea, Manchester City and Liverpool, to say that Real Madrid rode their luck would be an understatement. They were the better team in none of the ties, and relied on very brief spells at both ends to gain implausible outcomes. Some of that luck was earned via great goalkeeping and great finishing (particularly from Karim Benzema), but much of it was plain old dumb luck. Any club that has to rely on their goalkeeper making a string of world-class saves has lost the tactical battle, lost the fight, lost the control – but sometimes that's all it takes to win a game. It's just not sustainable. The bigger worry for Liverpool would have been to have been outplayed or outclassed, as you used to see against Spanish teams five-15 years ago. In essence, it felt like playing Burnley but with better players – albeit with an aura that can get into the minds of the opponents as the game wears on, and your team start to think 'what's with *this* team?'

Obviously, you always stand a chance of winning if you have a world-class finisher, a world-class keeper, a fast winger, an elite defensive midfielder and a couple of legendary playmakers (as part of a super-expensive squad), and you sit back and try to block everything – but as a team they were playing a style of football from a bygone era; again, almost a José Mourinho side, taking no risks, thrilling no hearts and winning no minds, and getting away with floodlight robbery.

'Plucky' £1.5billion Real Madrid

That Real Madrid should have been allowed to enter the final as plucky underdogs was a kind of obscenity, given their lavish spending over the years, much of which still underpinned their squad; a club that just tried to offer a player a record-breaking figure, and to unveil him ahead of the final in Paris. Days before the final, Tariq Panja of the *New York Times* wrote: "Real Madrid, a 13-time European champion, had given Mbappé a contract offer that would have made the 23-year-old forward the highest paid player in its history. Its offer included a signing bonus of almost $140 million, a net salary of more than $26 million every season and complete control over his image rights."

Mbappé also says he *spoke* to Liverpool (his mum is a fan), but those kinds of figures, and what he ended up taking from PSG to stay there, were four times what Liverpool (up to then) paid their top-earners, *before* even considering the crazy signing-on fee. (As an aside, which is something also seen at City with Erling Haaland, where the £42m paid to the Norwegian's agents and family needs to be added to a transfer fee, considering that they almost double what's being paid: combined it makes him almost a £100m signing). We're talking obscene amounts of money, above and beyond what seems rational.

Liverpool, as a club, share out their money more meritocratically, to help team unity (not a concern at PSG, as there is none) and because the budget is not limitless; Real Madrid also still try to collect superstars. Liverpool – or *Liverpool with everyone fit and time to prepare* – were the better team, clearly. Before the game, and on the day. And far better than the team Madrid beat in the 2018 final, and also the injury-hit side they knocked out of the previous season's Champions League, where Ozan Kabak and Nat Phillips started both games at centre-back.

Yet in Paris, Madrid still had the greater budget and the greater experience. They had a costlier team and squad, and bigger revenues. The underdog status felt wrong, especially in a big one-off game.

Six Days

For the Reds, six days is usually *just about* enough. It was longer than any time to prepare for a game in months, after all. Indeed, I think it's *usually* the perfect turnaround time for a Jürgen Klopp side. Analysis I did a couple of years ago showed it to be ideal, but that did not take into account a game being the *sixty-third* of a season, or the 16th in less than two months (with those 16 games all being *massive*: to stay in with a chance of the title; to reach cup finals; to win cup finals). This was not just any old six days, but six days at the end of a gruelling campaign, with players pushed beyond their normal limits, and others not up to match speed. It was a season where the reward for Liverpool (and Egypt and Senegal) for success was to play even more games.

In Paris, as the second-half wore on, Liverpool's decision-making looked poor, as it had at times in the recent do-or-die league games (in which they'd *found a way*). Heads were foggy, limbs were heavy. They gave it their all, but there wasn't quite enough left in the tank. A sub who might have made a difference against a deep defence was Divock Origi, but he was out injured, and as such, had already said farewell to the club as a player, ahead of a move to AC Milan. He was only there as an onlooker, a supporter, with the non-playing squad members.

Originally, Origi's best position was out wide, using his searing pace to get to the byline. But in time he became a secret weapon as a centre-forward against low blocks: the one player who could mix it up physically (to some extent), back into defenders, make sharp turns and win headers. It's not a style Liverpool need to rely on too much, as usually they pick their way through via other means (hence why he wasn't used too often), but against Everton in April it was the introduction of the Belgian that turned a 0-0 draw into a late 2-0 win. It's something Darwin Núñez can offer, and more besides.

With five subs allowed, Origi could have come on; in the end, only three were used by each manager. He was also a 'lucky' player – one who made things happen in big games when coming off the bench; a player who made others remember that anything was possible. It was just one more bad piece of luck, to not have that clear point of difference. This was, after all, *an Origi game*. He played just 17 matches in 2021/22, starting just five times; but scored six goals, including a vital last-gasp winner at Wolves; away at AC Milan in another win; an important late goal at West Ham (to get the Reds back in the game at 3-2 with seven minutes to play, even though it proved insufficient); and his perennial late game-killer against Everton. As a starter or as a sub, most of his goals came after the 75th minute. If Real Madrid were relying on their fairytales, Origi was Liverpool's Hans Christian Andersen. Unfortunately, when injured, he was about as useful as Hans Christian Andersen.

Of course, the cost of Real Madrid's squad should have quashed all talk of plucky underdogs, even if, like a mega-expensive Mourinho side, that's how they played. Football will continue to move forward, and outdated styles will generally fail; but every now and then, playing dull-but-effective football like Leicester did in 2015/16, or Greece at the Euros in 2004, will work. The difference is that they were genuine outsiders, rank underdogs. Ancelotti deserves to go down as one of the game's greats, but just as he was unlucky in Istanbul, he had four-leaf clovers coming out of his ears in Paris.

Billionaires
Adjusted for football inflation (using the Transfer Price Index), and as such comparing prices only with the Premier League rate, Real Madrid's 2021/22 squad cost *almost* £1.5billion to assemble: £1.48billion. (And that was with them offloading a couple of big names in 2021.)

The mind-blowing squad cost was partly down to the mega-signings Gareth Bale, who rarely played, and Eden Hazard, who had just returned from injury. But even without their two costliest signings, the rest still topped £1billion. Luka Modrić and Karim Benzema may be old, but they're still elite, and they cost an absolute fortune when signed (both well over £100m in 2022 money). Hazard was signed in 2019 as an elite player, too.

To put it into context, Liverpool's entire squad cost £825.5m to put together, adjusted to 2022 prices. Or just over half the cost.

Real Madrid's starting XI, so *excluding* Bale and Hazard (and other subs Luka Jović at £77.2m and Isco at £84.8m), still cost £600m when adjusted for inflation; getting close to Man City's 2021/22 average of just under £700m, and already fairly close to the overall cost of Liverpool's *entire squad*.

Liverpool's starting XI came to £527.9m – around 15% less than the Spaniards' – but the difference on the subs bench was astronomical; Madrid's *bench* cost far more than Liverpool's starting XI. Indeed, just three players on their bench – Bale, Hazard and Isco – came to a combined £560m.

For all the wealth of the Premier League, and of the petrodollar/ oligarch clubs springing up all over the place, it's worth noting that Madrid are still in a massively strong financial position – at least in terms of the squad at its disposal. Now, whether it's sustainable or not is a different matter; how many training grounds can they sell to pay off their debts, after all? After the final, they beat Liverpool again, this time paying €100m for the French midfielder Aurélien Tchouaméni, who Klopp coveted.

Maybe Madrid also sold their soul to the devil, and he came up trumps with the heaps of good fortune.

You Don't Always Get What You Deserve in Life, So You Have To Learn To Enjoy the Ride

After Liverpool lost the final, in a brief foray onto Twitter (to post links to my article rather than bathe in the bile) I stumbled across a Newcastle fan laughing his head off at Liverpool and Jürgen Klopp. "Getting manager of the season for winning two cups on penalties and bottling the Champions League and Premier League", he noted, albeit I added the correct capital letters, to make it look more like an adult typed it.

It bears repeating: Liverpool won 49 games in 2021/22. Newcastle only *played* 40 – and won less than a third (13). Obviously there's no point arguing with idiots on the internet, but it sums up the increasing modern obsession with schadenfreude over self-respect and self-awareness.

People can belittle what was won in the end, but as a body of work – a season of 63 games – it was a *masterpiece*.

Perhaps the stupidest 'take' in the aftermath of defeat in Paris was that, in 2021/22, Liverpool somehow only 'achieved the same' as the Arsenal team from 1992/93, which – by removing the context – is like saying that the Man United team from 2009/10 (Edwin van der Sar, Gary Neville, Patrice Evra, Rio Ferdinand, Dimitar Berbatov, Wayne Rooney, Ryan Giggs, Park Ji-sung, Nemanja Vidić, Michael Carrick, Nani, Paul Scholes et al) was only as good as the Birmingham team from 2011, as both won only the League Cup.

That United side, who made the Champions League final the year before and the year after, lost the title on the final day by a single point (to Carlo Ancelotti's exciting Chelsea, ironically); Birmingham were relegated. Yes, Birmingham winning the League Cup was a bigger achievement than that Man United team winning the League Cup, but it would be comparing apples with oranges. And even then, United's 2009/10 did not achieve anything historic. Liverpool in 2021/22 *did*: most games ever won by England's most successful club in a single season; longest attempt at keeping the quadruple alive, and one of only a handful of clubs to play every game possible; a points tally that would have won the title more often than not in the history of English football; the first English team to win all six Champions League group games; the only time, apart from when they did so in 2019, that a European team got more than 90 points domestically when also reaching Europe's major final; and much more besides.

Arsenal in 1992/93 finished 10th in the league and didn't even play in Europe. Anyone comparing Liverpool narrowly losing the Champions League final after winning 28 league games (losing just two) when finishing 2nd, with Arsenal winning a measly 15 (from 42 games, not 38) whilst playing none in Europe, is being really weird. It's a weak kind of sophistry.

Despite playing four more league games, Arsenal managed just 56 points in 1992/93 to Liverpool's 92 three decades later, and even if you can't easily compare eras, then don't make specious comparisons designed to denigrate unfairly. Arsenal lost four times as many games in the league as Liverpool lost *across four competitions*.

Despite two long cup runs, Arsenal won fewer games in 1992/93 across three competitions than Liverpool won in the league alone; as well as the Gunners facing the 'mighty' Sheffield Wednesday in both domestic finals, rather than the reigning European champions. And it's not like Arsenal were some small club at the time: they won the title in 1989 (lest we be allowed to forget) and 1991. What they did in 1992/93 was partly possible as they clearly didn't put much effort into the league, and obviously required no effort for Europe. To go back to an example used earlier in the book, *Penny Lane/Strawberry Fields* only achieved the same in the charts (no.2) as Shane Richie's cover of

Wham!'s *I'm Your Man*, but that doesn't make the two in any way comparable.

Also, a few journalists and football writers who really should know better were seeing a flaw with the fact that Liverpool did not beat Manchester City, Spurs or Chelsea over nine games (sometimes throwing in Real Madrid to make it ten), with the exception of a cup win against Pep Guardiola's men; so, just one win in those games, even if two more were won on penalties.

Yet City likewise didn't beat Liverpool, and more startling (if you want to make this kind of tenuous point), City lost twice against Spurs, who finished 4th, while Liverpool were unbeaten against them. That's five games against Liverpool and Spurs for City, with three defeats and two draws. And, if you want to again focus on just the clubs where Liverpool dropped points, you could do something for Man City and create a mini-league including Crystal Palace, Liverpool and Spurs, and they would be bottom, having won none of the seven games, and lost four. But that's not how football works. There will always be teams, like Chelsea and Man City for Liverpool and Crystal Palace, Liverpool and Spurs for Man City, where a clash of styles might negate what would be considered the better team on paper, as well as any misfortune on the day. Had City not staged their late comeback against Aston Villa, no one would mention the points Liverpool dropped against Spurs; and everyone would instead focus on Spurs doing the double over City as proof of something inherently wrong with Guardiola's team.

Liverpool, in addition to getting 92 points, had a European run where they beat AC Milan twice, Inter Milan (Italian champions and last year's champions), Atlético Madrid twice (reigning Spanish champions), Villarreal twice (reigning Europa League champions) Porto and Benfica – with the Portuguese league not elite, but also, traditionally relatively strong. They also tore City apart at Wembley in a semi-final, to go 3-0 up at half-time.

If making random mini-leagues, or looking at other top six teams – the Big Six, it transpired again, just in a slightly different order than other seasons – then Liverpool beat Arsenal twice (three times if you include the cup) and thrashed Man United 9-0 across the two games. For all their extra money, Man City finished one point ahead, won fewer trophies and didn't get as far in Europe. It doesn't say too much about them, and what they're made of, that they lost both games against Spurs, took just a single point against Crystal Palace, and could not beat Liverpool over three games – or that they lost to Real Madrid on aggregate. They got 93 points to Liverpool's 92.

Once you're past 90 points then you're really splitting hairs to focus on games *not* won, given that 90 points means relatively few have been dropped, and total perfection remains impossible. To get 90+ points – historically almost always enough to win the league – and to find fault is a bit like griping that Liverpool didn't beat Crystal Palace 10-0 in 1989 instead of 9-0.

Clichés! The Cynic Never Fails, Never Cries, As He Never Loves, Never Tries

You may have heard these before, but in the hours before the final I contemplated the healthy reaction to any disappointment, should it arrive, later that evening. Narratives, I feared, would be formed on the basis of one game, and everything that came before would be ignored.

Better to have loved and lost than never loved at all.

Arriving is not the best part of a fantastic journey.

The chase is better than the kill.

And so on.

Better to have reached finals and been within touching distance of the title than to, I don't know, get knocked out early or finish 16th. Better to have a chance of the title in the second half of the final game of the season than to not even be on the ride; to sneer and say that only idiots subject themselves to such high drama and tension. Better to be in the Champions League final than to watch it hoping a rival loses.

The week leading up to a final, it occurred to me, remains special, something to savour. The day of the final (if not being attacked by riot police) is usually full of thrilling anticipation. Beaten finalist hurts, but it's better than beaten semi-finalist, beaten quarter-finalist. Better than not-even-qualified.

I've only been to two Champions League finals – Istanbul and Athens – and while the former remains one of the best two days (and one night) of my life, the latter was great fun too, with a group of about ten Reds, beautiful weather, drinking and eating al fresco, and full of hope and anticipation in the Greek sunshine. (There was obviously another UEFA cockup over ticketing and accessing the stadium, but I'd luckily managed to steer clear of that.)

Liverpool played well in 2007 – actually outplaying Carlo Ancelotti's AC Milan (after only outplaying them for six minutes in 2005) when losing 2-1 – but again, such is football. In 2022, Liverpool weren't just the better team but were utterly dominant from start to finish.

Another cliché: you need to buy a ticket to win the lottery. In 2021/22, Liverpool bought a shedload of lottery tickets for the fans.

Basically it proved a lottery-ticket-tastic campaign; a lottery ticket *every game*. No single game had been meaningless, beyond when the 'group of death' was won early.

My favourite quote for life is from the ancient Stoic philosopher Seneca:

We suffer more in imagination than in reality.

With a few exceptions (being mangled alive in some horrific machining accident, having Roy Hodgson as your manager), it rings true.

Losing hurts, but rarely as badly as you expect, at least once the initial sting wears off. It hurts like hell but then, in contrast to a loved one dying or a long-term relationship ending (or even a beloved pet needing to be put to sleep), it passes quickly. There's always another season, another game, another win, just around the corner. Other big chances to win trophies, too, if you're lucky.

Of course, you can make it worse if you've been a dickhead all season on social media and people are now coming back to haunt you; or, if just unlucky, you run into the arseholes, online and in the streets or pubs, from other clubs, whose fans go out looking for innocent Reds to abuse and mock. For all those who laugh at Liverpool losing, it proved far better than the chloroformic pall of dead seasons, over by January, sleepwalking until May when some weirdos will then focus on winning the transfer window (ever since the January one slammed shut).

Few seasons were this exciting, this much fun. Few will be as memorable.

The key sentence of this book is repeated a few times. Here it is again. Teams are not always duly rewarded for their brilliance, but they are *remembered* for their brilliance.

I've mentioned them before, and I'll mention them again. Holland 1974, 1978. Hungary 1954. Brazil 1982. Dortmund 2013, even, and Spurs 2019 – certainly more memorable than the Juande Ramos-won trophy of 2008. England in 1990, which, with Gazza's tears in the Italian summer, has been mythologised. (I can't say I'll remember much about recent England performances as I stopped watching them about ten years ago.)

The best Liverpool teams since I first went to a game in 1990 are the 1995/96 side, who won nothing the season after the 1994/95 team won a cup – but Roy Evans' team was so exciting a year later; Gérard Houllier's 2001/02 team was probably better balanced than the treble-winning team of 2000/01, albeit we'll always remember that treble-winning side with great fondness. The 2008/09 team was better than either of Rafa Benítez's sides that reached the Champions League final; yet Fernando Torres, Fábio Aurélio, Álvaro Arbeloa, Yossi Benayoun and Javier Mascherano won nothing with Liverpool, and Pepe Reina, Daniel Agger, Lucas Leiva and Dirk Kuyt won only a domestic cup or two. Djimi Traoré, inferior to them all, won a Champions League, a League Cup and an FA Cup.

The chaotic brilliance of 2013/14, with Luis Suárez settled and unstoppable, was better than the cup-winning team of 2012, albeit Kenny Dalglish's team almost completed a memorable cup double.

Yet it would be wrong to define Jürgen Klopp's team by its narrow failures, or to call it one of the best teams to never win certain things. Indeed, unlike the mythical Holland and Hungary sides (which admittedly had fewer opportunities), this is a Liverpool team – with just a few altered faces – who have won the Champions League, the Premier League, the FA Cup, the League Cup, the World Club championship and the European Super Cup. Its greatness is secured in those successes and moreover, the football played, the points tallies racked up in the league, the runs to major finals, the beautiful ride, the joyous journey. It all goes into the mix.

On the site, TTT subscriber *Robert* noted: "One of the best and most beloved baseball teams of all time was Jackie Robinson's Brooklyn Dodgers. They challenged every year, but only won one World Series in 1955. They are immortalised in a wonderful book, *The Boys Of Summer*. That team had men of remarkable talent and character. Our Reds are cut from the same cloth."

Again: teams are not always duly rewarded for their brilliance, but they are *remembered* for their brilliance.

Further Context
In the aftermath of the season, subscriber Peter Danes noted:

"When you compare this season to what is possibly the best seasons in English football (for each club) Liverpool in 1984 (treble), United 1999 (treble) and Arsenal 2004 (Invincibles) you have to say our season stands up incredibly well."

As he laid out, Liverpool in 1983/84 racked up 38 wins: League: 22 (in 42 games, 1st, 80 points); FA Cup: one (4th Round); League Cup: seven (winners); European Cup: 8 (winners). The Arsenal of 2003/04 also won 38 games, with their 26 victories in the league actually two fewer than Klopp's latest vintage. And in 2001 – which included quite a lot of weaker opposition given the nature of the cups – the Reds picked up 39 wins.

By contrast, Manchester United's 1998/99 side won just 36 games in the season, compared to Liverpool's 49 in 2021/22. Chelsea won 42 in 2004/05 (José Mourinho's first season) which looks like it was the best prior to this season. Manchester City bagged 41 wins in 2021/22, eight fewer than Liverpool.

(That said, they did win 51 games, including shootouts, in the best season under Pep Guardiola.)

Parade

The open-topped bus parade had been organised weeks in advance, and would go ahead whatever happened on the final weekend of the league season or at the final in Paris. The Reds had won two cups and the women's team had won promotion. There was also the chance to make up for the lack of a similar event in 2020 due to lockdowns. As ever, fans of clubs who won nothing, challenged for nothing, mocked the parade – because of course, no one else should be allowed to enjoy themselves. Thankfully, Liverpool fans were still in the mood to show their appreciation.

"Lose the Champions League final the night before and the people arrive here in the mood they are," Jürgen Klopp said. "It is absolutely outstanding. This is the best club in the world. I don't care what people think. You have to plan these kind of things. I hoped we would find something like this, something incredible.

"Yes we lost the last two trophies but these people don't forget. They know exactly what shift the boys put in. It is such a boost for everything that will come. I am proud of these players but I am proud of these people – unbelievable.

"When you see the eyes of the people, it's incredible. You don't have to win, you just have to put all that you have in and the people of Liverpool love you.

"I'm not drunk," he added. "Just emotional."

Final Thoughts

The American sports analyst, author, podcaster, and sports writer Bill Simmons, writing a few years ago, summed up how I felt on the eve of the Paris final, when the joys of success were still a possibility:

"… Then I remembered something. Sports is a metaphor for life. Everything is black and white on the surface. You win, you lose, you laugh, you cry, you cheer, you boo, and most of all, you care.

"Lurking underneath that surface, that's where all the good stuff is – the memories, the connections, the love, the fans, the layers that make sports what they are.

"It's not about watching your team win the Cup as much as that moment when you wake up thinking, 'In 12 hours, I might watch my team win the Cup'. It's about sitting in the same chair for Game 5 because that chair worked for you in Game 3 and Game 4, and somehow, this has to mean something.

"It's about leaning out of a window to yell at people wearing the same jersey as you, and it's about noticing an airport security guy staring at your Celtics jersey and knowing he'll say, 'You think they win tonight?' before he does."

And hell, he was not even writing about *football*.

Most subscribers to *The Tomkins Times* are old enough to have lived throughout the entire fallow period that began in 1990, albeit even then, there were highs along the way, up until the 2018 overdrive. (While we welcome younger subscribers, the site is not exactly full of TikTok videos, bantz and skilz.)

Some on the site started watching Liverpool in the early Bill Shankly years, in the second tier, a club drifting when the Scot arrived. A handful of our subscribers even predate Shanks, albeit like WWII veterans, that great generation cannot go on forever. We're not always right in what we say, but there's wisdom onboard, in its crowd. We know an amazing team when we see it. Maybe some young fans or new fans are too unaware of the dark days; indeed, dark *decades*.

We know that the cynic never loves. He never allows himself to.

The cynic never falls off the bike, as the cynic never rides the bike. He'll never get back on the horse, *as he wasn't even on the horse in the first place*.

As Theodore Roosevelt said more than a century ago:

"It is not the critic who counts; not the man who points out how the strong man stumbles, or where the doer of deeds could have done them better. The credit belongs to the man who is actually in the arena, whose face is marred by dust and sweat and blood; who strives valiantly; who errs, who comes short again and again, because there is no effort without error and shortcoming; but who does actually strive to do the deeds; who knows great enthusiasms, the great devotions; who spends himself in a worthy cause; who at the best knows in the end the triumph of high achievement, and who at the worst, if he fails, at least fails while daring greatly, so that his place shall never be with those cold and timid souls who neither know victory nor defeat."

Savour it, as this is a rare frequency of forays to this final. It happened once before for Liverpool, 1977-1985 (five finals, four won). Then there were the two finals, 2005-2007, before more drought.

Now we've just had three in five seasons, 2018, 2019 and 2022 (with Covid not helping to keep that streak even hotter.) This is a level not seen in generations. If a generation is 20-or-so years, then this eclipsed the excellent period (two finals) 20 years after Heysel ended the original domination. And that first spell in the club's history commenced one full generation (22 years) after the European Cup/ Champions League became a thing in 1955.

Some clubs are lucky if they make it to one Champions League final, even with spending that's literally off the charts (PSG, Manchester City). They stack the deck, *and they still can't do it*. If their fans are happy, then all power to them; it's not my place to rain on their parades. But buying success is not as much fun as *earning* it.

The pain and disappointment will pass, sooner than expected. Life will move on, and football will begin again, because the football never ends.

Jürgen Klopp and his team will get back on their horses, as these are winners – winners of more games this season than in any in the club's history, winners of every trophy going since 2019 – who will *sometimes* stumble, but will climb back on and, starting at dawn (with the wine purely metaphorical), ride, ride again.

Acknowledgments

Thank you to all our subscribers, staff and contributors, who somehow keep the site going in difficult financial times, rife with stiff competition. Also, thank you to everyone who answered questions for this book, not all of which made the cut, but I'll try to put the rest online in due course. As ever, thank you to Daniel Marshall for the wonderful cover design.

Printed in Great Britain
by Amazon